T0418517

All Play and No Work

PAUL GAGLIARDI

All Play and No Work

American Work Ideals and the Comic Plays
of the Federal Theatre Project

TEMPLE UNIVERSITY PRESS
Philadelphia • *Rome* • *Tokyo*

TEMPLE UNIVERSITY PRESS
Philadelphia, Pennsylvania 19122
tupress.temple.edu

Library of Congress Cataloging-in-Publication Data

Names: Gagliardi, Paul, 1978– author.
Title: All play and no work : American work ideals and the comic plays of
the Federal Theatre Project / Paul Gagliardi.
Description: Philadelphia : Temple University Press, 2024. | Includes
bibliographical references and index. | Summary: "This book examines how
comic plays of the Federal Theatre Project challenged work norms
promoted by the federal government during the Great Depression"—
Provided by publisher.
Identifiers: LCCN 2023013330 (print) | LCCN 2023013331 (ebook) | ISBN
9781439922156 (cloth) | ISBN 9781439922163 (paperback) | ISBN
9781439922170 (pdf)
Subjects: LCSH: Federal Theatre Project (U.S.) | American drama
(Comedy)—20th century—History and criticism. | Drama—Social
aspects—United States. | Work in literature.
Classification: LCC PN2270.F43 G34 2023 (print) | LCC PN2270.F43 (ebook)
| DDC 812/.05230900904—dc23/eng/20230811
LC record available at https://lccn.loc.gov/2023013330
LC ebook record available at https://lccn.loc.gov/2023013331

Printed in the United States of America

9 8 7 6 5 4 3 2 1

To my grandmother and uncle.

Contents

Acknowledgments

I am beyond grateful to the many people, more than I can remember, who supported me in the completion of this project. First and foremost, Jason Puskar, my mentor and dissertation advisor, was the driving force in seeing my nebulous idea transformed into a viable research project. To be frank, I would never have completed my dissertation without his guidance. I am also grateful to Gregory Jay, Josephene Lanters, Mark Netzloff, and Robin Mello, who provided guidance on this project—and often had to tolerate a then toddler looking for something to draw on in their offices. I want to thank Julie Burrell for her advice on crafting arguments and readings, especially in Chapter 4. I also want to thank my "comrade" Amy Brady who has supported this project since we met on a NEMLA Roundtable on the FTP in 2013. And Adam Ochonicky has not only been a dear friend for years but also has been an invaluable guide to the book publishing process. And I would be bereft if I did not thank my friends, colleagues, and mentors for their continued support over the years, including Jessica Dorman, Ron Felten, Tim Galow, John Gennari, Nathan Hackman, Pat Johnson, Chad Jorgensen, Bridget Kies, Tasha Oren, and Ali Sperling. My colleagues in the English Department at Marquette University have given me an intellectual home to complete this project and provided the support to see it through. Amy Blair, Cedric Burrows, Lilly Campell, Gerry Canavan, Leah Flack, Steve Hartman-Keiser, Grant Gosizk, Ben Pladek, and Jacob Riyeff have all been more than giving of their time and thinking on this project. I also want to particularly thank Liz Angeli, Jason Farr, and Jenna Green for their encouragement, kindness, and friendship. My sincerest thanks to the anonymous readers of the manuscript and Shaun Vigil, William Forrest, and everyone at Temple University Press for their tireless work.

Without question, I owe a debt to various archivists and researchers for their assistance in locating materials for my research, including Paul Allen Sommerfeld and the rest of the staff of the Music and Performing Arts Reading Room at the Library of Congress, John Waggener from the American Heritage Center at the University of Wyoming, Paul Civitelli from the Beinecke Library at Yale University, Sharon Gissy from the Chicago Public Library, and the researchers from the University of Iowa and George Mason University.

I owe special thanks to my family who have supported me in this long endeavor. Perhaps my biggest thanks go to my parents who encouraged me while—I suspect—barely enduring near-endless trips to museums, battlefields, and libraries of the mid-Atlantic states when I was young. And I want to thank the newest people in my life, my in-laws and stepsons, Roy and Otto, who have been such a wonderful addition to my world.

I want to save the final words for two important people: my daughter, Zigana, who has been an inspiration to me throughout her life, and my wife, Bridget McCann, without whose love I could not have finished this work.

All Play and No Work

Introduction

The genesis of this project was, to be perfectly honest, accidental. In an early draft of a graduate school research proposal on comedy of the Great Depression era, I had included a throwaway line about the dearth of scholarship into comic plays of the Federal Theatre Project (FTP). While I wanted initially to do a broad analysis of the need for laughter during the 1930s, my advisors at the University of Wisconsin–Milwaukee found that throwaway line to be far more workable for a dissertation, and after reflection, I came around to their point of view. The following summer, I spent a few days examining FTP playscripts and materials in the Performing Arts Reading Room at the Library of Congress. I had narrowed my focus of comic plays to those that were most often performed by FTP, and as I read the archival materials, I began to see an odd pattern: many of the plays had interesting portrayals of labor at a time when access to work and jobs was rather important. In a play about a group of struggling actors in Puritan Massachusetts, some actors simply give up acting rather than deal with the pitfalls of acting. In another, a Black man refuses to work and instead dreams about financial success while sitting on a riverbank. One play even focused on a man who simply walked into a bank and pretended to work there without any business training. On my yellow notepad that I had brought with me, I wrote "work and antiwork" over and over and over. In a meeting with my advisor after my trip, he reflected on my findings and suggested, "You could even call the project something like 'all play and no work' or something along those lines."

All Play and No Work is an ironic title in some respects. A pun on the maxim of "all work and no play makes Jack a dull boy," it overlaps with several cultural views of work and theater. One is the long-standing view of the actual work of the stage, long diminished as the antithesis of "noble" labor by everyone from the Puritans to many of the critics of the FTP itself. In another sense, the title refers to the emphasis on work over leisure that has long been engrained in American society. But more for my purposes, the work represented in the plays examined in this project often directly contradict the promoted ideals of work found in American society, culture, and within the broader New Deal itself. David M. Kennedy perhaps offers the most succinct observation about American society during the Great Depression. Describing Harry Hopkins's Civil Works Administration (CWA), one of the first relief agencies of Franklin Roosevelt's presidency, Kennedy argues that the prevailing principle of the program could be summarized so: "The operative word was work."[1] As part of a federal response to arguably the worst economic crisis in American history, what does it mean that many plays produced by the FTP celebrated forms of labor like speculation and swindling?

I argue that many FTP comic plays concerned with work promoted views of labor that critiqued work norms of American society as well as the New Deal itself. Backstage comedies critique the FTP's promotion of radical theatrical labor but also defend the organization's existence. Middle-class work plays challenge mainstream views of work-relief and gendered labor as well as the consumerist impulses of the nation. Comedies of speculation promote forms of chance as labor especially for marginalized communities. And the con artist comic plays of the FTP not only reveal the prevalence of swindling in American society but also how it could be used to provide agency for workers in the Great Depression. Taken together, these comic plays complicate the ideological tenets of the New Deal and afforded audiences and performers opportunities to challenge the norms of labor during the Great Depression.

In analyzing work comedies of the FTP, this project locates the concepts of work, governmentality, and comedy through how all three become both repressive and liberating forces. Work has long been a fundamental component of human life, but the rise of industrial capitalism enforced the conceptualization of wage labor to Western societies, fundamentally altering discipline and time for workers. For Karl Marx, this paradigm of work was repressive and alienating, a view that has influenced a range of social scientists. For Max Weber, Marx's writings on labor were useful, but whereas Marx focused on the economic superstructures that enforced wage labor, Weber saw a religious component to the rise of capitalism. In *The Protestant Ethic and the Spirit of Capitalism*, Weber argues that the various doctrines of Protestantism—especially Calvinism—encouraged workers to seek their fortunes through their own enterprises and helped explain the rise of market capitalism in northern Europe. In turn, those workers began to look for signs in their work that signaled divine grace. In time, the calling of work would come to dominate every facet of life in places like Germany and America. However, from Weber's perspective, the work ethic had come to repress individuality and spirituality. As he famously commented: "The Puritan wanted to work in calling; we are forced to do so."[2] While ideally the "calling" would manifest in the "highest spiritual and cultural values," in the United States, work had become particularly devoid of any asceticism, merely a "mundane" passion with the "character of sport."[3] While Marx saw the freedom from the alienation of labor through revolution, Weber, who generally had a gloomy view of modernity, did theorize a less radical way society could escape the iron cage. Positing in "Politics as a Vocation" that new political prophets could arise with "passion and perspective," new political intellectuals and experts could invigorate society with a "great rebirth of old ideas and ideals" that could help alleviate the struggles of alienated citizens and, perhaps, workers.[4]

While Weber's observations about work and the nation-state have generally not been connected to the New Deal, many progressive reformers argued for a reorientation of social changes that were led by skilled technicians and political prophets. And for the progressive and pragmatic members of the Roosevelt administration, one of the central aims of the various work programs of the New Deal was not only to provide work to the unemployed but also to, in a Weberian sense, infuse work with the moral, spiritual component that had long been missing from work. Much of the work promoted by the New Deal adhered to conservative norms of working, and Franklin Roosevelt often evoked moralistic language in detailing work programs, emphasizing the restorative power of work for the souls of Americans. Rather than provide direct relief to Americans, the programs of the New Deal promoted work-relief (with some exceptions), that in theory would restore traditional work values for the unemployed. Moreover, federal work relief projects like the Civilian Conservation Corps (CCC) and the CWA provided projects for their workers that aided the greater good. Harry Hopkins, who would lead the Works Progress Administration (WPA), which would house the FTP, went further than Roosevelt in believing in the restorative power of work relief, claiming that the work of the WPA could enact a new work-life paradigm for Americans. Hopkins believed the programs of Federal One—a series of humanities-based work programs—would be able to alleviate much of the economic and social angst Americans were facing.

This belief in the power of work relief to change the country was also espoused by Hallie Flanagan, head of the FTP. As leader of the Federal One program that was the most controversial, Flanagan often defended and promoted the FTP as an organization that would give theater to the people and revolutionize the art form. Throughout her tenure, Flanagan promoted her vision that the FTP should not just entertain audiences but also create theatrical communities in which actors and directors could both celebrate culture and challenge audiences. And many of the FTP's most celebrated productions reflected these ideals. In places like New York, Los Angeles, and Seattle, audiences saw living newspaper plays that, through a combination of nonnaturalistic acting and mixed-media sets, promoted social action. In Harlem, Orson Welles staged his famous *Macbeth*, which featured an all-Black cast. And on October 27, 1936, at theaters across the nation, the FTP staged an adaptation of Sinclair Lewis's novel *It Can't Happen Here* that drew national acclaim. However, the FTP also garnered a great deal of criticism for not only its cost but also the leftist themes in its productions. As John Frick notes, "from practically its first day of operation, conservative critics challenged its collectivist approach to social issues, scrutinized its productions, and attempted to exercise social controls over its offerings."[5] Indeed, many Republican critics of the FTP, such as Texas senator Martin Dies, chairperson of the House Un-American Activities Commission, charged that the FTP was nothing more than a communistic organization and one more link in the vast New Deal propaganda machine. Just four years after the program began, the FTP was cut from the 1940 federal budget and the experiment in federally subsidized theater ended.

This vacillation between repression, restoration, and liberation can also be seen with comedy theory, and while my primary focus with this project is locating these plays within the ideologies of the New Deal and work, I do want to acknowledge comedy theory here briefly. As Michael North observes, one of the most "intractable debates in modern comic theory pivots on the opposition between release and domination." For those who subscribe to the idea that comedy is anarchic and even revolutionary, like Sigmund Freud does at times in *Jokes in Their Relation to the Unconscious*, the art can free its audiences and subjects "from the reign of sense" as it is not simply, in Freud's mind, a straightforward indulgence but a relief that those emotions need no longer be suppressed. For others, like Henri Bergson in *Laughter*, the "release is illusory or contradictory, given the power of humor to punish those who deviate from the dominant norm."[6] Even though Bergson acknowledges the joy and flexibility in comedy, laughter "is above all, a corrective" and is "intended to humiliate [and] make a painful impression on the person against whom it is directed."[7] North sees a great amount of overlap between the two theorists' extended treatises on laughter and comedy and reads Walter Benjamin's work on film comedy as an attempt to resolve this dichotomy. The Frankfurt School critic would often be ambivalent about the state of film technology but also be sympathetic to seeing comedy as a defense mechanism for people victimized by technocracy.[8]

This intersection between comedy and its function as a defense mechanism as well as form of resistance is echoed by James C. Scott. Writing in *Weapons of the Weak: Everyday Forms of Peasant Resistance*, Scott examines how lower-class groups resist the tenets of middle- and upper-class norms in various societies. Of particular interest to him is analyzing how "peasants fashion from their experience," meaning "their 'offstage' comments and conversation, their proverbs, folksongs, and history, legends, jokes, language, ritual, and religion," the degree to which the lower class accepts the social order propagated by elite society. Scott notes broadly that it is an empirical matter whether social norms—like work—"find support or opposition within the subculture subordinate classes." He writes, "If bandits and poachers are made into folk heroes, we can infer that transgressions of elite codes evoke a vicarious admiration. If the forms of outward deference are privately mocked, it may suggest that peasants are hardly in the thrall of a naturally ordained order. If those who try to curry the personal favor of elites are shunned and ostracized by others of their class, we have evidence that there is a lower-class subculture with sanctioning power."[9] This resistance among the lower class is not universal, Scott notes, as subordinate classes interact with dominant culture in different ways. He concludes with his observation that these cultural trends often do not have any revolutionary ethos, but function as symbolic of people's modest economic and social goals.[10] He concludes his work by noting that while these forms of resistance do not signal revolutionary change, the weapons of the weak—namely, acts of self-preservation like ridicule, truculence, irony, petty acts of noncompliance, disbelief in elite norms—should be celebrated.[11] In my mind, Scott's overview of resistance and humor serves as a helpful lens for reading the comic plays about work here in this project: they are not revolutionary acts of humor but function as small-scale acts of resistance for some audiences overwhelmed by the repression of work, economic calamity, and the general alienation of the era.

While studies of the FTP have generally downplayed comedy as a focus, this project places itself with a broader emphasis on the interplay between the temporary resistance of the stage and the political and social restraints placed on the FTP and its productions. The traditional narratives on the FTP have examined this interplay as relating to the more radical productions of the FTP. For example, in her analysis of the FTP in comparison to national theaters in Europe, *The National Stage: Theatre and Cultural Legitimation in England, France, and America*, Loren Kruger argues that the FTP went further than similar programs in England and France in "articulating a popular theatre that might be 'national' in scope and 'democratic in attitude.'"[12]

For her, the productions that exemplified this "national" theater were "canonical" living newspaper plays like *Triple A Plowed Under, One Third a Nation,* and *Injunction Granted.* But other studies have shifted away from such "canonical works" to examining more popular and commercial texts. In her study of the Negro Units of the FTP, *Blueprints for a Black Federal Theatre,* Rena Fraden examines lesser-known productions of that unit like the musical *Run, Little Chillun* and the Negro Unit's adaptation of Gilbert and Sullivan's *The Mikado,* entitled the *Swing Mikado,* and how these plays operated against dominant racialized structures in the FTP. In addition, recent studies such as Elizabeth Osborne's *Staging the People: Community and Identity in the Federal Theatre Project,* Leslie Elaine Frost's *Dreaming America: Popular Front Ideals and Aesthetics in Children's Plays of the Federal Theatre Project,* and Macki Braconi's *Harlem's Theaters: A Staging Ground for Community, Class, and Contradiction, 1923–1939,* have studied less-examined plays and also focused on the exchange between those plays and the social anxieties of Depression audiences in various communities across the country. Moreover, as scholars like Jane De Hart Matthews and Loren Kruger detail, local FTP theaters often staged productions that contradicted the aims of the program at large. By extension, this project draws heavily from the work of scholars like Rena Fraden, who notes in her analysis of the Negro Unit that productions in Chicago and New York presented themes that complicated both WPA hiring practices and American views of race. Additionally, this project also follows the lead of scholars such as Barry Witham and Elizabeth Osborne who illustrate how the themes of many FTP plays coincided with the ideological positions of New Deal programs like the Tennessee Valley Authority or the FTP itself.

My general approach to analyzing these plays is to consider the breadth of their production history, focusing more on a broader, more literary analysis based on extant playscripts. Given that several of the plays here in this book—namely, *Ah, Wilderness!, Help Yourself,* and *Mississippi Rainbow*—were produced dozens of times by the FTP, I feel that a broader, more national approach to analyzing the plays is prudent. However, I do focus on specific production history with several plays as smaller case studies of the complicated reactions to these productions. When detailing *A Moral Entertainment,* I focus on that play's negative response by Boston-area critics who question the rationale of the play as well as its portrayal of Puritan culture. I posit that the Raleigh, North Carolina, production of *The Torch-Bearers* signals a more nuanced understanding of theatrical labor, while I draw heavily on Braconi's work on the Harlem Negro Unit's production of *The Show-Off* to examine the interpretations of that play to different communities. In addition, I consider how the Chicago production of *Mississippi Rainbow* illustrates larger concerns over the play, especially if that play permitted Black audiences the space to undermine white working norms. These performance histories are based on production reports and audience surveys from the Library of Congress and other archives as well as other primary textual documents, such as the lengthy correspondence between the playwright of *Mississippi Rainbow*, John C. Brownell, and the director of the Chicago Negro Unit, Shirley Graham.

While I generally apply a more liberating reading of the comedy in these plays, I do allow for the possibility of alternate readings. As Umberto Eco famously complained, there are far too many different things that make people laugh, and as North notes, context changes precisely what makes an audience laugh.[13] In turn, comedy is inherently "conservative" in its narrative structure, representation, and ideological tenets, and comedy is bound to its historical conditions: to make an audience laugh, a comedy must align with the broadest tastes of that audience, ranging from characterizations to ideological constructions and even the references embedded within the text. And comedy of the Great Depression, especially popular comedy, was often cemented in mainstream political, social, and cultural norms that are affronting to contemporary values. As I acknowledge in each chapter, a great many of the plays I examine here can certainly be read as aligning with other problematic representative patterns seen in 1930s media and literature. The plays were all written or adapted by white playwrights, many of whom would go on to long, successful careers in Hollywood and on Broadway. As such, many of these plays offer a window into the comic sensibilities of the 1920s and 1930s, as certainly some audiences would have responded to elements in these plays by reverting to the dominant norm to laugh at situations or characters. Moreover, the plays here were not necessarily on the cutting-edge of comedy during the Depression, as there are little to no traces of the popular slapstick, anarchic, parodic humor seen on the stage and screen during the era in these plays (for the most part). Indeed, most of the plays in *All Play and No Work* can trace their performance histories to the 1920s, and their approach to humor partially reflects a more conservative, genteel tradition of comedy. Yet as the Jazz Age and its hedonism morphed into the anxiety of the Depression, no doubt the reception of these plays changed for certain audiences as different productions tweaked the meaning of the plays and their humor for varying means and audiences.

To broaden the interrogation of the plays I write about, I utilize an interdisciplinary approach to my research, drawing on fields like literary, cultural, and film studies to better contextualize the comedies of the FTP. Following the models of scholars like Sean McCann in *Gumshoe America: Hard-Boiled Crime Fiction and the Rise and Fall of New Deal Liberalism* and Michael Szalay in *New Deal Modernism: American Literature and the Invention of the Welfare State*, the chapters herein connect to theories and historical constructions of work, ranging from New Deal work relief, professional acting work norms, middle-class views of labor, consumerism, speculation, and swindling. In turn, the chapters here contextualize the plays within the context of the ideologically complicated New Deal, especially how its programs like the Social Security Act straddled progressive ideals and conservative, capitalist norms. The chapters also place the plays within a broader cultural context. In my chapter on confidence artist plays, for instance, I connect *Help Yourself* and *The Milky Way* to longer cultural traditions of the confidence artist in American literature of the nineteenth century as well as popular entertainment in the 1930s like various screwball comedies and professional wrestling. I also make connections between the plays to film studies. In Chapter 2, for instance, I draw parallels between self-reflexive musicals and the backstage comedies produced by the FTP. I also apply the idea of the star persona to film adaptations of some of these plays to theorize about audiences' receptions to those specific plays.

In cataloging these plays, I have settled on four genres to examine in the following pages: backstage comedies, middle-class comedies, comedies of chance, and con artist comedies. To be fair, my approach here is problematic in that these are not stable genres recognized by other scholars or by producers and audiences of the 1930s—apart from the backstage comedy, which parallels the traits of the backstage musical. And there are several elements of these genres that overlap with one another: two of the backstage comedies focus on characters positioned as middle-class, while several characters of the comedies of chance carry hallmarks more closely associated with those con artist characters. But what I do see, retroactively, are several narrative and thematic connections in these plays that offer some stable indications for not only the characterizations in the play but also the narrative expectations for audiences. Backstage comedies result in the diegetic staging of a play and promotion of theatrical labor; the middle-class comedies subvert elements of middle-class views of labor; comedies of chance feature characters embracing speculation to achieve their financial goals; and con artist plays emphasize swindling as a means to an end.

Chapter 1, "The Work of the New Deal and the Federal Theatre Project," examines the complicated space of work and work relief during the Depression. While pinning-down the ideological view of the New Deal is difficult, the Roosevelt administration's general view of relief was based on the promotion of work relief rather than the more direct-relief of other welfare states. Many members of the administration believed that only work could restore the soul of individual workers and promoted such a belief in a range of programs including the WPA and Federal One. While the programs were inherently conservative in nature, both politically and socially, Harry Hopkins and Hallie Flanagan promoted the revolutionary potential of programs like the FTP to establish a new mode of work and life in the country. The work within the FTP was often a point of contention, however, as Flanagan struggled to balance a range of charges for the program, as well as competing visions of what type of theatrical labor should be promoted by the FTP. For many theater professionals, this was a model of work in line with the demands of commercial theater, and they resisted the urge to promote more modernist types of performance.

Chapter 2, "Backstage Comedies," asserts the backstage comedies of the FTP function as their backstage musical counterparts in film and on the stage, especially like the self-reflexive musicals that became increasingly popular in the 1930s, 1940s, and 1950s. These plays both promote the necessity of the FTP itself and condemn some of its tendencies toward theatrical aesthetics that endanger the security of employment. George Kelly's *The Torch-Bearers* advocates for the professional stage by presenting noncommercial theater as inferior, while acknowledging that theater is one of the few venues that permits agency for women. Allen Boretz and John Murray's farcical *Room Service* presents theater producers as willing to do anything to protect their acting troupes—even engaging in fraudulent behavior—while portraying the struggles professional actors encounter. The play also shows that overly political works endanger theatrical workers, a theme also expressed in Richard Maibaum's *A Moral Entertainment*, which centers on an acting troupe that is arrested by a magistrate for performing Shakespeare in colonial Massachusetts. Showing both the tribulations of actors as well as the dangers of overtly political theater, *A Moral Entertainment* advocates for the necessity of the FTP and warns of the political repression that actors could face if they overly embrace political theater.

Chapter 3, "Middle Class Labor," examines two plays that challenge middle-class work norms during the 1930s. After decades of having their work promoted as "different" than that of lower-class laborers, the fact that many middle-class workers experienced mass unemployment caused broad social and psychological anxiety among the middle-class workforces. At the same time, many programs of the New Deal sought to restore the stability of middle-class life in a variety of forms. Within this larger context, two plays attempt to placate a variety of social anxieties over middle-class life and work. Eugene O'Neill's *Ah, Wilderness!*—with its nostalgic view of small-town life and work—was especially appealing to conservative audiences of the era and seemed to promote values that resonated with middle-class audiences. Yet O'Neill's only comedy is rife with concerns over the middle-class view of social programs and attitudes toward issues of alienation and alcoholism. In George Kaufman and Marc Connelly's *To the Ladies*, business culture is satirized, but so is the dominance of the male workforce as the men in the play are not the stalwart breadwinners seen and promoted in 1930s culture. The performances of the play seem to signal an undermining of New Deal hiring norms by showing women as more capable than their husbands.

Chapter 4, "Comedies of Chance," examines two plays and their relationships to the concepts of chance and security during the Depression. Chance was often placed in opposition to work, especially with the forms of chance and risk that bore no resemblance to the hallmarks of work and frugality. Of course, this degradation of chance did not apply to the risk-taking involved with capitalist work. The cultural appeal of "illegitimate" chance and "legitimate" chance grew more pronounced with the onset of the Depression, as there was an increased interest in forms of labor that intersected with illegitimate chance—games of chance, gambling, insurance fraud—while the federal government began to encourage Americans to reengage with legitimate chance. George Kelly's *The Show-Off* features a character named Aubrey Piper who loves the thrill of chance as it relates to the sport of business but also overly embraces risk; this contrasts with his working-class family-in-law, who not only adhere to traditional work norms but also reject risk by embracing the security of social insurance. John C. Brownell's *Mississippi Rainbow* centers on an unemployed Black man who—much to the chagrin of his family and community—avoids finding work and instead dreams of his "big idea" all day long. Written by a white playwright, *Mississippi Rainbow* is one of the most problematic plays performed by the FTP as it outwardly reinforces many stereotypes of Black labor. Yet many Black performers and audiences found the play compelling, as it became a site of resistance where white labor norms could be subverted through Black characters embracing the tenets of speculative work.

Chapter 5, "Con Artist Plays," focuses on plays centered on confidence artists that show how the dominant economic system perpetuates swindling and is tolerated by society. The con artist plays feature characters who outwardly engage in "noble" confidence schemes. In Lynn Root and Harry Clork's *The Milky Way*, a milkman accidentally knocks out a boxer during a routine milk delivery, and the boxer's manager conceives of a plan to promote the scrawny milkman as a legitimate contender. The narrative speaks to the need for mythologizing of the underdog, but also the importance of the audience embracing the con presented before them. Paul Vulpius's *Help Yourself* centers on an unemployed man named Chris Stringer who wanders into a bank without employment there and begins to work at said bank. Playing to the performative nature of office work, Stringer concocts an investment between two banks out of thin air—and, despite his swindle, is promoted at the end of the play. The play certainly speaks to the antibanking ethos of the 1930s and satirizes the supposed stability of banks but also functions as a warning about how the banking system is still rife for fraud—a stark reminder for audiences about the dangers of the capitalist system.

The Work of the New Deal and the Federal Theatre Project

R elief work for theater workers, artists, and historians was controversial to many Americans (and remains so).[1] To combat the controversy around the relief work of Federal One, Harry Hopkins, along with Eleanor Roosevelt, began to actively campaign for the WPA and Federal One during the 1936 presidential election. On one train trip, Hallie Flanagan held her first serious discussions with Hopkins about the FTP, and she was particularly struck by one stop at Iowa State University where Hopkins dealt with some rather vocal dissent about the programs of Federal One. After one of the assembled yelled, "Who's going to pay for all that?" Hopkins, as Flanagan recalled, calmly responded to the objection by admitting that the taxpayers would be paying for it as the program would benefit all Americans:

> Then he said, "You are." His voice took on urgency. "And who better? Who can better afford to pay for it? Look at this great university. Look at these fields, these forests, and rivers. This is America, the richest country in the world. We can afford to pay for anything we want. And we want a decent life for all the people in this country. And we are going to pay for it."[2]

Hopkins's whistle-stop campaign was part of a concerted effort by the Roosevelt administration to persuade the American public that its work programs would restore the virtues of traditional work ethics. By temporarily providing work to the unemployed—qualified unemployed it should be noted—the

Figure 1.1 *From left to right*: Virgil Geddes, Hallie Flanagan, and Harry Hopkins at a May 1936 production of Michael Gold and Michael Blankfort's *Battle Hymn* at the Experimental Theater in New York City. *(Box 1214, FTP LC.)*

administration believed they could not only invigorate the economy, but also provide nourishment to workers' souls. Drawing on long-standing views of work relief as well as pragmatic reform, the work of the New Deal was problematic as it was ideologically strained between progressive values and a broader desire to restore capitalism. Yet people like both Hopkins and Flanagan believed the WPA could also enrich the lives of all Americans through providing art—including theater—to those who could not afford it. Like the broader New Deal, the FTP also balanced its pragmatic function with ideological concerns over work, especially in terms of professional acting work norms. Over the course of its history, the FTP attempted to balance its aim as an employment organization with broader aesthetic ideals but ultimately succumbed to internal and external pressures—but not before staging plays that interrogated issues of work within the broader New Deal (see Figure 1.1).

The New Deal Work Ethic

As the historian David Kennedy has observed, the New Deal has become a touchstone of "American political argument, a talisman invoked by all parties to legitimate or condemn as the occasion requires" as the programs of the New Deal are awash in competing, ideological mythologies. Commentators can view the New Deal as a failure by not overturning the capitalist system at the moment of the country's worst economic crisis or the New Deal as an overextension of the government into the private sphere.[3] Kennedy notes that it is better to realize what the New Deal did not do—it did not radically redistribute income, nor did it achieve full economic recovery—and nor was it communist in nature. But Kennedy also notes it is helpful to consider, in evaluating the programs of the Roosevelt administration, that the programs were driven by two concepts: security and work.[4] And certainly, work was on the mind of Roosevelt as early as 1932. In accepting the nomination for president of the United States, he was rather blunt about one of the central aims of his candidacy:

> What do the people of America want more than anything else? To my mind, they want two things: work, with all the moral and spiritual values that go with it; and with work, a reasonable measure of security—security for themselves and for their wives and children. Work and security—these are more than words. They are more than facts. They are the spiritual values, the true goal toward which our efforts of reconstruction should lead.[5]

Work, of course, was also on his mind as Roosevelt sought an economic system that would enable people to work and avoid the "dole"—something that he personally despised. Throughout his presidency, Roosevelt was consistent in condemning direct-relief payments: in 1934, he declared that he had "no intention or desire to force either upon the country or the unemployed themselves a system of relief which is repugnant to American ideals of self-reliance" and while "dependent members of the community who are unable to work" would not be expected to work, the "needy unemployed . . . can give adequate return for the unemployment benefits which they receive."[6] He also declared that he "was not willing that the vitality of our people be further sapped by the giving of cash" as "we must preserve not only the bodies of the unemployed from destitution but also their self-respect, their reliance and courage and determination."[7] And in 1938, he noted that work was always preferable to the dole as the latter only provided the bare minimum to keep "body and soul together."[8]

While there were few commonalities between the various programs of what we loosely term the New Deal, this emphasis on work might be the most consistent thread between the programs. But in many respects, the types of work Roosevelt tended to promote were familiar to traditional adherents of laboring, especially those who promoted a mode of labor that aligned with the hallmarks of the Protestant work ethic as well as long-standing views of charity and relief. While government policies were often more conservative in terms of labor, the rhetoric of the administration, as well as some of its programs, focused on the spiritual benefits to work that resonated with many Americans. Indeed, many of the work programs of the 1930s appear to have been influenced by progressive programs that were concerned with restoring workers' faith in capitalism. Working against long-standing American attitudes toward relief, Roosevelt promoted the idea that temporary work-relief could benefit the American worker. Additionally, other New Dealers saw the work of their programs as having more revolutionary benefits. WPA chief Harry Hopkins claimed that the programs of his program, including those of Federal One, could uplift the spirits of all Americans. For both Roosevelt and Hopkins, government and bureaucracy could restore the spiritual values of work for workers during the Depression.

One of the challenges faced by New Deal planners was promoting work programs to the American people. Historically, Americans, influenced in part by Puritan and Protestant views of charity, have long had a problematic relationship with relief to the unemployed, viewing governmental aid as either "earned" or "unearned" and recipients of aid as "deserving" or "undeserving."[9] The deserving poor were composed of the sick, the widowed, and the weak, while the undeserving poor were composed of women who bore children out of wedlock and any able-bodied men. In nineteenth-century workhouses and farms, there was little distinction between poverty and criminality. Many overseers subjected dole recipients to routine floggings as a means of building "proper" work habits in the underemployed workers.[10] Moreover, the only way for the "undeserving poor" to receive relief was through public and "clearly useless" work such as "digging ditches and filling them up again or moving piles of stones from one side of a workyard to the other and back." Such a provision for relief was intentional, as many believed that such public demonstrations would discourage "anyone who could possibly work for wages from going on relief."[11] These views of relief as earned or unearned have become a hallmark of American social policy, ranging from the "earned" pensions for Civil War veterans to the "unearned" welfare associated with the Child and Welfare Dependent Acts. In her study of the social provision movements of the nineteenth century, Thea Skocpol details how male bureaucrats and politicians focused their legislation on not workers but soldiers and mothers. While attempts to extend such benefits to the broader populace generally failed, "the federal government and forty-some states did enact social spending, labor regulations, and health education programs to help American mothers and children along with women workers who might become mothers."[12]

Like nearly every aspect of the New Deal, the model of work relief adopted by the federal government during the Great Depression was born out of a complicated exchange of an embrace, rejection, or modification of European and Progressive social programs.[13] Of particular interest to many New Dealers was the German Elberfeld system of socialized aid, whose aim was "the cornerstone of an overall strategy of increased discipline of the poor, intended to force an orientation to the labor market and to combat welfare dependency."[14] Aid was not permanent, only a short-term reprieve. By stressing the temporary nature of this aid, proponents of this model believed that workers would develop a stronger sense of self-reliance and would be encouraged to seek employment. While the German system was not devoid of the moralizing that often plagues relief organizations, adherents of the Elberfeld system sought to buoy the spirits of displaced workers. In some cities, the local relief boards even gave more generous support to out-of-work laborers (but not the destitute poor) believing that treating workers with respect would bolster their self-esteem and make them feel as if they were not receiving a handout.[15] By borrowing many ideas from German relief models, as well as similar aid programs from American urban centers of the late-nineteenth century, New Deal work programs convinced many Americans that work relief was a viable solution to economic deprivation. These programs, as Edwin Amenta argues, demonstrated that work relief could function as social welfare without the stigma of the traditional Protestant and Anglican "dole."[16] While work had been a component in some capacity throughout the history of relief, the promotion of temporary aid and/or relief that was only obtainable through work eased the concerns over relief for both the public at large and the unemployed.

Yet the rhetoric and purpose of these work-relief programs often served to both reinforce conservative views of the labor market and unequal hiring and work practices. The purpose of these programs was not simply to ease the burden for the unemployed in the United States, but also to restore aspects of capitalism. Following in line with both the Elberfeld System's aims and most other New Deal programs, the primary driving goal of work relief programs was to prepare its aid recipients to return to the free-market labor system.[17] In a parallel to other New Deal programs that I discuss in Chapters 3, 4, and 5—all of which tried attempted to balance between reengaging and reforming systems like the middle-class economy, the speculative market, and the banking industry—many work-relief programs were tailored to the desires of the larger capitalist marketplace or older models of work-relief. While the CCC provided much-needed environmental improvements and beautification projects across the country, it drew criticism over its relatively low pay[18] and how it aligned with an idea of "the old labor colony" that "had not yet lost its appeal" among not only planners in the United States but also similar programmers in Germany, Britain, and France.[19] Similarly, unions that had long resisted "government adjudication" now "turned to the state to broker new pacts between labor, government, and stability-seeking employers" and found relief in new legislation like the National Labor Relations Act of 1935; it can be argued that the federal government partially "bought off labor's demands for jobs through public works" projects and "emergency makeshifts of resuscitation and relief."[20]

The Roosevelt administration's first attempt of work relief was the Federal Emergency Relief Administration (FERA) in May 1933. Building on the Hoover administration's Emergency Relief and Construction Act and based on the grant proposals of Robert LaFollette and modeled on New York's relief operations, FERA distributed federal aid to individual state relief agencies to "provide both cash aid and aid in kind to all manner of needy family heads and individuals." FERA was increasingly concerned with not only eliminating direct-relief and replacing the dole with work relief programs but also diversifying the type of work offered by the government. In some cases, work relief programs focused on producing products for unemployed or struggling workers who could not afford basic supplies, such as a mattress-making project that would use surplus cotton to produce mattresses and comforters for others on work relief rolls.[21] And after studies commissioned by Hopkins revealed a high percentage of unemployed white-collar workers on relief rolls, FERA began to promote education agencies, domestic projects, and other work programs for women and middle-class workers. But because of the structure of the overall program, and its inability to directly control how states and organizations spent the money, the Roosevelt administration developed two subagencies to further enhance work-relief. The first was the CCC, arguably one of the most popular of New Deal programs. Employing young men in a variety of work projects in fields like forestry, flood control, anti-erosion, conservation, transportation, and recreation development, enrollees would be enlisted for a year in their assigned camps and remit money home to their dependents.[22] The second was the Civil Works Administration (CWA), a more centralized program that would provide work for the winter of 1933–34 to workers on emergency relief and unemployed workers unwilling to apply for work relief. The CWA provided labor-intensive projects that did not utilize the useless "made work" of older work relief models. Instead, CWA work consisted of projects "falling somewhere between constructing sewage systems and the collection of garbage." And although most often CWA workers found themselves "building roads, a wide variety of workers with varied skills were employed" by the program.[23]

By the time of the passage of what many historians have called the Second New Deal in 1935, Roosevelt and Hopkins understood the need for a form of work relief that was not simply about the "made work" of the CWA or the park projects of the CCC. Their new WPA would focus on projects geared toward the public interest (not unlike other New Deal programs), and the WPA built schools, hospitals, roads, airports, hotels, post offices, and monuments across the country, including the Tennessee Valley Authority. Unlike other decentralized programs, the WPA "brought national control over the selection of labor-intensive projects, which were to be proposed mainly by state and local authorities." Moreover, these projects could not compete with private business, and there would be overt attempts to win over support for the project from organized labor by offering workers a prevailing wage rate.[24] But unique to the WPA was also an emphasis on professional work that tailored to the needs of many long-term unemployed in white-collar fields, or, as William F. McDonald termed it, "the white-collar program." Federal Project Number One (often shortened to Federal One), consisted of the Federal Writers Project (FWP), the Federal Art Project (FAP), the Historical Records Survey (HRS), the Federal Music Project (FMP), and the FTP. While prior to the New Deal there were localized agencies in various cities that did provide public projects and aid for unemployed white-collar workers, the idea of national programs that catered toward professional workers was first experimented in the CWA, as bands and chamber ensembles performed free concerts, artists assisted teachers in public schools, and actors gave plays in public parks.[25] In course, each program would produce government-funded art for the general populace and labor opportunities to qualified workers in those fields: the FWP would produce travel and historical guides; the FAP would develop public art and the FTP would stage free to low-cost plays across the country.

Despite its structural limits, the WPA was a lightning rod for attack from the Right. Much of the criticism leveled toward the WPA and its agencies focused on the alleged work ethic (or lack thereof) of its employees. The WPA became the preeminent whipping boy of the Republican Party, as congress-people like Martin Dies made their careers by disavowing its sanctity. This furor was hardly tempered by Hopkins's steadfast support of the agencies, even after the strong accusations the WPA was nothing more than a massive recruiting tool for the Democratic Party heading into the midterm elections of 1938. As Republicans slowly began to win back their losses from 1932 and 1936 and regain political leverage, the WPA was placed under the press of a series of congressional inquiries and reports. Many of these inquiries would argue that the work ethic was suffering under the control of the government. As McDonald reports, many congressional or investigating committees trumped-up accusations of "boondoggling" and claimed that government money was wasted on poultry surveys and eurythmic dancing, and the conservative anti–New Deal press reported accusatory testimony at face value without any critical lens. Perhaps the most famous example of this was the front-page headline of the April 4, 1935, *New York Times*: "$3,187,000 Relief Is Spent to Teach Jobless to Play" with the subheadline of "BOON DOGGLES MADE,"[26] with lurid reporting emphasizing the anger of council members amid claims of graft and waste of taxpayer money—despite the defenses of teachers and workers.[27] The next year, the *New Yorker* cartoonist Robert Day would publish a cartoon in the magazine equating boondoggling with the WPA: in the foreground, several WPA employees stand resting their bodies on their shovels as they snicker at a newly hired worker furiously digging into the ground. Mocking the newcomer, one worker notes that "it's his first day. He's certainly making an ass of himself." New Deal policymakers also had to fend off attacks that their labors were too German, too Soviet, or too un-American in nature. Granted, some of the outcry over the New Deal was the same arguments brought against progressive legislation for decades—the programs were "inefficient and ineffectual . . . they weakened the springs of moral and economic action, that they whetted the appetite of a leviathan state"—but during the 1930s, the accusation of "un-American" lobbed toward New Deal policies was rampant.[28]

But like many New Deal programs, the WPA was also open to criticism from the Left as well. Many prominent intellectuals found the New Deal and its agencies to be as disorganized as American capitalism, exemplary of the confusion and ideological equivocation of Washington. Lewis Mumford lambasted not only the WPA but also the entire New Deal when he argued that the administration's policies were nothing but "aimless experiment, sporadic patchwork, a total indifference to guiding principles or definitive goals, and hence an uncritical drift along the lines of least resistance, namely the restoration of capitalism." Figures like James Burnham and many members of the Communist Party of the USA (CPUSA) equated Roosevelt's policies with the rise of fascism in Europe. Others within the CPUSA "opposed the five-billion-dollar WPA program, arguing that it would reduce wages below the already inadequate limits set under the NRA (National Recovery Act) codes and provide business with a convenient source of cheap labor." The *Nation* and the *New Republic* also criticized Hopkins's program, arguing that it was "just another emergency measure, underfinanced and severely restricted from competing with private enterprise."[29]

But the programs of the WPA, especially Federal One, also ran into hostility from administrators of other New Deal programs—even within the WPA itself. Hopkins's archnemesis Harold Ickes, head of the Public Works Administration (PWA), decried the WPA as a program "based upon an economic and social fallacy" with a goal of putting "men to work, regardless of what they were being put to work at" and because of its "absurdities, its inefficiencies, its bunglings and its graftings" would cost the president the election.[30] This sentiment was echoed by many state WPA administrators who, while happy to accept work relief, but only under "certain conditions" as "they thought primarily in terms of the unskilled laborer and partly because manual labor approached the nature of a work test, which represented their philosophy of relief." Broadly speaking, these administrators also preferred construction projects because they resulted in physical, public projects that could be easily sold to the general populace (certainly, while other programs of Federal One were esoteric in nature, the public murals of the FAP and the Travel Guides of the FWP helped popularize those programs in ways that were more concrete than the FTP had available to it). Moreover, for many administrators, the tendency of these programs to hire women and minorities also increased their general hostility to them.[31]

Additionally, these programs—never adequately funded—often upheld many gender and racial inequalities in American society. While these programs did provide work and jobs for those the marketplace had failed, such as the aged or single female caretakers, giving both groups public support that had been rare in decades past, the limitations of these programs cannot be ignored. Like other nations, the American approach to New Deal work relief was embodied by the "liberal type of welfare state, [one] deemed least favorable to citizens [and] . . . devoted to making markets run smoothly, by making public spending low in amount and degrading in delivery."[32] Policies, even in the WPA, anticipated one family breadwinner, who was presumed to be male in most instances and, in turn, often limited women's access to government work. Presuming that most private sector work was incredibly scarce, in many states local administrators and governments reworked stipends for working women to reinforce gender work stereotypes. As Linda Gordon notes, the New Deal work programs helped cement a bifurcated welfare state that marginalized women, especially single mothers who could not take advantage of unemployment relief.[33] For Black Americans, especially in the years of the First New Deal, work relief was rare, especially in the South, where local administrators barred work opportunities to Black workers. To be fair, WPA hiring policies prevented discrimination and Black workers constituted 14 percent of WPA employees in 1939. But while WPA programs afforded more work opportunities for Black workers than the private sector, work was harder to come by for Blacks in the South, especially in rural areas, suggesting blatant discrimination. Black women were doubly disadvantaged, "suffering racial discrimination as well as the program's biases against female family heads."[34]

As controversy surrounded the programs of the WPA, especially Federal One, Hopkins became one of the program's biggest advocates and often laid out a revolutionary vision for the WPA and Federal One. In addition to touring the country speaking on behalf of the WPA, Hopkins also penned a treatise on the benefits of the Second New Deal entitled *Spending to Save: The True Story of Relief.* In that book, Hopkins stresses the importance of New Deal legislation and the idea that the work of its programs could uplift the spirits of Americans from the rigors of the Depression. In the chapter dedicated to the WPA, Hopkins adamantly argues that people who demonstrate talent and skill have the right to earn a wage for their labor. And just as farmers or factory workers have the right to procure living wages, so do the skilled professionals of the arts and humanities. Hopkins argues that it is the labor of teachers, historians, artists, and performers that provide the "greatest contributions" to American society, even if those contributions are less tangible than the public works projects of other agencies.[35] Hopkins also connects these workers' dedication to their craft with the calling of the Protestant work ethic:

> If it is more ironical for one person to be on relief than another it is seen in the fact that scientists, writers, musicians and all the rest of those persons, who by the virtue of gifts and discipline have arrived in that upper fraction of the people ... should find themselves without recognition, livelihood, or any means to continue the benefits which only they can bestow.[36]

By emphasizing their virtues and gifts, Hopkins argues that these workers can transform American society. While manual laborers can produce creature comforts in a modern society, the artist can improve the quality of life of the American populace. Art can envelop the senses and offer beauty to the people and writers can assist the government in creating educated men and women or, as Hopkins terms them, "thousands of new literates." In his grandiose language, Hopkins would further suggest that WPA workers of Federal One could assist in an "upward movement of labor." This new movement would alleviate the suffering of workers by filling their lives with "something more than the competitive struggle for existence." Hopkins concludes his chapter on the arts programs of the WPA by envisioning a new work paradigm: "If leisure, once the privilege only of the rich, is now to belong to everybody, one objective of any move to share the world's wealth has already been accomplished. It would be curious if we found that the mastering and enjoyment of this leisure, which was forced upon us under such economic stress, would be the means of easing that same stress." He concludes by noting that frequently war was often the solution for unemployment but that this new paradigm may prove more effective than "blood-letting" to ease unemployment.[37]

For New Dealers, the solutions to the Depression and, by extension, the repression of workers were the federal attempts to restore Americans' faith in work. As Roosevelt often noted, the temporary work given to the unemployed during the 1930s was as much about restoring the self-worth of workers as it was about reinvigorating the economy. At the same time, figures like Hopkins believed that the ultimate benefit of specialized work programs would be a dramatic shift in the work experiences of all Americans. While Hopkins's belief in the more radical possibilities of New Deal programs was very likely not shared by Roosevelt, many of the heads of Federal One programs felt that their work could contribute to a great shift in the American experience. And perhaps no leader felt as strongly about the capacity of a program to accomplish Hopkins's aims than Hallie Flanagan.

Acting Work and FTP Work

One of the most frequently mentioned anecdotes of the FTP concerns Richard Wright's work as a publicity agent with the Chicago Negro Unit, a time he did not reflect on kindly. Writing in his memoir, Wright recalled advocating for an evening of one-act plays, including Paul Green's *A Hymn to the Rising Sun*, but the unit almost immediately fractured over the content of the play, with an actor, to Wright's recollection, claiming the play "indecent" and preferring work that would "make the public love us." Scoffing at their reasoning, Wright comments that Black actors should be tired of being forced to don the "stereotypes of clowns, mammies, razors, dice, watermelons, and cotton fields." After researching their work records in the office, Wright found that most of the actors "spent their lives playing cheap vaudeville" and now were protesting "legitimate theater" because, in his reading, the actors were "scared spitless at the prospects of appearing in a play that the public might not like, even though they did not understand that public and had no way of determining its likes or dislikes."[38]

While I return to the Chicago Unit in Chapter 4, this anecdote serves to illustrate the often bitter splits that would occur within the FTP at both the unit level and nationally as many disagreed over what type of theater it should produce. For many within the FTP, the theater staged by the program should embrace a more radical aesthetic, but for others, the FTP should promote theater that had remained popular with audiences and proved commercially viable. In this sense, the actors who advocated for the latter paralleled larger, more conservative New Deal views of work with their own sense of theatrical work: drawing on the evolution and general acceptance of acting in the United States, they understood their own work ethic as one that ran counter to the more radical work promoted by others in the theater program. But even then, there remained a great deal of ideological vacillation as much of this work both advocated for and challenged the FTP and the New Deal overall.

Historically, acting and work were considered antithetical concepts in many circles, perhaps most notably with Puritan culture. As Jonas Barish shows, the Puritans saw the stage as symbolizing "a whole complex of attitudes anathema to the sober burgesses" of proper Londoners. For the Puritan, the stage "stood for pleasure, for idleness, for the rejection of hard work and thrift as the roads to salvation. Its siren song held prentices from work and fickle parishioners from the church pew."[39] This antitheatrical view was carried to the United States, as there remained a very strict reading of the work of actors as eponymous with vile aspects of society—equating prostitution with acting as well as other criminal elements with actors themselves. But the general importance of acting and its prominent role in American culture—especially in urban areas—began to shift the sensibilities of Americans away from strict moralist readings. This changing view of theatrical labor can be explained, in part, by how theater functioned on a micro level as a representation of democratic participation. Around the time of the Civil War, the theatrical realm was a leisurely communal space where a motley collection of artisanal republicans and members of the middle and upper classes engaged in "directing actors on stage, demanding encores . . . or booing people off stage."[40]

These views became more codified as the profession began to be more integrated into the capitalist space. As railroads allowed more traveling productions to tour the country and as local theaters (both professional and amateur) flourished nationally, audiences began to see the value of theatrical labor in all forms ranging from variety shows to broad melodrama (an impulse that would increase with the rise of film and then radio). Theater was "becoming less a process of discovering what will appeal and more a plan for inventing the product and creating the audience."[41] Producers "operated primarily as venture capitalists" who could not only market a product to an audience but also sell their larger-than-life personas to align with grand narratives of American capitalism.[42] Meanwhile other capitalists like B. F. Keith and Edward Albee, as well as film studio bosses, attempted to "create networks of business entertainment that integrate[ed] all aspects of the industry into an expansive, unified system of production, distribution, exhibition, and reception." By gaining control of all aspects of the system itself, these figures became entertainment robber barons.[43]

Similarly, there was an overlap between the world of consumerism and leisure—approaches to life that were often already intertwined—and the placement of acting and theater within those confines. There was a connection between "the display of merchandise" and the "consumption" of spectacle borrowed from the realm of entertainment. The "merchandising of desire was already a theatrical rule of operation" and shopping was simply "the continuation, by other means, of the public delight in curiosities, spectacles, and feats of wonder that were offered up in the world of entertainment." And when patrons went into theater buildings or movie houses, they were "even more splendid displays, from spectacular scenic wonders in melodramas to continuous shows at the vaudeville houses, where each performer seemed more striking and curious than the one who went before."[44] This consumerist bent then transferred into the broader consumption of leisure itself, wherein the spectacle of what was placed before a person was slowly being understood as a form of labor being presented to a spectator. One of the major ways in which acting began to be more broadly accepted by Americans was a reconditioning in how most Americans understood the concept of entertainment. While entertainment and leisure had often been promoted as participatory in nature—as evidenced by the litany of philosophers and intellectuals who preached the value of work as leisure—by the 1920s, Americans began to consider singing, dancing, baseball, and other activities not as something to do but as something to watch. And increasingly, the nature of that entertainment was not just professional sports like baseball, boxing, or horse racing, but performative fields like commercial theater, cinema, vaudeville, and the night club circuit—all of which afforded the leisure of entertainment to people from all class backgrounds.

Moreover, actors and other theatrical professionals had utilized the burgeoning mass media to both promote theatrical performances and themselves, as publications provided their readers information about actors' personal lives, displays of their homes, descriptions of their personas, and estimates of their incomes. This crystalized the sense that performers were exceptional personalities unbound by traditional social restraints, and this interest would also fuel the rise of backstage musicals and comedies to placate the public's growing interest in the infrastructures of acting and celebrity.[45] These public personas helped cement a cultural expectation for modeling on the stage and on screen that would exemplify social and cultural norms, and slowly acting became, more and more, intertwined with positive representations of middle-class life. As Mark Franko argues, the precision of a chorus line in a large-scale Broadway show evoked the ideology of Taylorism; as such, conservative commentators were more accepting of such performances as labor because they represented a connection to certain social and cultural norms.[46] Similarly, many commentators praised comic texts—like the sentimental work of Chaplin or many of the comic work plays examined in this project—that represented the values and ideological perspectives of the upper and middle class.[47] And even more broadly, theatrical and cinematic labor became symbolic of more modern views of working—especially in the 1920s as "actors embodied a different ethic, one that harmonized with an urban society that was no longer convinced of the older virtues." As more and more people became enamored of leisure, consumption, and personal image, actors and their celebrity became "paragons of freedom . . . models of lifestyle" that represented a shift from "an ethic of strict moral demands to one of permissive self-fulfillment."[48]

This reinforcement of model norms was also found in community theater movements of the era. Upholding Progressive Era–genteel values, many theater groups often served as the training ground for many female professional actors, while college theater programs helped train young women actors for future nontheatrical professions. As Dorothy Chansky argues, the rise of higher-education theater programs helped convince Americans that women could earn a respectable living as educators with theater training. While theater studies students constituted a small percentage of the overall college population, Chansky asserts that there was a surge in the employment opportunities for unmarried women in high schools for teaching theater courses. In the minds of many reformers of the era, trained professional women who could teach theater would "persuade insiders and outsiders that theatre . . . could serve America's needs," as women could both provide students with a work ethic and "impart the building blocks of citizenship within an industrialized world characterized by systematized schemas for nearly everything from the production of goods to ideas of personal hygiene."[49] This belief that the teaching of theater, with its emphasis on acting, set design, and cooperation, would help students adjust to a new work environment was part of a larger cultural movement that sought to manage the "practical" and the "creative" in education. By the mid-1920s, this model of teaching theater had helped give theater and other creative arts an increased cultural legitimacy.

Despite the broader acceptance of acting labor in American culture, there were increasing divisions over the nature of theatrical work within acting spaces. Perhaps the biggest divide that would carry over into the FTP were the competing visions between modernist approaches to theater and commercial acting. Beginning in the late-nineteenth century, many playwrights and directors wanted to either remove some of what they perceived as blatant, commercial excesses from theater—the overbearing producers, vain stars, and hackneyed playwrights—and reform theater into a different space. Even more aggravating to many modernist thinkers was how the theatrical experience—especially the randomness of an individual audience—was distracting from what they privileged more than anything else: the sanctity and complexity of the script.[50] By the end of the Great War, plays began to appear on the Broadway stage that were written by playwrights who were influenced by European theatrical movements and the works of Ibsen, Shaw, and Chekov. As James Fisher notes, as the work of figures like Eugene O'Neill, Robert Sherwood, Lillian Hellman, and Thornton Wilder became more prevalent, some celebrity actors began to both resent and challenge this new generation of playwrights, preferring to instead gravitate toward fare they deemed more economically viable. Perhaps the most outspoken of these figures was George Cohan, who not only strove to engage in fare that was "pleasing" to "an older generation of playgoers" but also publicly condemned the newer plays. Writing in *Liberty* magazine in 1936, Cohan admonished newer Broadway works that ignored what he felt was an essential credo of theater: "when you're in the entertainment business, you must realize that the first rule is never consciously to offend anybody" and that "our latter-day trouble is that our so-called problem plays focus on one problem—sex in its vagaries." Casting blame at Ibsen, Cohan lamented that "writers of less eloquence but far more impudence have grown bolder step by step, until to create new sensations and shocks . . . the boys have had to drag out homosexuality and heaven or hell knows what next."[51] It should be noted that these views would not preclude Cohan from appearing in a production of O'Neill's *Ah, Wilderness!* (more on that in Chapter 3), but nevertheless, there remained an impulse among many professional actors to engage in work that was more focused on pleasing an audience rather than engage with the more problematic elements of society. This conflict also extended to views of comic performance as more modernist, gag, or vaudeville comic performers were positioned in opposition to more traditional forms of comic acting. Through the latter-half of the nineteenth century, "legitimate theater" emphasized the displacement of the audience and performers as seen in melodrama or other forms of theater and placed the emphasis on crafting a sense of a homogenous verisimilitude in performance, shifting away from an individual performer's ability to "stop the show" and toward an ensemble "group art" where every actor embraced their place in the overall performance. The old-star system was now considered antagonistic to realist theater, as many producers and theorists felt that attracting too-known an actor—especially in stock companies—permitted audiences to attach themselves to one performer, and even curtain calls, save for the close of a show, were discouraged.[52]

Exacerbating the divide within acting over the nature of theatrical work was the dire employment situation for theater workers in the 1920s and 1930s. Indeed, the professional theater market had been struggling even before the Great Depression began, as even in the 1910s, increasing transportation costs, as well as rising costs in materials and wages, forced many traveling companies to cut back on their circuits, "eliminating more and more of the 'one-night stands'" in cities. In turn, many theatergoers began to complain about poorer-quality productions coming their way, and many began to invest their time in the growing Little Theatre Movement.[53] The major factor in the closing of theaters or the reduction of bookings for theaters was the growing popularity of cinema. Whereas in the nineteenth and early twentieth centuries, traveling shows and commercial theaters in most cities had allowed many Americans to see many of the same theatre productions nationally, by the 1930s, theater had become a far more localized experience as community theaters filled the void left by the growing dearth of professional theaters. In addition, those cities where professional theater still maintained its foothold—New York, Chicago, Philadelphia, and similar cities—theater became increasingly an extraordinary event for its patrons, not a more routine occurrence as theatergoing had been in previous decades. This was of course in contrast to cinema attendance, which was not only more affordable to audiences during the Depression but also in many ways far more democratic in its appeal. But an industry that was already unhealthy became that much worse post-1929, as, for instance, 213 of 253 companies in New York had closed or suspended operations by May 1932, while members of Actor's Equity saw a 50 percent drop in employment during the same time.[54]

Nor was it just commercial, realist theater suffering with the onset of the Depression, as forms like both vaudeville and amateur, modernist theater also struggled. Vaudeville circuits struggled with declining attendance throughout the era, as larger venues in New York and Chicago struggled financially and smaller venues often outright closed. Moreover, many comic artists that had become synonymous with vaudeville circuits, such as Eddie Cantor, W. C. Fields, and Mae West, had long left for Hollywood, better pay, and reduced traveling schedules, while other performers who had only recently become stars on the circuit—Abbott and Costello, the Three Stooges, Milton Berle—transitioned into cinema or radio.[55] The Depression was also a challenge for many amateur theaters in the United States, which had also been struggling through the 1920s. Recounting the rise of the Little Theatre Movement, Karen Blair notes that the movement itself was in considerable disarray with the breakdown of the Drama League of America in May 1931, as the organization was, for all intents and purposes, bankrupt. While amateur theater remained strong in various parts of the country, especially in the Midwest, nationally the system had suffered from its own success. Volunteers who had built and supported the Drama League were often replaced by professional directors and workers looking for opportunities within Little Theatre or replaced by women university graduates who had studied theater in school—a goal born out of the view within the Little Theatre Movement of expanding university opportunities for women interested in theater. Amateur theater also suffered from the competition from cinema—a fact that many within the movement began to recognize: "One writer, for example, observed the seemingly irreconcilable tension between the little theater's wish to challenge mass culture and its hunger for mass support. Helen Deutsch admitted that her peers in the little theater movement 'expect little theatres to be experimental.' Most audiences simply wanted plays to be fun."[56]

To run the FTP and provide relief to theater workers, Hopkins selected Hallie Flanagan who would, in many respects, share his view of the capacity of art to enact a new work paradigm. A former classmate of Hopkins at Grinnell College, Flanagan had developed a theater program at the Iowa university and later worked with George Pierce Baker at 47 Workshop at Harvard. After becoming the director of Vassar's experimental theater program, Flanagan became the first woman awarded a Guggenheim Fellowship to study European theater. She was particularly taken with post-Bolshevik Russian theater, which, while propagandistic, could elevate "the stage beyond mere entertainment or luxury to become a vital center for community building."[57] Flanagan carried these experiences and her own artistic ideology to the FTP, believing one of the aims was to bring high art to the masses:

> Was it not true, however, that for the worker in the theatre as well as for the painter, sculptor, or musician, connection with a much wider audience must be established? Was it not our function to extend the boundaries of theatre-going, to create a vigorous new audience, to make the theatre of value to more people? Over the past decade free concerts and free musical instruction in the schools, not to mention radio and recordings, had made it possible for everyone to hear music. . . . But theatre instruction in schools was limited, and aside from a few community theatres throughout the country, there was no way in which people could go to the theatre.[58]

While the FTP would provide theater to audiences that had no access to quality productions, Flanagan also envisioned a new model of theater. For her, the FTP should be "socially and politically, aware of the new frontier in America, a frontier not narrowly political or sectional, but universal, a frontier along which tremendous battles are being fought against ignorance, disease, unemployment, poverty and injustice."[59] She envisioned a national theater that was both listening to the needs of the American people and remaking the work and art of the stage. In her mind, the work of the FTP was not to satisfy the tastes of the "first ten rows" of theater patrons on Broadway but to engage new audiences across the country. This impulse grew from her initial conversations about the program with Hopkins. As Hopkins would advise Flanagan after she accepted the job: "It's got to be run by a person who isn't interested just in the commercial type of show. I know something about the plays you've been doing for ten years, plays about American life. This is an American job, not just a New York one."[60] Indeed, Hopkins's dictate encouraged Flanagan to emphasize theatrical work that sought to both change the minds of audiences and to create a new relationship between audiences and the stage. She was both very aware of the challenges facing theater, which had been superseded by radio and film, as well as the need to recapture the prominence that theater had in the nineteenth century. To achieve this, she reasoned, theater must move away from the commercial and traditional. Flanagan noted that "theatre must wake up and grow up" and move away from its clinging "to melody, to the facade, to the sentimentality" and listen to the "age in which men are whispering through space."[61]

In enacting this vision for new theatrical labor that could uplift the spirits of audiences, Flanagan enacted several structural elements that problematized her vision. Partly inspired by the words of Eleanor Roosevelt, who suggested that quality performances could be on par with her Vassar work sans the budgets of Broadway productions, Flanagan implemented this vision in the broader structure of the FTP itself. This was especially true in the hiring of regional directors, only a few of whom had commercial theater backgrounds. For example, Flanagan selected E. C. Mabie from the University of Iowa to oversee the Midwest, Thomas Wood Stevens for Chicago, and John McGee of Birmingham little theater to head the South region.[62] As Lauren Rebecca Skarloff notes, "the selection of directors was based on their ability to envision the theater beyond a commercial institution," and as various controversies over specific productions would show, this "initial emphasis on the noncommercial aspect of the project would later lead many in Congress to question the economic purpose of federal relief programs."[63] This was part of a broader confusion over the aims of the program, all of which contradicted one another and caused vexation among directors and administrators. On October 8, 1935, the recently appointed regional directors met with Flanagan and WPA staff in Washington, DC. In this meeting, Flanagan "proceeded to contrast the passing of individual patronage [commercial theater] with the new emphasis upon the theater as an agency of democratic education," and then representatives from the Treasury and the WPA explained governmental procedure. At the end of these meetings, one regional director immediately resigned and "others were dissuaded with difficulty from following his example." What these regional managers saw was the promotion of a regional, democratic, and avant-garde theater that required "something more than actors whose background was exclusively professional."[64] Indeed, when the directors listened to Flanagan, "they were persuaded to think in terms of a new art theatre"; when they read *Instructions* (a guidebook published by the FTP outlining protocol) "they were persuaded that a permanent community theater was the aim"; and when they interacted with WPA officials, regional directors "concluded that the sole purpose of the project was the employment of professional actors."[65]

Despite the need for the FTP, many in the professional theater community resisted the national program. Some of this was born from a broader resentment toward the program from workers not employed by the FTP. For these workers, especially those working in the larger theatrical markets, the FTP posed competition by offering many productions of plays that were still being staged on Broadway with low-cost or free attendance (generally, the FTP would stage their more experimental plays in major markets for this reason). And many professional actors and producers felt that the productions and the talent in the FTP were hardly high quality.[66] The Broadway playwright and screenwriter Sidney Howard clearly made his opinion of the FTP known to Flanagan in a letter he sent to his Workshop 47 classmate: "I do feel . . . that by far the greater part of our unemployed actors should be hurried out of acting a [sic] quickly as possible . . . and relieved of the constant misery of encouragement in a profession for which they are not qualified."[67] The charge that the agencies of Federal One were hiring unqualified (amateur) workers was a common refrain throughout their histories. In particular, the Federal Dance Project (a subagency of the FTP) was accused of hiring amateur dancers by the professional National Dance League.[68]

Moreover, many FTP employees, especially those actors trained on the New York and Chicago stages and theater directors who had been successful in regional and stock theaters, resisted Flanagan's aesthetic vision. As Jane De Hart Matthews notes, the FTP was dominated by a "New Deal cultural elite" whose tastes favored experimental theater and conflicted with not only the tastes of many audiences but also the theatrical professionals performing the plays.[69] While Flanagan and many of her colleagues advocated for the performance of experimental and avant-garde plays to liven up the dead horse of professional theater, many of the very people Flanagan was to hire— theatrical professionals—were incredibly hesitant to engage in overly political theater. Not only were many commercial theater workers hesitant to change their approach to acting, but they were also concerned that the overt political theater would endanger the program itself.[70] This was especially true in cities where community and Little Theatre companies had succeeded by producing mainstream plays.[71] Moreover, many avant-garde or high-modernist theatrical groups of the era were financial failures. While such groups as the Theatre Guild and the Group Theatre found varying levels of success with less commercially viable works, groups like the New Playwright's Theatre or the Theatre Union struggled financially.[72] And as nearly every history of the FTP has noted, the emphasis on political theater endangered it at a national level. Living newspaper plays often promoted leftist principles and drew the ire of conservatives, while a children's play like *The Revolt of the Beavers* was condemned by Republicans and anticommunists as propaganda aimed at indoctrinating youth to be agents of Moscow.

Flanagan, to her credit, often attempted to downplay such concerns that the FTP was only focused on staging radical plays and hiring undeserving or underqualified talent. Partially as a response to criticism from Broadway circles that most of the workers employed by her program were untalented, Flanagan argued that her job was to work with all her workers on relief. As Mark Franko asserts, the FTP relied on an expansion of the term *professional worker*—as critics long equaled "professional" with a "critical and commercial evaluation of skill" while "worker" meant "an egalitarian standard" or "unemployed."[73] Franko argues that Flanagan's position "does more than characterize unskilled labor: it generates theatrical power." He writes, "By recognizing the power of performance to inhere in experience as much as training, her statements turned professionalism on its head . . . the transferential working-class body as a theatrical vehicle devoid of skills but demonstrating something perhaps as important as skills."[74] But such attempts to reframe the narrative surrounding the work of the FTP only went so far: many FTP employees resented the implication and connection to other workers, and the program continued to be attacked from both the political right and left.[75] Both Flanagan and Hopkins felt that they had to placate the Right in Washington and in the press, especially after 1938, and appointments were made to conservative theater producers in New York City. Meanwhile, Flanagan also grew tired of attacks from the Left within the program as artists complained about censorship and unions called for strikes and protested job cuts. As the program dragged on, Flanagan became much more embittered privately even if publicly she remained optimistic.[76]

Structurally, the FTP struggled with a range of internal issues that also endangered the work of the program itself. One of the major problems facing the FTP was its cost and bureaucracy. Because the program was required to spend 90 percent of its budget on labor and just 10 percent on productions, any budgetary cut (or specter of budget cuts) created serious problems for productions and generated unease among casts and workers. Moreover, the amount of bureaucratic effort to stage a play was often daunting as state directors had to submit forms for salaries and other funds in a confusing sextuplicate system. Such bureaucratic inefficiency did not endear the program to many administrators who ended up resigning than deal with such hassle.[77] In turn, the more democratic approach to governance, while standard for WPA operations, led to several problems for job stability for actors as many regional and local theater directors took the ethos of "free, adult, and uncensored" theater to heart and staged plays that did not attract local audiences. Recounting the failure of the Milwaukee FTP, Flanagan notes that Milwaukee had a plethora of talented actors who had trained at prestigious theaters like "the London Gate Theatre, the Moscow Art Company, [and] the Dublin Abbey."[78] Yet the plays chosen by director Laura Sherry were "too special for the wide diversity of people our company, if it wished to succeed, must attract."[79] Plays like *The Mask and the Face*, *Old Heidelberg*, and *Three-Cornered Moon* were not "appropriate to Milwaukee" and were "reminiscent of a Little Theatre season."[80] She offered a similar critique of the unit in Omaha. While the Nebraska Federal Theatre was cut after the FTP's overall budget was slashed in 1937, it garnered critical support from the press and a massive letter writing campaign from locals who were determined to save it. But even with the relative success of the unit, Flanagan bemoaned that such theaters were not challenging their audiences. In reference to Omaha and the excitement generated locally by the Nebraska Federal Theatre, Flanagan wrote that "we did no classics, no originals, and none of the 'interpretations of the political and social trend of the times.'"[81] Due to increasingly poor play choices by regional offices, political pressure, charges from the press, and other WPA agents who accused the FTP of only staging overtly leftist productions, Flanagan understood that she needed to exert control over what plays were being performed by the FTP. In 1937, she established the National Service Bureau (NSB). This "umbrella" organization was charged with duties ranging from streamlining costs to transferring costumes and scenery from unit to unit. In addition, the bureau would be "the sole negotiating agency" for the entire project, drawing up contracts with playwrights to produce their plays and ensuring the Play Policy Board, one of the NSB's subagencies, would have greater control over play selection.[82]

The interventions over play choice by the program also signal another issue with FTP work: the overriding role of the government as an "author" in the productions and the subsequent impact that would have on both play stability and the nature of actors' work. While the FTP promoted the ethos of "free, adult, and uncensored," there were a range of considerations over the political impact of plays and their content therein. Two of the most infamous incidents of FTP government censorship center on two canceled productions: the first was of the living newspaper play, *Ethiopia*, which caricatured Benito Mussolini and critiqued Italy's invasion of that African nation—a fact that caused the US State Department to protest the planned production, fearing the repercussions of a government-produced play that openly mocked a foreign head of state. The second was John Houseman and Orson Welles's production of Marc Blitzstein's *The Cradle Will Rock* in 1937. While the play was officially shut down due to a combination of union issues and cost, many felt (and many critics still assert) that the play was canceled due to its strong pro-union message. And while Flanagan herself was generally more open to a range of plays being produced by the FTP, even if she wanted challenging fare, many local theaters struggled to appease the whims of state WPA administrators—many of whom interfered with or restricted productions. A notorious instance of this was in California where Donald "Colonel" Connelly, the local WPA administrator, was found to be editing content out of several plays or closing productions that he felt were too controversial for his state, such as when he shut down a production of Elmer

Rice's critique of fascist Germany, *Judgment Day*, because he believed the play to be communist in nature.[83] Within the broader WPA this dynamic led, as Michael Szalay argues, to federally funded artwork that bore no semblance of political radicalism or liberation but a new standard of conservatism that diminished the role of the artist and promoted digestible art to consumers on behalf of the state. Focusing on the FWP, Szalay argues that many of the writers who applied for work with that program were not interested in dynamic political or social reform but merely wanted security from the demands and dangers of the marketplace. Federal One, by extension, functioned akin to the Social Security Act, providing writers opportunities to engage in work that was "no longer dependent on the public's response to what in fact the labor did produce."[84] While this employment bargain did free writers from the demands of the marketplace—Szalay notes that many employed by the FWP were high modernists whose work did not resonate with the public—the quality of the Travel Guides produced were inconsistent and simply regurgitated information consumers already knew and understood.[85] In exchange for providing writers the opportunity to be "free from the perils of the marketplace" and to, on occasion, give particular voice and style to their product, the various government agencies controlled the message and the space of the author's product as "He was a professional writer and a client of the state, but decidedly not an author."[86]

But this is not to say the work of the FTP could not balance the conflicting governmental elements and differing views of labor to present ideologically complicated plays. Despite attempts to control the content of plays, actors were still able to project political arguments in their performances. This stood in contrast to a project like the FWP wherein project head Henry Alsberg could edit or rewrite an offending passage in a guidebook before publication, but an FTP performer could, in "actual performance," inflect political intent even if a script had been edited.[87] But of particular interest to me was the expectation for many of the programs of Federal One, including the FTP, to work in conjunction with other New Deal agencies to promote those programs. The plays performed by the FTP had a complicated ideological relationship with the broader New Deal, as performances often served to promote other New Deal legislation and programs—but this was not universal. Without question, planners of the WPA saw the capacity of the arts programs to serve as vehicles to promote federal reform or other agencies. Perhaps the most far-reaching of these approaches were posters produced by FAP artists that not only promoted performances of the FTP but also helped recruit workers for the CCC, and touted the accomplishments of the TVA and other programs. Woody Guthrie was also hired by the Bonneville Power Administration to write songs promoting hydroelectric power, while Rexford Tugwell of the Resettlement Administration commissioned Pare Lorentz to film the documentary *The Plow That Broke the Plains*, which illustrated the causes of the Dust Bowl.[88] Despite the repeated objections of Flanagan to critics that the program was not engaged in New Deal propaganda, many FTP plays promoted New Deal ideological positions. For instance, the play *Power*, which shows characters who argue for the public ownership of utilities and portrays how access to electricity is controlled by trusts and capitalists, was performed at the height of the debate over the Tennessee Valley Authority. As Barry Witham notes, "even a cursory reading of the play" is startling to "the degree to which the private sector is hounded and vilified" and facts become "'dramatized' into New Deal propaganda."[89] But there was a tradition of FTP plays voicing some skepticism of New Deal policies, even in living newspaper plays, which skewed more politically left. *One Third of a Nation* concludes with the argument that New Deal legislation would help America in fighting its slums, yet the play mentions that the stripped-down Wagner-Steagall Act will only provide limited resources for the poor. *Triple A Plowed Under* documents the struggles of the agricultural industry but also openly critiques the Agricultural Adjustment Administration (AAA), especially that organization's treatment of Black sharecroppers and the high prices of meat and other goods because of the AAA's strategy of supply reduction.

As Leslie Frost notes, the work—in this sense the plays staged—of the FTP were too vast to fit into one stable definition. While many agents and administrators within the program wanted to dispense with "the usual products of Broadway and Hollywood, no matter how good," and focus on the work of Shaw, Peters, Anderson, and Green, the program overall often focused on fare that was "classic, comfortable, and familiar" as units often staged Moliere, Gilbert and Sullivan, and Shakespeare.[90] This duality within the program was born not simply from a "New Deal cultural elite" but also of different competing visions over the work that the program should do—and for many professionally inclined theater workers, that vision was reinforced by changing views of theatrical labor. But just because such views were more commercial and less modernist in scope, that does not mean these performances were apolitical.

Backstage Comedies

Detailing the musical revue *O Say Can You Sing*, Elizabeth Osborne illustrates a litany of changes made from the play's first script to its production script—including the toning down of a nefarious theatrical producer who bore some resemblance to Hallie Flanagan as well as a Russian theater director character who wanted to stage a modern adaptation of *Uncle Tom's Cabin*.[1] But the play also presents an awareness of work relief and FTP politics. In the musical's finale, entitled "Out of the Red and Into the Blue," actors sing about their status as workers and communicate pro-American sentiments by projecting themselves not as ardent leftists or dole-abusing workers: instead, they promote a more conservative vision of laboring while reminding their audiences that the work of the FTP is merely temporary; relief is simply a stepping stone for more permanent work for these actors:

> *And we'll sing the praise of better days in view—*
> *There'll be no more grief—*
> *We'll forget relief—*
> *When we're out of the red and into the blue!*[2]

Reading the lyrics, it is difficult to not read the overall tone of positivity, especially the "can do" attitude, of the performers that parallels the rhetoric of traditional work norms. And the phrase *out of the red* signals an awareness of both the "red" deficit of Keynesian economic spending as well as a winking acknowledgment of the FTP's own alleged communist infiltration. Any interest in leftist philosophies is merely temporary—just as the relief work of the FTP and the rest of the WPA is just temporary labor.

The performers in "Out of the Red and Into the Blue" still demonstrate a need for the work they do—and this chapter examines three backstage comedies that both wrestle with the complicated nature of theatrical work in the FTP and argue for theater itself. In productions of George Kelly's *The Torch-Bearers*, performers satirize tenets of amateur theater while also advocating for the opportunities afforded women in the arts programs of Federal One. Advocacy for economic security is also promoted by productions of Allen Boretz and John Murray's *Room Service*, wherein theater workers are shown living in near-poverty conditions. But *Room Service* also suggests that overt political content can endanger the production of a play. These thematic issues coalesce in Richard Maibaum's play *A Moral Entertainment*, which focuses on a troupe of actors arrested by Puritans in colonial Massachusetts for endangering the morals of the town. The play demonstrates the importance of job security for actors but also acknowledges the threats to the acting profession posed by government security, overt political performance, and a hostile audience that reads political content in every performance. Taken together, these plays argue for both the existence of the FTP and assert reforms to the program for its survival (see Figure 2.1).

An Overview of Backstage Comedies

In her essay "The Self-Reflexive Musical," Jane Feuer examines musicals produced primarily at the height of the studio-system in Hollywood that affirm their own value as an art form to their audiences. These films, primarily within the backstage space of a theater (or the broader infrastructure of theater), feature performances that both fail to and later succeed in satisfying audiences to "create a myth about the musical entertainment permeating ordinary life."[3] For Feuer, these mythmaking strategies serve "to give pleasure to audiences by revealing what goes on behind the scenes in theater or Hollywood," thereby demystifying the art. But these films also reconstruct the art by presenting three other modes of mythmaking: myth of spontaneity (a performer's joyous embrace of performance), the myth of integration (how an individual can be integrated into a community where high and low art can merge), and the myth of audience (how audiences are shown to be enjoying the diegetic performance in a film to show the film audience how to respond to the musical overall). These tropes, Feuer argues, function within these musicals as a ritual celebration, specifically to "reaffirm and articu-

Figure 2.1 Roslinda (Patricia Mackin) is placed under arrest during the trial scene of the Boston production of *A Moral Entertainment*. *(Retrieved from https://www.loc .gov/item/musftpphotoprints.200223124/.)*

late the place that entertainment occupies in its audience's psychic lives."[4] These films seek to "perpetuate rather than deconstruct the codes of the genre" and demonstrate that the musical can withstand social and cultural forces that threaten its status as an important art form.

While Feuer's analysis mainly concerns postwar films, her arguments about self-reflexive musicals serve as a template for my reading of the back-stage comedies of the FTP. To be certain, there are some significant differences between these texts and those Feuer discusses—namely, differences in genre and medium, as well as the myth of spontaneity present in the films she discusses. But despite these differences, the backstage comedies of the FTP function in much the same way as the self-reflexive musicals: they both serve to entertain their audiences and reinforce their status as an art form in the face of changes and threats to the art form. But whereas innovative technology like television was threatening the musicals of the 1950s, the FTP backstage comedies are dealing with the environment of the 1930s. These plays vacillate between reinforcing dominant mythologies and ideologies of the stage and demystifying those same viewpoints. Moreover, these plays are not simply advocating for the need for theater but also are responding to internal divisions over theatrical labor within the FTP, as well as the conflict over overtly political theater in the program itself.

Unlike the other genres of plays examined in this project, backstage comedies are part of a stable broader genre, sharing a great deal in common with the backstage musical. In general, both forms focus on the infrastructure of theater and its productions, especially on the lives of its performers and directors. The primary motivation for the characters is the professional need to "put on a show," and overcome a series of problematic challenges to the performance within the play. Aside from their generic differences, the genres split over their treatment of the play within a play. Traditionally, theatrical backstage texts remain primarily focused on the overarching show as the play within a play is performed offstage, while the backstage musical builds to a more developed play within a play. Additionally, backstage musical films add another element that differentiates them from most backstage theater texts: the audience. In cinema, the audience of the film is privy to the backstage antics of the film as well as the musical within a film but also to the reactions of the diegetic audience in the film; this stands in contrast to the lack of audience onstage in either the backstage comedy or musical.[5]

The rise of backstage texts—a loose term for both nonmusicals and musicals—grew, in part, out of reactions to both Hollywood and a growing interest in the lives of performers. Rick Altman argues that in response to the ability of Hollywood to create a star system that promoted both the on-screen persona of actors and their off-screen lives, playwrights and producers began to populate the Broadway stage with a range of plays and musicals that concerned the offstage lives of performers—especially for the risqué lives of showgirls and chorus girls as evidenced by 1919's *Golddiggers*.[6] In the wake of that play's success, the 1920s saw an "unending series of plays concentrating on the entertainment profession, its problems and joys," and increasingly an emphasis on the sordid aspects of theatrical life and an inherent interest in what happens "behind the curtain" and the effects the entertainment professions had on their performers.[7] By the advent of talkie films and the subsequent embrace of musicals in cinema, backstage musicals dominated the cinematic landscape as Hollywood demonstrated its willingness to adapt the texts and themes from Broadway for the financial success of its studios.[8] With the onset of the Depression, Hollywood embraced this philosophy of the backstage narrative and applied it to musicals, as a convenient way to incorporate spectacular set pieces and dance numbers into the narrative structure of the film and "cast a protagonist's frequent bursts into song or dance as a natural side effect of their profession."[9] With the success of *The Broadway Melody* (Harry Beaumont, 1929), musicals became an integral part of the Hollywood scene and incredibly popular with audiences as "their upbeat messages of group effort and success, as well as their visual lavishness offer[ed] a stark contrast to the realities of economic impoverishment" to Depression audiences.[10]

Yet while they were a popular form of entertainment in the 1920s and 1930s, backstage texts—especially film and Broadway musicals—were becoming increasingly less popular through the 1930s.[11] One of the issues facing these texts were narrative shifts in how musical and dance numbers were integrated into film. Studios began to point musical films in a new direction, wherein an overarching plot served a vital role rather than simply a means to loosely hold together musical numbers. Musical film productions dipped to their lowest levels in 1938,[12] and both Hollywood and Broadway began to shift toward more "realistic" narratives. Popular entertainments began to embrace grittier stories of performers struggling behind the scenes in shady venues, and by the American entry into World War II, musicals were experimenting with "plots inspired by current events, an increased sense of realism, hardened protagonists, and subtle (or sometimes not-so-subtle) inflections of patriotism."[13] Indeed, as Altman notes, the musicals that began to appear as Hitler overran Europe not only embraced grittier themes, they also downplayed the driving ethos of "the show must go on." Musicals now had an "expression of shared exuberance" where the "staging of a show grows out of the practical problems of a community of young people" and a benefit show or a musical provide communal relief for their community.[14] To be fair, the reputation of many backstage musicals—especially prior to the enactment of the Hays Code—was of texts that offered audiences titillation and fantasy as evidenced by, perhaps most famously, the Busby Berkeley films. Yet even films like Berkley's that featured over-the-top musical sequences, such as *42nd Street, Golddiggers of 1933*, and *Footlight Parade*, still held other elements that offered rather pointed or disturbing social critiques such as the "My Forgotten Man" sequence at the conclusion of *Golddiggers of 1933* or the suicides in *42nd Street*. Sheri Chinen Biesen details that the genesis of what she terms the noir musical, where the film noir and musical overlap, can be traced further back into the history of cinema with such fare as D. W. Griffith's *The Musketeers of Pig Alley* (1912) featuring backroom bars and a struggling musician mugged by mobsters.[15]

Of particular interest to me is how these plays engage in debates over the nature of theatrical labor. One way in which the texts engage over issues of work is in their treatment of gendered theatrical labor as they often privilege masculine theatrical labor—a criticism often leveled against the more popular backstage or reflexive musicals. This is perhaps most evident in *Room Service*, where not only are there a couple secondary women characters but also the theatrical labor presented in the play is firmly grounded from the perspective of men; additionally, there are strong male-emphases in both *A Moral Entertainment* and *The Torch-Bearers*. The general privileging of male theatrical work in these texts can signal both a conservative reinforcement of male labor or power—this is especially true in aspects of *The Torch-Bearers* with John Ritter's demands on his wife—and perhaps an assertion to audiences of "the forgotten man" of the theater space. It is not difficult to hypothesize about a growing fear over the viability of men actors professionally given increased opportunities for women in that space, as illustrated by the hyper-successful run of Claire Booth Luce's *The Women* in 1936. However, as Adrienne McLean shows, women could undermine the male hierarchy of a text by placing themselves at the center of the performance, and in my mind, *The Torch-Bearers* and *A Moral Entertainment* afford women characters and performers the opportunity to place their labor at the forefront of the plays. Focusing on Rita Hayworth's work in the 1948 musical *Down to Earth*, McLean argues that the women performers in the film compete with the male characters in many of the film's numbers and "win" as they are the primary protagonists and performers, and they can break into a near-perfect performance at any time—whether that is a polished performance or spontaneous in nature: "Entertainment is not only found or naturalized, but it is also created by calculation."[16] The women in the film solicit the attention of the diegetic audience in the film—as well as the text's audience—and in essence, outshine their male counterparts at every instance. For a program that was one of the few of the New Deal that afforded women a great deal more economic and labor agency in comparison to most work programs (which were inherently far more conservative in nature), the ability of women characters and performers to recenter the focus of the plays onto their labor signals an acknowledgment of the importance of the FTP to themselves.[17]

There is also an embedded tension in these plays over what constitutes theatrical labor, one that reflects a frequent rift within the FTP itself. In particular, the comedies illustrate an antagonism between professional actors who worked in entertainment-driven venues and theater workers who were advocating for more overtly political or avant-garde work. As detailed in Chapter 1, one of the central issues within the FTP was the conflict between the workers that were supposed to be employed by the program—professionally trained actors and playwrights—and the aims of many others within the FTP to promote more radical or experimental theater. For many professional actors, certainly operating through their experiences in the troubled commercial theater of the last decade, other forms of theatrical labor did not align with their own goals as theater workers, nor did these other approaches to theater align with the goal of the FTP for employment security. In contrast to the plays being promoted and performed by the program, these comedies suggest a need for performers to stage plays that have proven successful for broad audiences and are, at least outwardly, devoid of the experimentation and political content that could make audiences shy away and endanger the work.

One may presume that given this conflict over the nature of theatrical labor, these plays emphasize the "product" of a play and its consumerist potential over any embedded politics. And to an extent, the plays examined in this chapter do promote considerations over the final "deliverables" to an audience, especially in terms of considerations over political content (*Room Service*, *A Moral Entertainment*) or quality of production (*The Torch-Bearers*). In this regard, these collected works align with the stated goal of many other backstage narratives: that the play, or musical's successful staging is the aim of the theater troupe. This is particularly true in *Room Service*, in which we see Gordon Miller willing to do whatever it takes—deceit, theft, changing of characters' names—to stage his play successfully. And moreover, we as audiences are aware that the products produced by the theatrical workers are received positively by the diegetic audiences contained in the plays themselves. While there is not the same visual representation of the audience as is seen in film musicals, the plays do feature some element of in-play diegetic audience (even *Room Service*, in which most of the acting labor and performance takes place offstage, still features characters commenting on the positive performances). More to the point, *The Torch-Bearers* and *A Moral Entertainment* both feature audiences reacting to the play or performances within the plays themselves: in the former, we hear the audience within the play respond to the production of the amateur players; in the latter, we see the townspeople cheer the acting of the traveling players at various points of the play. The plays collectively signal the need for their own existence by showing the pleasure they afford people and, in turn, illustrate to their audiences how it is acceptable to enjoy the entertainment afforded them.

But this is not to say that these plays merely reify the consumerist or professional bent of other backstage musicals or comedies. Indeed, the plays also present the very real labor and working conditions of the actors and other theatrical workers present within the texts. While delivering the production as a product still dominates the characters' motivations, there is also an important need to stage the product to procure the financial and economic security for the actors. As such, while we do see segments of the plays-within-the-plays here in these works—even *Room Service* gives us some small glimpses as to what the production of *Godspeed* is—we are presented more with the lives of the actors behind the scenes, and those lives, especially in *Room Service* and *A Moral Entertainment*, are anything but glamorous.

The Torch-Bearers

In the 1920s, one of the most prominent comic playwrights of the Great White Way was Philadelphia native George Kelly, who won a Pulitzer Prize for his play *Craig's Wife* and wrote *The Show-Off* (discussed in Chapter 4) and *The Torch-Bearers*, which was a mainstay of both professional and amateur theaters across the country. But Kelly the playwright was something of an enigma. Coming from an acting and sporting family (his brother Walter was a vaudevillian; his other brother, John, was an Olympian and boxer and would later head the US Olympic Committee; and his niece was Grace Kelly), Kelly was often very secretive about his professional and personal life, was averse to giving interviews, and maintained a curmudgeonly, conservative persona in public. His reluctance about interviews stemmed from the fact that he was a closeted gay man, which was an open secret in the Kelly family, and led to him burning all his correspondence before his death in 1974.[18] But Kelly also maintained several reactionary views throughout his life, refusing to share a stage as an actor with Black performers and, at times, blaming his less-than-successful career as a Hollywood writer on Jews.[19] While Kelly was sympathetic to the Actors Guild, in general he held labor unions in contempt and "deeply resented the influence of left-wing playwrights like Clifford Odets, who, he felt, were attempting to change the theater from a temple of morality to a raucous political arena." A staunch Republican, Kelly was no fan of Franklin Roosevelt or the New Deal: Kelly despised FDR and "viewed the Democratic party's social legislation as nothing more than a senseless giveaway of his tax money to those who were unwilling to work as hard as he."[20] Given his conservative politics, it seems a touch odd that Kelly would grant a program like the FTP permission to stage his plays.

Because of the lack of primary material from Kelly himself, it is mere speculation on my part as to why Kelly's works were staged by the FTP. But given his interest in professional theater, it is reasonable that he may have seen Flanagan's organization as an opportunity for actors that were not available at the height of the Depression. In a rare interview he gave to Bosley Crowther in 1936 as his play *Reflected Glory* premiered on Broadway, Kelly sees the need for some further professionalization for actors. For Kelly, actors need "experience to do it upon a stage" and "that, I think, is the greatest danger confronting theater today—the lack of opportunity for youngsters to gain experience. In the past, when we had the road, the young actors came along until they were spotted by New York scouts as the possessors of real talent. Today, a genuine artist has so little opportunity to develop that we find very few promising new ones and the movies get those." Kelly further sees the "consequence of so little theatrical activity, in comparison to other days, is that directors, too, are denied the opportunity of learning the art of the theatre." "It is," Crowther writes, "all a vicious circle which Mr. Kelly thinks revolves around the economic axis and the only solution will be the return of 'better times' with a consequent increase in theatrical activity." Kelly also, tellingly, understands that "films have alienated a vast audience which formally patronized the cheaper theatrical productions" and while Kelly feels that true theater patrons prefer the stage, "it is a question whether our audiences today are developing their tastes as they should."[21]

For a play with a long legacy as a satire of the Little Theatre Movement and other amateur acting, *The Torch-Bearers* would seem to be simply one that appealed to conservative audiences in terms of its treatment of overzealous actors and women who threatened the stability of the domestic space. And while it is unquestionable that many audiences would have interpreted the play as such, I think it bears noting that the play's various performances—as well as a prominent film adaptation—undermine such readings. Moreover, its FTP performances serve to reinforce the need for theatrical opportunities, even if they occur on literal amateur-professional stages or the stage of a federally subsidized theater.

Kelly's play was originally produced as a one-act play entitled "Mrs. Ritter Appears" in 1916 that is the third act of *The Torch-Bearers* with only a few subtle differences. The play within the play of *The Torch-Bearers* are lines of dialogue from another of Kelly's one-act plays entitled *One of Those Things* (originally copyrighted in 1913 as *Dr. Arlington's Wife*), a blend of farce and melodrama that centers on a convoluted scenario: a husband believes his wife is unfaithful to him, and she, in turn, believes he wants his freedom from their marriage. When the husband declares his commitment to the marriage, the wife suggests they head to the theater and see a comedy because she can still laugh (this is all contained in the downtown doctor's office of physician the married couple knows). For the feature-length play, Kelly borrowed the term frequently used by women involved in women's clubs in the late nineteenth and early twentieth centuries to describe how they viewed themselves and their work: *torchbearers* refers to "the concept of leading others to the highest ideals, a concept which presupposes women's ability to march to a purer drummer than the men around them." This term was rather, as Kathy Blair notes, mercurial to the user: "To some, the clubwoman who carried the light widened a path toward new roles for women. To others, the torchbearer's light represented the effort to protect an ancient path."[22] And to others, the torch-bearing women, such as those portrayed in Kelly's play, represented a threat to the status quo, a perspective often embraced by audiences and producers in the play's history.

The Torch-Bearers takes place in an unnamed small town and centers on a married couple named Fred and Paula Ritter. One day, Fred returns home to find his wife practicing for the rehearsal of a community theater production—which is surprising to Fred since his wife had never really voiced an interest in acting. Paula notes that a role has opened for the newest local amateur production because a woman withdrew from the company after her husband died from seeing her terrible acting. While he remains skeptical about her involvement in the play, Fred tepidly encourages his wife's interest. However, Fred's tone shifts once he must deal with Mrs. Pampinelli—the director and manager of the local little theater. Pampinelli declares to everyone that her job is to cultivate the talent in the town—especially Paula who she feels will be a star. This rankles Fred who believes that this work will distract his wife from her domestic duties.

Paula participates in the formal production the next night, and every aspect of the production falls apart: actors forget lines, mustaches on actors fall off, doors do not open, and the curtain fails. Despite nearly everything going wrong in the performance, when the cast does their curtain call, the audience breaks into thunderous applause.

The final act of Kelly's play shifts tonally and becomes something of a domestic melodrama. At the Ritter home, Paula and Fred get into an argument over the production: when Paula asks what her husband thought of the play, Fred proceeds to viciously criticize every aspect of the performance—especially his wife's acting. Undeterred, she tells Fred that Mrs. Pampinelli believes that she should head to New York to become a professional actor, and Fred is beside himself with the implication, noting that Paula has a job already: caring for him and their home. Mrs. Pampinelli arrives, and she and Fred get into an argument: the director notes that Fred has long been in favor of the little theater in their town and if actors cannot cut their teeth on the amateur stage, how can they become professionals? Fred retorts that every person should know their place. Fred leaves, and soon after, the phone rings: the speaker claims to be representing a film studio and demands to sign Paula to a contract. But it is apparent to Paula that the film company representative on the line is just Fred pretending to be the man, and Paula is even more upset. Mrs. Pampinelli leaves, but not before trying to convince Paula to attempt her hand at the professional stage; however, Paula doesn't like the idea, reasoning that Fred would be left alone. As her husband reenters, Fred, in another drastic character shift, encourages his wife to leave for New York, but she resists; they come to an agreement that one night of her acting will be enough for both. The play ends with Fred reassuring his wife that her performance would be remembered by all.

For decades, the legacy of the play has focused on its satirical jabs at amateur theater and the Little Theatre Movement overall. When the play premiered on Broadway in 1922, reviews were positive, with many praising the comedy embedded in Kelly's work as well as his satirical tone toward amateur theater, even if the former vaudevillian struggled in the transition from sketches to a full-length play. But several reviewers, most famously Alexander Woollcott, accused Kelly of backing off his satirical take on amateur theater. Woollcott was annoyed by what he perceived as the playwright getting cold feet at his satire and then accused Kelly of fearing potential repercussions from the Little Theatre Movement itself: "And then quite suddenly in the last act, *The Torch-Bearers* dies. It is really a case of murder in the first degree, and last night's audience watched the crime, stiff with horror, as at the wanton slaughter of something to which they had grown quite attached. The misfortune sets in when the author begins apologizing for this play." Woollcott continues: "The good spirits of the onlookers ooze away during an incredibly long dialogue in which the spineless Mr. Kelly explains in detail that he really thinks the Little Theatre Movement is perfectly lovely and that he doesn't want to discourage any one by all his spoofing and that he is sure that an amateur performance 'in the right hands' would be good for the community and so on and so on. This craven interlude appears to have been written in at the last moment for fear the Drama League would get angry at the play or that Mr. Kelly would be severely spoken to by the *Theatre Arts Magazine.*"[23] But if Kelly did offer some more nuanced takes on the play's premiere, later in life he seems to have embraced both a skeptical view of amateur actors and the Little Theatre Movement, decrying the latter in a 1971 interview: "There was a great flowering of the little theater groups at the time. Everyone who had a chicken coop had a little theater" the aging playwright told Foster Hirsch.[24]

Whatever his intended framing of amateur acting, Kelly's play soon became popular in amateur theaters across the country and produced, as Dorothy Chansky argues, a conservative receptive space that developed a problematic gender dynamic for women actors. Many of the plays produced by little theaters reinforced the idea that women were frivolous or not suited to the demands of serious theater. Chansky recounts that Frank Shay's popular anthology entitled *One Thousand and One Plays for the Little Theatre* heavily features male characters and the few plays that do feature more women's roles include such stereotyped fare as *Miss Myrtle Says "Yes"*, *Womankind*, *Dancing Dolls*, and *Why Girls Stay Home*. Increasingly, women could pursue the independence of acting through participating in community theater but by performing in plays that "criticized them for being too sexual, not sufficiently interested in supporting their husbands, too materialistic, or a host of other 'too's.'" These plays were often Broadway mainstays, thus resulting in this phenomenon of "Little Theatres s pursuing a version of mimetic sophistication by presenting recent commercial hits that depended for their arch knowingness on putting upper-middle-class women in their place."[25] In plays like George Kaufman's *Dulcy* and Kelly's *The Torch-Bearers* (popular especially between 1925 and 1929), little theaters offered their patriarchal audiences "ironic comfort" by belittling their workers through plays that critique strong women characters and "emphasize the primacy of women's domestic role and to see widespread feminist change as somewhere on the spectrum from impossible to deceptive."[26] Outwardly, we can read this control of theatrical performance as a reinforcement of conservative domestic norms, and certainly Kelly may have had such a rationale in place when he wrote the play; as Chansky writes, the play is in a tradition of viewing women as part of a "general" audience that reinforced "ideas of sophistication and business-as-usual for middle-and-upper-middle class white women" and as part of said general audience, women were "assumed to share a critical stance that was dismissive of women qua women."[27]

Given its production history and gendered spaces, *The Torch-Bearers* certainly had a legacy by the time it was considered for and staged by the FTP. Perhaps because of its reputation as a male-leaning play, its frequency of production, and Flanagan's desire to weed-out older productions, Kelly's play was staged just three times by the FTP: in New York City in August 1936; Raleigh, North Carolina in November of that year; and Atlanta in the spring of 1937.[28] And it is interesting to note that two of the productions were staged before the streamlining of play approval. Writing for the forerunner to the Play Policy Bureau, Dan Rush did not recommend Kelly's play for production, noting that the play was "no doubt very amusing" but he felt that the play's amateur theater performance history presented problems, noting that "as a production for amateurs, I am afraid it would be difficult to shade the acting to amateur and real performance difference." He further noted that the play painfully paints a "true picture of amateurs" and that he feared it "would be most unpleasant to them."[29]

Despite Rush's recommendation not to stage *The Torch-Bearers*, the play did manage some success in its Raleigh production, which merged amateur and professional theatrical labor. With some rare exceptions, the FTP in many southern cities faced a litany of obstacles that prevented much positivity for the program. Elizabeth Osborne argues that unlike Los Angeles or New York, "issues that were little more than nuisances in other regions expanded to become nearly insurmountable obstacles," and these smaller units struggled to manage these crises and were, in essence, ignored by national administration.[30] Furthermore, with productions like *Altars of Steel* that challenged the "social, political, and economic hegemony of the South," the FTP units in the southern states drew an extra level of scrutiny from politicians and the press, who feared the communist overtones of many plays and the presentation of racial issues to a still highly segregated South. Osborne posits that "the southern region seems to have regarded organized FTP units as unwelcome and dangerous intrusions (perhaps not surprising in a region occupied by federal troops during Radical Reconstruction only sixty years earlier)."[31]

However, the Raleigh FTP Unit was one of the few successes in the South during the program's run. Formed in 1935, the Raleigh FTP developed a unique arrangement: professionally trained actors would produce and perform plays that seemed to cater to the needs of the community, but they would work under the auspices of local amateur theater workers. In this sense, the Raleigh FTP and its little theater became one and the same (and the present Raleigh Little Theatre traces its roots to this venture). *The Torch-Bearers* was produced by the Raleigh Unit in November 1936, under the direction of Wilbur Dorsett. He sought to further develop the relationships between the FTP and the local community by holding workshop classes in play reading, writing, and general stagecraft as well as monthly meetings in which one or two one-act plays were staged by the troupe. In turn, he actively tried to find new actors to perform onstage or curious people who were interested in trying their hand at stage work.[32] While Dorsett may not have been as polished or dynamic as his predecessor, Kay McKay, an experienced director who had worked on Broadway and radio, Dorsett's play fit into the generally more dynamic and risk-taking approach of the first eighteen months of the Raleigh Unit (which also included its own Negro Unit—and likely was the only FTP Unit in the South that staged any productions with a mixed-race cast).[33] Conversely, as rehearsals began for the play, the local unit played host to a tristate conference on WPA women's and professional projects, and the conference was treated to a special performance of the play. After opening on November 10, the play was greeted with strong praise from the local press: one reviewer noted that the local unit had another hit on its hands, while Fred J. Mahler commented on the increasing importance of the unit in the community: "The Little Theatre has come to occupy a fixed place in the cultural as well as entertainment phase of Raleigh life."[34]

This combination of professional and amateur labor in the Raleigh production leads to some interesting questions about the status of *The Torch-Bearers* within the FTP. Certainly, directors wanted to stage the play for its long-standing popularity, but it is also likely that producers wanted to stage the play to promote professional performances while critiquing amateur theater—and perhaps even the FTP itself. The play within a play is shown to be far inferior to professional productions. In particular, Kelly critiques the women who run the theater itself who are shown to be nosy, dangerous, and self-important—no one more than Mrs. Pampinelli. Hirsch argues that Kelly adds bitterness to his portrayal of Pampinelli by having her misdirect "his own dry, understated one-act" *One of Those Things*. Kelly has Pampinelli misread the play's tone, trying for a fevered, melodramatic pitch at every moment in the play: "In fact, she sponsors all the tricks of the trade that Kelly's own muted, detailed, naturalistic direction tried to circumvent."[35] And, it is tempting to suggest the FTP performances of *The Torch-Bearers* making a subtle—or perhaps not-so-subtle—connection between Pampinelli and Flanagan. First, there is something of a parallel between Mrs. Pampinelli, the academically inclined leader of the troupe, and Hallie Flanagan (at least a vision of Flanagan that was portrayed by her critics).[36] Pampinelli is melodramatic, dictatorial, and pretentious, such as how she describes reading an article that reminds her of Emerson that has her "own thoughts returning to me from an alienated majesty."[37] Moreover, these performances of *The Torch-Bearers* on the FTP stage signal an acknowledgment of the status of the FTP in the public's imagination as well as the critical response to much of the program. In a meta and self-referential motion, by staging a performance of *The Torch-Bearers*—a play centered on an amateur theater constructed to be inferior to professional theater—the FTP productions address the critical critiques of the program as offering audiences inferior theater by presenting "inferior theater" onstage.

However, there are a few complicating factors that complicate such a reading. For starters, whatever the quality of the performance within the play, the play within a play is wildly received by the diegetic audience of *The Torch-Bearers*, signaling some promotion of the audience's acceptance of the performance. In turn, the Raleigh Unit had a history of tweaking standard productions and offering satirical takes on the plays.[38] There are also some intertextual considerations here as there were two film adaptations of *The Torch-Bearers* that presented a different take on the play. The first was *Too Busy to Work* from 1939, an installment of the Jones Family B-picture series that was popular in the late 1930s that appears to have been loosely based on Kelly's play.[39] But more in line with the FTP productions of *The Torch-Bearers* was the Will Rogers vehicle entitled *Doubting Thomas* from 1935. Originally given the working title of *The Torch-Bearers*, the film deviates quite a bit from the play itself. While the basic conflict of the play remains, one of the key differences is that there is a Hollywood screen test agent named Rudolph La Maze who is actively recruiting young actors and actresses to test for a career in Hollywood for the nominal fee of seventy-five dollars. This attracts the interest of Peggy Brown, the daughter of Thomas and Paula Brown (the Ritters of this version), who decides to screen test. Thomas, played by Rogers, recalls that his wife had the desire to act when they first met, and becomes infuriated when, after returning from a business trip, both his daughter and wife are acting in the local theater production. In the film, Thomas is more proactive in sabotaging the dreams of his wife and daughter. Attending a preproduction party, Thomas lets it be known to everyone that a famous Hollywood producer is coming to scout the play—and the actors are even more nervous than they normally are. In a review session, La Maze lambastes all the actors as talentless—save for Brown who has done a screen test (in the film, this provides Rogers an opportunity to reenact aspects of his vaudeville routine). In a nod to the confidence artist tradition, it is revealed that Brown has hired a local actor to play La Maze to demonstrate everyone's incompetence, which angers his daughter and wife.

Casting Rogers in the Fred Ritter role would seemingly soften the character, but by 1935, Rogers had engendered a complicated and at times controversial star persona that likely colored some audience members' reading of the character. While still a significant box office draw around the time of *Doubting Thomas*, Rogers had appeared in several films that had generated criticism from the press for their ideological content. In *David Harum* (James Cruzze, 1934), a film set in the Panic of 1893 wherein Rogers's character finds work as a horse trainer in a rural community, critics found the film's representation of optimism and promotion of the New Deal as too heavy-handed and unrealistic.[40] In addition, Rogers appeared in two of director John Ford's early films—*Dr. Bull* and *Judge Priest*, both from 1934—that garnered a range of controversy for the actor. In *Judge Priest*, Rogers plays the eponymous judge in a Kentucky town in the Old South who acquits a stranger despite pressure from the Ku Klux Klan. While the film is not overly progressive, its depiction of race relations (problematic as they are) worried Fox Studios, and for marketing in the South, the studio ordered Ford to cut a scene in which Rogers condemns lynching and racial apartheid in the former Confederacy. In *Dr. Bull*, Rogers played a crotchety old country doctor who held contempt for his patients, many of whom are portrayed as slackers and whiners.[41] Moreover, Rogers's persona to audiences was also informed by his incredibly popular syndicated newspaper columns and his radio show that began airing on the National Broadcasting Corporation in 1933. In his columns, Rogers often promoted the Roosevelt administration and the New Deal, though he did criticize the president, namely, FDR's sudden cancellation of national air mail service.[42] Nor was Rogers's popular radio program not without controversy. Recorded live and without a script, Rogers, who was often exhausted after filming movies all day, would pick a single topic and pontificate on that subject for each show's duration. While his topics would range from the humorous to the serious—he lambasted the American government's treatment of Native peoples in one episode—he garnered a great deal of criticism when during an episode reminiscing about ranch life, he referred to a popular cowboy song as a "nigger spiritual." The network was deluged with criticism, and Rogers apologized for his use of the term on the following week's program.[43]

Even if audiences of FTP performances did not carry their knowledge of Rogers's own complicated star persona, they may have seen parallels between Thomas Brown and Fred Ritter as both characters are concerned with what they perceive as existential threats to the stability of their domestic spaces. In both the play and the film, the male patriarch dominates and controls the labor of the women in his space. In the case of *Doubting Thomas*, Rogers's underhanded character is the driving force in controlling the performances of the other characters, especially those of his daughter and wife, while he is the one who permits himself to perform whenever he likes. Similarly, Ritter does everything in his power to undermine both his wife's desire to act as well as the little theater in his town. In one argument with his wife, Ritter hostilely decries the labor of the stage while reinforcing his patriarchal space: when Mrs. Ritter declares to her husband that she "ought to go on with the work,"[44] Mr. Ritter retorts that she should go on with "the housework."[45] In the play's conclusion, Mr. Ritter convinces Mrs. Ritter to stay, in part, by cynically claiming a willingness on his part to let his wife become the head of the household. He declares, "I've concluded that it's more important that the world should see you act, than that I should have a home to come to."[46] Mr. Ritter's manipulation of his wife signals that the real motivation for his hostility toward the theater is not an overriding concern for quality theatrical work. Instead, Mr. Ritter is only concerned with reestablishing social gender norms. Even if we grant Ritter the benefit of the doubt and read his endorsement of Mrs. Ritter's plan to become a professional actor as legitimate, Ritter himself is still controlling her theatrical labor by permitting her the opportunity to do so.

Yet the FTP performances of Kelly's play also overlap with shifting views toward Little Theatre among women actors. While it did afford women agency through education and acting opportunities, Little Theatre was beginning to be seen by many women as outdated and regressive. In the years immediately before the Depression, younger women actors were increasingly less invested in the Little Theatre Movement itself. This was borne, in part, out of a series of generational divides between younger women and founding members of Little Theatre—like Marjorie Ayres Best, who promoted a Progressive Era view of theater that emphasized social uplift, church-friendly work and "willingness to have members toil without pay or even official leadership positions."[47] For women of the 1920s and 1930s, such unpaid positions were hardly attractive, and women actors were increasingly looking for more professionally aligned opportunities such as university-training for education jobs or for professional theater work. What was once considered transgressive labor for women was now seen by younger generations as a hallmark of old-fashioned views of the labor market. With increasing male views that women's work should be confined to the home (especially among the middle class, as I discuss in Chapter 3) and that female camaraderie was old-fashioned and unnecessary, acting provided an opportunity for women who resisted these norms. Moreover, the amateur theater seen in *The Torch-Bearers* becomes synonymous with these patriarchal views: while Mrs. Pampinelli is hardly a regressive character, the amateur theater in the town appears to be the only outlet for the women to temporarily escape the gender construct they exist in. When Paula Ritter agrees to not seek employment on the professional stage, she symbolically and literally returns to the space that has dominated her. The Little Theatre Movement—as newer generations of women saw it—was simply an extension of patriarchal power.

I cannot discount that audiences seeing *The Torch-Bearers* on the FTP stage would have read the play as many audiences in the 1920s would have: as a reaffirming of patriarchal ideals and a satire of amateur theater. But both the text and its performances were often not as clear-cut. And while the production of the play would certainly have appealed to more conservative audiences based on its reputation, *The Torch-Bearers* performances on the FTP stage—especially the Raleigh production with its intersection of amateur and professional workforces—suggest a defense of theater in all forms. When Mrs. Ritter acquiesces to her husband as the curtains close, she is submitting to his will and, symbolically, the needs of a conservative society that wants the restoration of the male breadwinner. Yet while the performances reinforce that outwardly, they offer audiences the question of at what cost does that restoration come to the women who find moments of agency through their labor of the stage?

Room Service

At the first American Writer's Congress in August 1935, Kenneth Burke gave his famous (or infamous) address entitled "Revolutionary Symbolism in America." Delivered to an audience consisting of 216 of the most politically engaged writers of the era, Burke argued for his fellow leftists to rethink how they preached to the masses their aim of a "cultural front" for social change.[48] Encouraging his writers to disavow the propaganda of "the worker" in exchange for the propaganda of "the people," Burke argued that the duty of the propagandist was to avoid the signs of one's own political persuasion. To persuade an audience, the propagandist must include in his or her work the signs of the larger culture: "Let one encompass as many desirable features of our cultural heritage as possible—and let him make sure that his political alignment figures prominently among them. . . . And I am suggesting that an approach based upon the positive symbol of the people rather than upon the negative symbol of 'the worker.'"[49] While Burke's argument frustrated some attendees at the Congress, others took his central thesis to heart and found the argument compelling. And the circulation of Burke's ideas likely spread to the minds of both Allen Boretz and John Murray as they were writing *Room Service*, a play that would become a massive Broadway hit. After *Room Service*, Murray would move into writing for various radio comedy variety shows and eventually then television, while Borertz would work on several projects, including the Abbott and Costello vehicle *It Ain' Hay* (1943) and a musical version of *Room Service* called *Step Lively* (1944) that featured Frank Sinatra. But Boretz would have his career ruined by his blacklisting in the early 1950s in the wave of anticommunist hysteria in Hollywood. Toward the end of this life, Borertz would reflect on his time as a playwright and screenwriter, noting in an interview that there could be subversive content placed into a text—even the comedies he was known for: "My feeling about that was that [Marxist] content could be put in. I don't like to say 'put-in.' Content could be made an integral part of the structure of a film if it lived up to its dramatic purposes and was not inserted willy-nilly. Otherwise, it would stand out like a sore thumb. . . . It could be too strong, but it could also be too subtle, in which case it was useless."[50] In this vein, I think it is helpful to consider the political and subversive content of *Room Service*. Outwardly a farce, the play focuses on the economic toils facing theater workers at the height of the Depression and the lengths those workers must go to subsist on their meager earnings and to stage a play. But the play also signals the need for theater workers to embrace the cultural signs of the "people" to both promote ideological positions and, in the case of the FTP, maintain security for actors who need such stability.

Room Service takes place in a Broadway hotel room where Gordon Miller, manager of an acting company, is staying along with his coproducers and twenty-two actors, all of whom are charging room service meals and other services to Miller's account. It is revealed that Miller tends to take up residence in various hotels in the city and then skip out on the bills—a fact that concerns Miller's brother-in-law and manager of the Hotel Gribble. But Miller has promised him that his new play, *Godspeed*, will make everyone successful again. Then the playwright of *Godspeed*, Leo Davis, arrives, ready to make it big on Broadway and collect an advance from Miller. Adding to Miller's angst is that one Gregory Wagner is investigating the finances of the hotel and is continually threatening to evict Miller through any means necessary. Miller then proposes that he use the empty theater space in the hotel to stage *Godspeed*, but Wagner is indignant until both men become aware of a Mr. Jenkins, a representative for a wealthy man who is interested in financing Miller's play. Jenkins promises to give Miller the money for rehearsals. After a series of farcical scenarios, Mr. Jenkins returns and gives Miller a check for $15,000—but does not endorse the contract. The theater troupe members are deflated until they realize that they have five days until payment on the check can be stopped. That provides them, in theory, with five days to stage the play. After learning the financing is in the air, Wagner plots to have Miller and his cohorts arrested during the first production of *Godspeed* in front of a live audience, thereby ruining Miller. Taking a risk, the troupe convinces Wagner that Davis has committed suicide, and Wagner becomes nervous about the negative press the hotel might receive. The troupe manages to keep Wagner confined in the hotel until the play has finished, and then a Senator Blake, the secret backer, comes to the room and declares that the play will be a success—and Miller und Wagner will be partners for the foreseeable future.

When *Room Service* premiered on Broadway in 1937, it was a smash hit, running for five hundred performances at the Cort Theatre. Writing in the *New York Times*, Brooks Atkinson praised the production, labeling the play the funniest show of the season. He described its characters as guilty of "some riotous low-comedy antics" as they "fall silently and ravenously on a meal swindled off a temperamental waiter" and "improvise a bogus suicide to hoodwink a startled hotel manager."[51] And the play drew the attention of the FTP. For readers of the Play Service Bureau, the play certainly could be a win for the program—especially as they saw it as basically safe, apolitical fare. One reviewer praised the "many evident, hilarious situations" of the "simple and unimpeded" plot, and the dialogue was "cynical . . . terse, and crisp."[52] Marion Murray argued the play "is soundly constructed and will amuse any audience."[53] Another reviewer praises the reputation of the play on Broadway but warns it should not "be attempted by any company unless they are really masters at farce—and under the guidance of a director who knows every trick of the trade. It depends so much on timing and the proper casting of the types. A natural in any language."[54] After its recommendation by play reviewers, *Room Service* was performed six separate times across the country.[55] And in general, audiences and producers found the play to be enjoyable and, as suggested by various other reviewers, apolitical. Writing in his report of the 1939 Denver production, director Andrew Slane notes that the play is an "ideal commercial farce" and has "no great meaning" and the emphasis of any subsequent production "should be on its entertainment" factors.[56] Additionally, an audience member of the same production notes in their review that the play is so likable they would like to stage the play with the drama department of their high school.[57]

While other plays I examine in this project have some strong intertextual overlap with a major film adaptation, that does not appear to be the case for *Room Service* as the 1938 film adaptation featuring the Marx Brothers was a financial failure for RKO Pictures. Having paid Boretz and Murray a then record $225,000 for the rights to the play, RKO also procured the Marx Brothers, fresh off their successful *A Night at the Opera* (Sam Wood, 1935), to sign a three-picture deal with the studio. Zeppo Marx, acting as agent for his brothers, managed to procure a $250,000 windfall for his brothers to sign the contract (to which Groucho is alleged to have snarked that Zeppo could have gotten them $350,000).[58] Adapted by Morrie Ryskind, *Room Service* also featured Lucille Ball and a young Anne Miller. Their only film that was not a version of one of their Broadway shows or specifically written for the Marxes, their normal brand of anarchistic musical comedy is not found in the film. There is no Groucho dance number, no Harpo harp sequence, no Chico piano moment. Moreover, the brothers were not allowed to go off script—a dynamic that Chico would declare that he and his brothers were simply not good at.[59] The film also became an economic loss for RKO and was the first cinematic flop for the Marx Brothers, who would soon return to Metro-Goldwyn-Mayer (MGM) for another series of films.

While screenwriter Morrie Ryskind was under orders from RKO to limit changes of the play for the screenplay, there were of course some tweaks to the film version.[60] While some of the changes were minor—some dialogue tweaks, the name of Davis's play becomes *Hail and Farewell*, and the addition of a flying turkey—other revisions change the ideological content of the play narrative. One of the significant differences lies in how the film constructs Gordon Miller. As Sebastian Trainor notes, the initial Broadway production featured Sam Levene who had cultivated a reputation for portraying "gritty, harassed heroes."[61] In contrast, Groucho Marx's portrayal draws more on his own persona of playing characters who are far more self-serving in their nature than determined (as Gordon Miller is constructed in the play). Groucho is still recognizable in his "Groucho" attire and audiences would be drawing on his other various film roles. For Joe Adamson, the nihilism of Groucho's persona overwhelms the character of the play: "Gordon Miller, who sincerely cares about the fate of his production and the people involved in it, being played by Groucho Marx who sincerely cares about nothing at all."[62] Other changes seem to have been made for more overtly political purposes. Screenwriter Ryskind was a conservative who in February 1944 became one of the founding members of the Motion Picture Alliance for the Preservation of American Ideals (MPA), "an aggressively anti-Communist organization founded to combat what they perceived as an inflation of communists (such as Allen Boretz) into the infrastructure of the American filmmaking industry."[63] Trainor suggests that several of the changes to the playscript of *Room Service*—namely, the removal of Senator Blake, the southern politician who owns the hotel—undermines the principal polarity of the play between the Russian waiter, whom the farce presents as the savior of the plot, and the senator, who is "the play's ultimate fool." Moreover, while the 1938 film still retained a theme of the mockery of authority, the removal of the senator character in Ryskind's screenplay downplayed the political elements of the play, canceling out not only the satire of a dimwitted politician but also his demands to make alterations to the play that read too much like communist allusions.[64] Trainor posits that there is in the adaptation process of *Room Service* an "ideological sanitization" that is present in the 1938 film and even more pronounced in the 1944 musical adaptation featuring Frank Sinatra.[65]

Where the stage versions are more overt is in the economic distress the theater professionals experience in *Room Service*, forcing them to forgo food, engage in swindling, and pawn their goods to survive. And in the context of the FTP productions, these representations remind audiences of the need for economic security afforded to workers by the program. In one scene, Miller and his main cohorts fantasize about food, seeing their toothpicks they use for chips in a poker game morph into hamburgers in their ravenous imagination. Even Miller confesses—or brags—to Davis that he has "gone without eating for days" and, in a clear jab at the previous presidential administration, notes, "President Hoover says it [not eating] is good for your stomach."[66] For Miller, the aim of any deception or "fast one" is the preservation of his troupe and his fellow workers follow suit (not unlike the con artists in Chapter 5). In a bit of allegorical "nuance," one of Miller's right-hand men is literally named "Faker" who adopts the persona of a British doctor in the play. This need to erase the lines between roles and personas in order to find a level of security is exemplified by not only Miller's actions—moving between hotel rooms and scamming various hotel managers—but also through the rest of his troupe, where actors adopt the roles of kitchen staff and wherein neophyte playwright Leo Davis has to embrace swindling as a rite of passage. After being convinced by Miller to "fake his death" to prevent the troupe from being kicked-out of the hotel, Davis relishes this turn, exclaiming: "You wouldn't think I came from Oswego five days ago!"[67] When their desperate attempts to order food from room service fail, Miller attempts to convince the room service department that he is the hotel doctor and they need to feed the ill Davis who is suffering from a tapeworm (in one of the funniest lines in the play, Miller notes that the room service manager says the tapeworm must register at the front desk before it can be fed). Things routinely become so desperate that actors frequently consider taking things from their hotel rooms to pawn, and several of Miller's workers fight over the possessions of Davis when he first arrives. The actors pawn a silver frame of his, take change and chocolate from his person, and hawk Davis's typewriter—an object not only important for his writing but also one that Davis has fallen-behind on his payment plan with (a crossover with the issues of debt faced by actors and, as we see, middle-class workers in Chapter 3).

But while there are some subversive leftist elements in the play, there remains a great deal within the play that echoes both Burke's new norms of propaganda and serve as a tepid reminder to the FTP about incorporating radicalism into art. Whatever the political allegiances of Allen Boretz or whatever ideological issues Morrie Ryskind may have read in the playscript, the fact remains that Gordon Miller is keen on tweaking his play to fit the demands of his potential audiences. The central conceit of this Burkeian approach to propaganda lies with the play within a play in *Room Service*, *Godspeed*. As readers, we receive little information about the play itself, but we can infer it is a combination of a social realist polemic and a historical narrative—a merging of forms favored by many FTP productions, including Sherwood Anderson's *Valley Forge* and Michael Gold and Michael Blankfort's *Battle Hymn*. Centering on a Polish immigrant miner who bemoans his social status, the play within a play outwardly parodies a great deal of the working-class ethos present in proletarian texts of the 1930s, especially many elicit leftist plays of the era. We get a glimpse of *Godspeed*'s content when Sasha, a Russian actor working as a waiter in the hotel, auditions for the play in front of Miller. Sasha says, "All my life I dig coal. Go to sleep couple hours—get up—dig coal again, and what I got? Three children no good—not worth a two-cent piece. Tomorrow, I dig coal again . . . dig . . . dig . . . dig." These leftist elements in *Godspeed* are contrasted with another aspect of the play that delves into the more fantastical: in the play, the Polish miner, after an argument with his family, falls asleep and dreams about "all the great figures in American history . . . and every man turns out to be [his] son." The miner (played by Sasha the waiter) then declares, "Konrad, I work hard. Make you something. I think some day you be great man. Like Washington, Lincoln."[68] If we are to read *Godspeed* as something of a political polemic typical of 1930s radical theater, then the inclusion by Davis of this character dreaming of the great figures of American history signals an awareness of one of Burke's key arguments in his speech. For an author to broaden the appeal of their work, they should incorporate shared cultural signs of both the worker and the people, and having a character symbolic of proletarian theater/art dream of the great men of American history signals an embrace of this approach to political art.

Moreover, Miller demonstrates a clear desire to amend his production to the desires of his audiences. One can read his tweaks as "selling out" to the demands of the market, but for Burke, this is a key tool of propaganda. Moreover, this becomes a clear signal to the FTP for the need to navigate to the demands of the audience. Again, returning to his speech delivered to the American Writer's Congress, Burke compares the role of the propagandist to that of the advertiser: "He [the propagandist] speaks in behalf of his cause, not in the ways, of a lawyer's brief, but by the sort of things he associates with it."[69] While he downplays the connection, Burke, in effect, argues that for both the propagandist and the advertiser, the goal of the art is to elicit positive emotions and sensations in the subject. And throughout the play, Miller demonstrates both a willingness to flatter the sensibilities of a potential audience and alter the content of the play to meet the ideological demands of another audience. In an early instance of his approach, Miller flatters the bourgeois sensibilities of a potential financial backer, noting the backer exudes "taste and discrimination" and that the backer could be supporting an original and potentially noteworthy play as Miller, hollowly, suggests "the average producer might think that *Godspeed* too artistic."[70]

While Miller is willing to flatter the aesthetic taste of a potential financial backer, he is also willing to neuter any overt political content from *Godspeed* to further illicit positive reactions in his audience. There is no better example of this than when Miller encounters Senator Blake, the southern politician who owns the hotel and its theater. After seeing the premiere performance of *Godspeed*, the senator declares it such a great play that "it will be here two years, if I'm any judge."[71] But the senator does offer one point of constructive criticism: "I'd like to change the name of the hero in the play ... I don't like Konrad, it sounds too much like *comrade*."[72] And of course, Miller is more than willing to make such a change to the play. To be certain, we can read Miller's flattery and editing as simply the hallmarks of a competent theater producer—if the "money" for a production demands changes, well, one should make such changes. In turn, it is easy to read these moves as hollow and performative on Miller's behalf: there's a suggestion that he cares not for the content of the play itself, but merely is concerned with the financial windfall for his acting troupe and he will go to any length to produce the play—artistic integrity of others be damned. And of course, Miller's readiness to change "Konrad" because of its homophonic connection with "comrade" also becomes a self-aware commentary of the accusations lobbed at the FTP from conservative spheres of plays ripe with communist propaganda. In this vein, this subtle-but-not-so-subtle joke aligns the play with other texts that offered similar commentary on the communist overtones of the FTP.

For me, I feel Miller's embrace of the need for editing the play speaks to both an embrace of the need for Burkeian propaganda and becomes a model for how producers and the FTP should deal with political content. Again, while it is easy to read Miller's removal of "Konrad" from the play because of its association with "comrade" as a form of government-imposed censorship, the senator's suggestion of one small change in a play that appears to have more radical content suggests that the political content within the play still exists. Moreover, a key part of Miller's rationale for making such changes or flattering potential investors is that he wants the play staged to provide security for the actors under his employment. The conclusion of the play seems to suggest that tweaks to the content of plays are necessary for the greater good of the profession and while Miller's own approaches to making those decisions are, at times, unethical, he nevertheless makes such choices.

It is difficult therefore to not read the performances as suggesting to the FTP to bear in mind the need of balancing overt political theater with subversive content or simply eliminating the overt political content altogether. If a simple tweak of eliminating comrade from a play ensures success, this becomes a guideline for the rest of the FTP to follow.

A Moral Entertainment

In their 1937 short film for Columbia Pictures entitled *Back to the Woods*, the Three Stooges play criminals in seventeenth-century England who are sent to the Massachusetts Bay Colony as punishment for their deeds. Once in the colony, the judge expects the Stooges to be used to fight Native peoples in conflict with the colonists living there. Upon arriving in the home of the colonial governor, the Stooges encounter his three daughters, all wearing stereotypical Puritan clothing, named Faith, Hope, and Charity. As they often do in their shorts, the Stooges each pair off with one of the three women the characters. As Moe flirts with Faith, Curly and Larry jostle over Hope; when Curly suggests that Larry take up with Charity, Larry responds: "I need not Charity—I'm on the WPA." After Curly asks what that is, Larry, clearly biting his lip to keep from laughing at the joke, takes a moment before retorting: "The Willing Pilgrims Association."[73]

Back to the Woods parallels Richard Maibaum's *A Moral Entertainment* in several ways: stereotypical views of Puritan life, clichéd and highly problematic views of Native Americans, and a connection between work as both something lauded and a form of punishment. It is this last point that I find the most interesting. Maibaum's play vacillates between presenting work in all forms, including theatrical labor, as repressive and dangerous and then praising labor—whether on the stage or in a store—as noble. In my reading, *A Moral Entertainment* seeks to display and justify theatrical labor while, at the same time, comparing it to other forms of labor—especially the struggles facing workers in other fields.[74] In turn, drawing on the long-standing views of Puritanism in American culture, it presents the very real dangers faced by theater workers from not simply the depravations of the theatrical labor market but also the accusations thrown at them from political figures. At once, the play advocates for the necessity of the FTP to provide work for actors—lest they seek out other forms of employment. But the play also suggests that there might be little the FTP can do to fully protect its workers from the rigors of the marketplace and the paranoia of audiences who see political radicalism in every performance.

A Moral Entertainment is set in 1690 in a small, fictional Puritan town named Maundy in Massachusetts. Peregrine Pillputt,—the minister as well as doctor and magistrate of the town—is dictating a letter for his sister to his nephew, Deodate. After lecturing his nephew on witches and sin, Pillputt is informed by his right-hand man, Experience, that a flyer for a production of *Romeo & Juliet* was found and there is a group of actors heading toward the town. Pillputt becomes incensed and sends Deodate to order the actors to leave. Meanwhile, outside of town in a deserted barn, Tony Ashton's company of players begin to set up for a performance of *Romeo & Juliet* that features his daughter Roslinda. The actors have been traveling all over New England, and most of their discussions focus on the dreams of what they will eat once they are paid. Several of the actors are willing to mutiny and leave the troupe—but Roslinda convinces them to stay and put on the performance. At this point, Deodate appears onstage and informs the players that they should not perform their "moral entertainment" of *Romeo & Juliet* or else they will be punished by the town elders. But before he leaves, Deodate appears to catch the eye of Roslinda. Despite his warnings, the players begin their performance, and when Pillputt arrives at the barn, he orders his nephew to arrest the actors.

Imprisoned in the town's jail, the actors become celebrities, attracting the flirtations of the single women in Maundy. This increases the ire of Pillputt, who orders most of the actors to be put onto a chain gang. The senior actors and Pillputt are concerned over the growing romance between Deodate and Roslinda. Pillputt orders a trial for the actors, with himself acting as judge and prosecuting attorney. Pillputt charges the players with performing lewd, immoral acts, but Roslinda offers an eloquent defense of acting in rebuttal. Speaking directly to the gathered townspeople, she notes that the players brought them laughter, joy, and song and begins to lead the crowd in a song and dance—which infuriates Pillputt. He orders his allies in the jury to render their verdict: they respond with "guilty" and Pillputt sentences the players to the stocks to have their ears and tongues cut. But then the dean of the commonwealth—a more moderate Puritan—orders the punishment suspended and offers the male players a choice: your sentences will be overturned if each man both marries a local woman and gives-up acting as a profession. And apart from Ashton and his colleague Ned, all the actors in the troupe agree to the offer. Enraged, Pillputt then declares that Roslinda be sent to Salem as a witch given that she has allured the townspeople.

As the play concludes, the married actors attempt to convince the holdouts to accept the dean's offer, but Ashton and Ned refuse. While Deodate plots to free Roslinda, Pillputt arrives at the jail where Ashton and Ned begin to enact a plan to escape. After failing to persuade Pillputt that they want to be saved, Ashton and Ned convince him that Roslinda would make a perfect wife for him and that he should sneak into Roslinda's section of the prison and embrace her. The actors then take the jail keys from Pillputt, lock him in the cell, and alert the villagers to see the minister's lustful nature. Roslinda and Deodate escape the town to live in Boston, and when the villagers accuse Pillputt of his own lustfulness, the minister declares that he's the victim of witchcraft.

Far better known for his work on most of the James Bond films from the 1960s to the 1980s, Maibaum attended the University of Iowa where various versions of his plays would appear onstage—including an early version of *A Moral Entertainment* in 1933. After graduating, Maibaum moved to New York and acted (he was the youngest actor to play Iago in *Othello* at the time) and wrote more plays, including *Birthright* in 1934, which is likely the first antifascist play produced in the United States. He also wrote *Sweet Mystery of Life* (which would be adapted by MGM as *Golddiggers of 1937*—more on that in Chapter 4) and would later have his biggest Broadway success with Harry Clork (cowriter of *The Milky Way* that I discuss in Chapter 5) with their comedy *See My Lawyer*, which ran for two years on Broadway and featured Milton Berle. By the mid-1930s, Maibaum had moved to Hollywood to work, and would write or cowrite several screenplays through the 1940s and 1950s.

While much of his legacy centers on the Bond films, Maibaum frequently wrote and produced films that addressed social issues, such as *Ransom!* (Alex Segal, 1956) and *Bigger Than Life* (Nicolas Ray, 1954),[75] and his concern over larger social issues can be seen in two of his plays. While attending Iowa, Maibaum wrote *The Tree*, which had a short run on Broadway in 1933, a play inspired by him being unnerved by the sight of a noose hanging from a tree in Iowa City (Maibaum was then appearing in a production of *The Hairy Ape* on campus). The play, which culminates in a Black man being lynched onstage by white terrorists while the Lord's Prayer is recited, was considered by critics—and Maibaum himself—too uncommercial for success. In *Birthright*, which he wrote also in 1933, Maibaum focuses on the Jewish German Eisner family who begin the play as a happy and prosperous group but who are persecuted by the rise of the Brown Shirts. Despite their culture and wealth, the Eisners struggle with their own sense of purpose and identity in the face of a reactionary movement. Reflecting on his early plays, Maibaum told a group of young theater workers that a playwright "has to be ready, emotionally and intellectually, to receive" inspirations for their work and then find an "incident or image" that triggers the writing: "In my own case, the sight of a rope dangling from the branch of a huge, blasted dead oak three (I think it must have been once part of a child's swing) started me thinking about the subject of lynching. . . . Seeing a group of young German Jewish refugees in London, one of them with his head bandaged, launched me on *Birthright*."[76] So, for a play written not long after both *The Tree* and *Birthright*, it makes sense for a fear of reactionary politics and movements to be present in *A Moral Entertainment*.

Whatever led Maibaum's play about Puritans to the FTP is unclear. In many interviews and speeches, Maibaum tended to focus on his experiences writing for the James Bond films—understandable given their cultural prominence. But, especially later in his life, he did reflect fondly on his theater successes of the 1930s, though he tended to focus on *The Tree* and *Birthright* and only sparingly referred to the FTP. But there are moments that I can glean of his interest and support for the program. Speaking to a conference of drama students and playwrights in 1962, Maibaum praised amateur theater for its lack of a professional aura that "creates an atmosphere of do-it-yourself in the best sense, which very often gives theatrical endeavor a vitality and an importance found nowhere else."[77] Asserting that the Robert Rossen–directed Broadway production of *The Tree* lacked the intensity of the Iowa City staging, Maibaum notes that some of the finest productions he has ever seen of his plays were not on Broadway but in Skowhegan, Maine; Iowa City, Iowa; and Roslyn, New York—site of one production of *A Moral Entertainment*.[78] Maibaum would again, indirectly, reflect on the FTP when attending the dedication of the E.C. Mabie theater in Iowa City, named after his mentor who taught at the university for decades: "We spoke about many things, and incidentally one of his great sorrows which he didn't speak about too [*sic*] many people was that the Federal Theater got mired down in politics and didn't outlast the Depression, because he felt in it the seeds of a truly great national theater that would have existed beyond the Depression."[79]

Maibaum's play was produced five times in 1938.[80] Within the FTP itself, the play was both praised and derided. In recommending the play for production, a reviewer for the FTP found the play excellent, as an "exceptionally droll piece of work" and "the first period comedy written in recent years at which I could do more than bat a jaundiced eye," even if "*Pursuit of Happiness* and one or two other alleged period comedies have met with some success on Broadway." Acknowledging that the play might be more difficult to produce than the average script given the three different sets and variety of costumes, the reviewer still felt the "the play is definitely worth the extra effort."[81] In contrast, Grace Fisher, reporting on rehearsals of the play in Hartford, was less than enamored of *A Moral Entertainment*: "My general impression was—mediocrity. The play loses its way and needs very expert and humorous treatment on the part of the director to bridge its structural lapses, particularly in the last act."[82] And paralleling the reviewers of the FTP, press reports were equally varied. A reviewer for the *Philadelphia Bulletin*, commenting on the Bryn Mawr production, found the play "brisk, manly fare" and thoroughly entertaining.[83] Yet for the most part, reviewers found the play frustrating or rudderless: reflecting on another production, William Kennedy dismisses the work as there is "nothing important about the play" and warns potential audiences there might be a few "moral lessons, but don't try to dig them out."[84]

The production of the play in Boston drew some negative reactions, part of which can be traced to the hostile reaction to the FTP and WPA in Boston itself. Workers for the WPA units in the city dealt with a great deal of stigmatizing, so much so that many who could have worked for the WPA did not.[85] Culturally, the city had a long history of reactionary censorship, gaining a reputation for campaigns against the works of figures like Upton Sinclair, Henrik Ibsen, and others. For the FTP unit, the issues began almost immediately for the organization with the production of Maxwell Anderson's *Valley Forge*. The play was selected, in part, due to the region's overall interest in history and while it generally reinforced American patriotism, it also contained scenes that showed historical figures as petty and cruel (especially when those scenes were taken out of context by hostile reporters). While later productions like *Created Equal* and *Lucy Stone* were able to tailor historical narratives to align with the interests of local patrons, there clearly was hostility toward the portrayal of Puritanism in *A Moral Entertainment* based on the reviews, especially what the viewers perceived as the mocking of colonial New England in the play. *Boston Herald* writer Elinor Hughes critiqued the play as "hardly humorous" and condemned what she saw as the stereotypical, ahistorical, unfunny, and backward view of Puritan punishment, including "slitting tongues, cutting-off ears and putting people in stocks, not to mention hanging and burning for witchcraft." Hughes also questioned the intent of the play, arguing that there was no clear perspective: "Was it really farce or a covert, serious treatment of Puritanism? The result was confusion in the writing and overall mood."[86] Another writer for the *Boston American* echoed Hughes's thoughts, noting, "There are times when it seems he [Maibaum] is at the point of saying something significant and pertinent to us, but he never does."[87]

Maibaum's portrayal of Puritan life draws on long-standing views of the religious order as paranoid, anti-art, and intolerant. As David D. Hall notes, it was during the 1930s that academic historians began to revise these views of the Puritans as stereotypically intolerant.[88] But this view of the Puritans as more nuanced did not fully translate into American popular culture, which drew on the works of not only Hawthorne but also nineteenth-century historians who reinforced the view that Puritans were intolerant toward the theater. But the primary new voice of anti-Puritan prejudice was H. L. Mencken in his essay "Puritanism as a Literary Force." In this work, Mencken condemned what he felt was the rise of a new-Puritanism in several social and cultural movements of the World War I era—especially Prohibition. These forces, Mencken believed, were detrimental to the vitality of American culture and would suck "in the Puritan spirit" and "enforce their fashion on the general public."[89] And without question, Maibaum's view of Puritan life reinforces these views of the religious group as killjoys and paranoid about the impact of theater and culture on the souls of the community; in doing so, both Maibaum and the performances of the play clearly connect to both the fear of new "Puritans" and likely critics of the FTP. Maibaum plays up the antitheatrical perspectives of Puritans as Pillputt condemns the players for luring "the mind from the contemplation of misery . . . , this citadel of pain and gloom in which we live," and for presenting "scenes of love, carnal love, [that] trick the mind into similar lust."[90] In addition, the Puritan characters espouse views that echo many conservatives who declared the FTP to be a boondoggle, as Puritans bemoan actors that "steal the honest wages of the poor" and declare the citizens of Maundy have better "things to do with hard won pennies than buy *their* wares."[91]

While the play critiques Puritan morality, *A Moral Entertainment* also shows the need for an organization like the FTP to provide some level of security for actors. Outwardly, the play makes it abundantly clear to its audiences that the acting profession is far from a stable labor: we are greeted with overt displays of the difficult working conditions facing the troupe as they travel around the countryside looking for any opportunity to work. Like the struggling actors in *Room Service*, the play shows theater workers struggling to eke out a livelihood. The characters complain about the lengthy traveling they have done with little success, a journey that has gone on so long that the soles of their shoes have given out. They are also on the brink of starvation; they have been in such a desperate state for food—and money in general—that they had to eat their horse and have "dragged the cart like a collier's dray" since.[92] Without question, the struggles of the actors onstage serve to remind audiences of the importance of security needed for these workers, and it is not much of a leap in logic to see this be an advocacy for the FTP itself.

Yet the more complicated conundrum posed by the play is what state-sponsored economic security looks like, since the play shows most of the actors finding security in other professions or within the town of Maundy itself. One of the clearest signals of this is how the men in the acting troupe are treated by the women of the town: the men are gifted pies, hams, sweet potatoes, and roast duck, and several of the characters voice a preference to this life as opposed to that of the stage. Like the contented Tramp in *Modern Times* who enjoys prison with scheduled meals, the actors here find a level of satedness that would be impossible while acting. Moreover, this section of the narrative seems to align with fears from artists and writers from both the political left and right who voiced concern over the affect security—especially security from federally funded work—would have on both the artist and the quality of their work. Granted the parameters are different here—the food security afforded the actors are gifts from townspeople, but it can be read as a metaphor of the "prison" of government-sponsored labor (or a conservative audience member could read these gifts as a metaphor of the "extravagances" given to actors on the government dollar). When the dean of the commonwealth offers the men "an acre of land, a horse, a goat, a pig, a cow, and . . . a wife" to leave the profession, several actors jump at the opportunity.[93] One actor exclaims, "I've always wanted a tailor's shop; I'll open one here!" Another actor declares that "acting's no life. The work's too hard. I'd rather fight redskins" than act.[94] To the actors who reject the deal, those who leave the profession are traitors, and in a sense, the play suggests that only those who are truly dedicated to the craft of acting will be willing to endure the struggles of acting. Yet the actors who give up acting have not only endured fights over whether their work has any merit but also struggled against a figure who demanded they adopt certain work norms. In turn, the dean's offer represents an alternative path to economic and job security, one by which an actor embraces labor that is not acting. In one respect, the dean's offer becomes the embodiment of work programs of the First New Deal, in which work was given to the unemployed not according to their respective training or skill but according to the need of the larger community. By showing actors leaving their profession for the greener pastures of other work, the play warns that the government might impact the acting profession, as many workers who do not necessarily subscribe to the radical notions of theatrical labor promoted by the FTP would be forced out of the program, thereby robbing the profession of some of its best workers.

While critiquing the allure of the state and nontheatrical marketplace, A Moral Entertainment also presents a complicated vision of theatrical labor itself, especially through its portrayal of Roslinda's acting. Certainly, the play shows her performance labor as carrying value for both herself and the communities she interacts with. Paralleling some of the female-centric backstage musicals of the 1930s and 1940s, Roslinda recenters the focus of the audience (both diegetic and real) on herself in moments like the trial scene, where she defends her troupe against the accusations lobbed against them by Pillputt. In turn, her defense of her labor becomes a not-so-subtle defense of theatrical labor overall, whether it be commercial or noncommercial in nature. Throughout her speech, Roslinda claims that the work of her troupe will bring "joy and honest pleasure to anyone."[95] Echoing this sentiment, she then turns to the assembled townspeople and asks them to consider how their world without theater—and joy—has rendered them alienated: "What have you let him [Pillputt] do to you? Laughter and song, where are you fled? . . . The spirit of joy and true delight! He's robbed it of you . . . and given you . . . what?"[96] She then asks the citizens of Maundy to witness a performance of her odes to love and to choose for themselves if they want to live under the repression of their souls or to enjoy life. The citizens begin to joyously dance and sing—spurring Pillputt to end the trial

Figure 2.2 Roslinda (*behind bars to the left*) looks out at her father locked up while several of the newly married ex-actors from the troupe stand to the right from the Boston production of *A Moral Entertainment*. *(Retrieved from https://www.loc.gov/item /musftpphotoprints.200223123/.)*

and convict the players (see Figure 2.2). Evoking language not unlike how Flanagan promoted the "uplift" that the FTP could provide audiences, as well as centering her argument on the joy and pleasure acting gives to audiences, Roslinda defends theatrical labor in a manner like other backstage texts.

However, this promotion of theatrical labor is complicated by the political implications of what Roslinda promotes. While her wording in her defense of theater seems politically neutral, some in her audience still read her performance as inherently political in nature—and more so, a direct threat to the stability of the community. Indeed, while Roslinda's speech encourages the townspeople, it also serves to further endanger her acting troupe. I suspect that Maibaum would have been keenly aware of the censorship movements in the 1920s, as many groups, drawing on nativist and anti-Bolshevik fears, began to seek out and censor any work that they perceived as dangerous to American norms of life. We can read Pillputt's condemnation of the stage as a parallel to politicians who condemned the FTP and its influence on audiences as subversive and politically radical. Even more so, we can see Pillputt as a stand-in for the censorship controversies that surrounded the FTP. As I detailed earlier, some of the most prominent productions of the program were both politically charged in nature and censored by administrators: the first living newspaper production of *Ethiopia* was shuttered by the Roosevelt administration, forcing Elmer Rice's resignation; *Stevedore* was banned in Boston; and the wife of the WPA director in Seattle thought that city's Negro Unit's production of *Lysistrata* was obscene.[97] And given this context, it is not difficult to see the parallels between *A Moral Entertainment*'s actors dealing with censorship and some of their audience finding their work, and the FTP, to be politically radical or morally objectionable.

But more pressing was the real-life "witch hunts" that were beginning to haunt the program as a whole: the investigations of the FTP and other agencies of Federal One for workers with communist and fascist allegiances. As Judith Brussell shows, the Division of Investigation (DOI), at the behest of the Department of Justice, delved into the supervisors of all federal arts programs for potential criminal prosecution. As she details, the DOI solicited any leads for potential communist and Nazi supporters through a variety of means—especially unsubstantiated accusations born of hearsay or through professional rivalries or attempts to curry favor with other government agencies. What is more, many investigators saw what they believed were suspicious financial boondoggles—the initial charge of the DOI—based on a lack of understanding of the nature of dedicated theatrical labor and the subsequent hours and overtime required of those workers.[98] And as investigators begin to morph their work into the political and ideological makeup of the FTP, vague or unnamed accusations of a person's political allegiances—often mixed with accusations of embezzlement—began to be leaked to the national press as well as other governmental circles, including the Department of Justice and, of course, the Dies committee.[99] Without question, workers would have been keenly aware of the dangers posed by selected witnesses to that body—especially as witnesses like Hazel Huffman, star witness to the Dies committee—told a fantastical vision of the political environment present in the FTP. Post-downfall of the FTP, Brussell argues that the DOI helped cement a "cold-war on culture," as it morphed from "an agency established to investigate fraud" to one that helped fuel "the long-standing persecution of persons in the arts and show business in America."[100] The play forecasts a symbolic and literal witch hunt for the FTP and for all other commercial and noncommercial theater. By the end of the decade, Hallie Flanagan was being questioned by the Dies committee about her program's promotion of communist ideals in plays that actively voiced such positions and in plays that did not. Despite its best intentions, the FTP was not able to protect its laborers from the audience, and by 1940, its employees were subjected to blacklists.

More than any backstage comedy, *A Moral Entertainment* presents the struggles of acting professionals and the need for economic security for actors. But as a play performed exclusively by the FTP, Maibaum's text becomes a parable for work conditions of the FTP itself. With its portrayal of desperate actors in need of work, the play advocates for the importance of the FTP in providing much needed employment for workers in need of a paycheck, suggesting that the program presenting the "work" to audiences was the solution. But the play is careful to acknowledge there are trade-offs with the allure of security offered by government with its overlapping of private enterprise and posits a fear of an artistic brain drain occurring in the acting space. And it presents a potentially harsh reality to the FTP itself: while warning, as *Room Service* does, overrelying on content that is too politically charged, the play argues that the very real danger facing the theatrical world in all forms is an audience predetermined to read the work as political in nature.

At the conclusion of most backstage musicals, films, and plays, the diegetic play within the play is staged, and the actors are praised by the diegetic audience—and the real audience as well. Whatever trials and tribulations the actors have suffered in the staging of a successful performance, they have reminded the real audience of the power and importance of the art form. In the backstage comedies I examine in this chapter, those tropes of their self-reflexive musical and backstage text brethren remain—but with important modifications. While certainly the staging of a successful production in *Room Service* drives the narrative, in the case of *A Moral Entertainment*, the production of a single play matters less than simply finding the opportunities for survival. In *The Torch-Bearers*, there is a question over the actual quality of the play produced. Moreover, these plays do function—like many self-reflexive musicals—with a conservative, ideological lens: women's labor is subservient to men's work, and domestic spaces are either restored or created at the conclusion of each play. Yet despite these complicated elements to the genre, the three plays here do demonstrate an aesthetic and ideological value to their assembled audiences—and at times, the FTP itself. *The Torch-Bearers*, although likely having a conservative appeal based on the play's performance history, demonstrates the need for the FTP for the promotion of women's work; *Room Service* signals the need for the FTP to recognize and modify its political content; and *A Moral Entertainment* shows the need for a program like the FTP to provide aid to theater professionals while, at the same time, demonstrating concern over the intervention of the state into art and the real danger facing its workers as a new moral crusade was beginning to endanger art professionals.

3

Middle-Class Work Comedies

The legacy of Charlie Chaplin's 1936 film *Modern Times* often rests on the overt leftist imagery in several of the film's most iconic scenes: the transition between sheep and workers hurrying to clock in to work, the Tramp's accidental arrest after picking up a red flag at a socialist demonstration, and, perhaps above all, the Tramp's literal entrapment by the machinery of capitalism as he gets caught in the giant gears of a conveyor belt. Yet the film is not as overtly leftist as its reputation suggests. Charles Maland argues that the film "guardedly affirms American middle-class values, particularly its optimism."[1] Take for instance a scene in which The Tramp and Gamin (Paulette Goddard) sit outside a middle-class home. They spy a husband and wife kiss as the husband leaves for work, followed by the wife skipping back into their home for "another apparently joyous day of housework." Yet this over-the-top, parodic moment is partially undercut by the fact that the subsequent daydream shared by the Tramp and Gamin about such a life "suggests their aspirations are remarkably similar to that of the parodied couple." Later in the film, Goddard's character luxuriates in an elegant fur robe like a typical middle-class consumer of the 1930s.[2]

While I tend to read Chaplin's portrayal of consumerist goals as slightly more satirical, the film's more complicated view of middle-class life and work connects to larger shifts in American culture toward portrayals of middle-class norms. While literary figures like F. Scott Fitzgerald and Nathanael West penned works that criticized consumerism and middle-class values, Hollywood began to shift its focus away from more morally ambiguous and

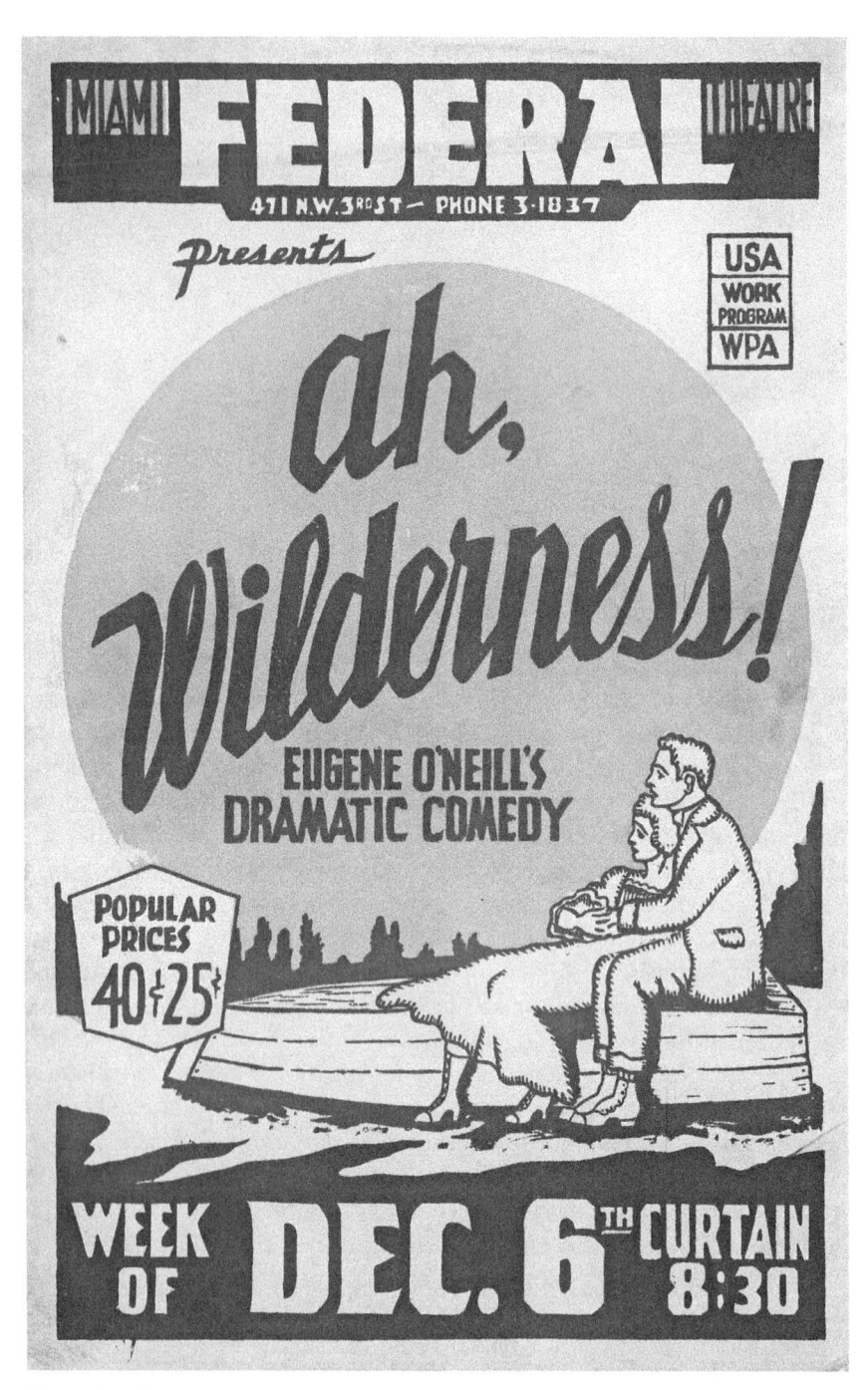

Figure 3.1 Poster for Miami production of *Ah, Wilderness!* that projects the play's nostalgic tone. *(FTP LC. Retrieved from https://www.loc.gov/item/musihas.200215809/.)*

ambitious characters like gangsters and showgirls that featured prominently in pre–Hays Code films to characters that were scions of middle-class values. As Morris Dickstein observes, "By the late 1930s, with economic fears somewhat allayed, success was associated with normality and ordinariness"—and American culture shifted an eye toward the postwar world of suburbia and prosperity.[3]

While Hollywood was beginning to promote more middle-class friendly fare, the FTP produced two relatively popular plays that problematized the middle class. In several respects, we can read the FTP productions of Eugene O'Neill's *Ah, Wilderness!* and Marc Connelly and George Kaufman's *To the Ladies* as plays that reassured middle-class, conservative audiences of not only the stability of middle-class life, but also that many of the tenets of middle-class labor—professionalism, gendered workspaces, consumerism—were also equally stable. And given that much of the New Deal was concerned with reestablishing the uniqueness and stability of middle-class work, it stands to reason that these plays functioned as reassuring texts for many audiences. Yet like the complicated views of middle-class working in Chaplin's *Modern Times*, the two plays I examine here offer a more problematic view of the work of the middle-class, especially in terms of the promises of labor and consumerism, and, I argue, go so far as to challenge the effectiveness of the New Deal's social and work programs (see Figure 3.1).

Middle-Class Labor and the New Deal

Writing in his 1935 tome *The Crisis of the Middle Class*, the Marxist philosopher Lewis Corey voiced his growing apprehension about the political and economic aims of the American middle class. Given his ideological allegiances, it is not surprising that Corey argued that the working classes and middle classes had a similar enemy in the "desperate capitalism"[4] that has denied work to millions "upon millions of manual and mental workers" even though there is an "abundance of the means and purposes of working."[5] Yet part of his concern was not simply how capitalism encourages "large scale permanent unemployment" but also the political ramifications of the conflict between the working classes and the middle classes.[6] Corey reasoned that part of the appeal of fascism in Europe was not simply the demagogic outbursts of political figures, but also the alliance between businessmen who "are involved in the all coercive relations of finance capital" and the middle class that abandons its ideals of individualism and free enterprise in the sake of more and total power.[7] For him, the paramount issue of the Depression was convincing the American middle class to not hold on to their economic power but to instead see the capacity of a new, revolutionary society.

Corey's work did not find an active audience in the brain trust of the New Deal. While there certainly were many Americans who advocated for a more leftist political shift in the nation, the Roosevelt administration did not—as detailed in Chapter 1 — embrace radical politics and social programs in the way their critics accused them of doing. And such conservative policies can especially be seen in relation to the restoration of the middle class in the New Deal: throughout the 1930s, various New Deal programs sought to both promote middle-class norms of work and reestablish the labor and consumerist aims of Americans who considered themselves middle class. Moreover, as the Depression continued into the late 1930s, the cultural reinforcement of middle-class ideology became more entrenched in American society, and there was a reactionary embrace of older models of class-identity and economic policies.

Defining what constitutes middle-class work is problematic. Partly, this is because by the first half of the twentieth century, many Americans began to subscribe most hallmarks of success—culturally, socially, economically—as part of a nebulous middle class. Marina Moskowitz charts how by the 1930s, many Americans began to simply see themselves as "middle class." And while several sociological studies of the era tried to categorize middle class through measurable financial criteria, many thinkers suggested viewing the middle-class identity beyond such strict terms as economic status. Many commentators began to note the increasing universality of middle-class norms across the nation, which "encompassed not only material goods but also access to education, leisure activities, the ability to save, and numerous other facets of social and economic standing."[8] And even if they exhibited a wide range of economic, social, or consumer goals, Americans were beginning to be connected by a national agreement on what they wanted. Buoyed by representations of middle-class life in radio, print, advertising, and cinema, Americans were able to share in a broad understanding of what it meant to be middle-class. Indeed, by the end of the decade, *Fortune* magazine had published a poll in which 79 percent of respondents considered themselves belonging to the middle class. And in his treatise on the political power of the middle class, Alfred Bingham suggests that the only real marker for belonging to the middle-class was a person or group's self-evaluation; if one considered oneself "middle-class," then one was, in essence.[9]

Despite the ubiquity of middle-class identification, for our purposes, I think it helpful to focus on a few hallmarks of middle-class labor in the early decades of the twentieth century. For Max Weber, one of the defining elements of middle-class identity was its outgrowth from the rise of the bureaucratic capitalist state. With the rise of the rational state came the demand for qualified experts who were trained and educated in specific fields—especially "technicians, clerks, et cetera" who obtained specialized degrees or passed examinations. Weber argues that such agency allows these specialized workers to intermarry with more notable families, to be admitted to new social circles, to qualify for social insurance, and "above all, . . . to monopolize socially and economically advantageous positions." This move toward professionalism is not, in Weber's mind, necessarily an "awakened 'thirst for education'" but a "desire for restricting the supply for these positions and their monopolization by the owners of educational certificates."[10] The rise of professionalization and specialization only continued with Taylorism. Often located as a hallmark of factory work with the simplification and routinization of work tasks, professional and managerial classes also faced the need for Taylorist specialization. This "further compartmentalization of knowledges, and the increasing authority" made the broad expertise of thinkers like William James or Silas Weir Mitchell next to impossible by the 1920s. In the case of Mitchell, his across-the-board medical expertise was "now split into the various fields and subfields of endocrinology, neurology, psychotherapy, family practice, public health, psychology, and others."[11]

The rise of professional, specialized work also began to morph how middle-class workers began to view their labor and leisure. For many of the middle class of the nineteenth century, the ideal work ethic was one based on leisure. However, as many members of the middle class began to enter various white-collar professions, many middle-class commentators began to promote the virtues of work to these workers.[12] But with this new dedication to work, middle-class workers began to experience intellectual alienation and physical exhaustion from their labor. The solution for this was the promotion of the concept of "hedonistic work." This was "a discursive trick that for the middle class, especially professions formerly associated with the leisure class—medicine, law, finance, art, scholarship—that work was a fundamental source of pleasure."[13] In hedonistic work, not only would one's health be improved, but also the process of working would supersede the value of one's production, in contrast to the labor theory of value. This promotion of work as a source of pleasure contradicted the traditional view of work as moral. As Tom Lutz argues, 1920s work was a reaffirmation of the work ethic, "not in its Weberian mode, as an iron cage, but in a spruced-up, boosterish, common-sense, fun-filled vein" seen in "cultural forums as diverse as 'success' pamphlets, industrial engineering journals, slick monthlies, and literary fiction."[14]

Another hallmark of middle-class life was the promotion of consumerism as a connection with one's leisure and work. Throughout the 1920s and 1930s, Americans increased their expenditures on items such as cars, personal appearance items, and a range of new commercial products despite growing economic turmoil. Advertisers embraced the idea of equating the consumption of goods with new, pleasure-minded ethics. Appliance advertisers promoted washing machines and vacuum cleaners that could "minimize the monotony and allow more pleasurable time with children and husbands, thus integrating mother's love with mother's work."[15] In the case of AT&T, advertising executives convinced the telephone company to discard its idea that telephones should not be used for "frivolous conversation" and embrace an ad campaign that promoted the convenience and comfort of consumers having "two to three telephone extensions" in a new, more stylized home.[16] Like the ads promoted to women that appliances could afford them the freedom to be better caregivers, ads like this one for AT&T emphasized the ease and leisure consumption could afford.[17] The early 1930s even saw politicians and producers cultivate a belief that workers needed more capital to spend on items to sustain the economy.[18] Immediately after the 1929 stock market crash, advertisers produced ads that blamed the Depression on a "buyer's strike" of workers unwilling to buy commercial goods, a viewpoint echoed in both the Hoover and Roosevelt administrations.[19]

As the Depression really began to impact the American economy in 1931, the long-standing sense of separation that middle-class workers felt about their unique work identity came undone as unemployment and class instability hit the middle class badly. In the words of C. Wright Mills, the Depression enacted a "status panic" on the middle class who had believed that their economic situation was inherently stable.[20] This was unusual given that in previous economic downturns, the workers most affected were laborers while the professional class was generally spared from any economic trauma. Not only did the Depression shatter the previously "easy" distinctions between the middle class and the working class, but it also undermined—or at least temporarily destroyed—the middle-class work ethic that had formulated over the course of the 1910s and 1920s. Work was no longer a place to find satisfaction with the pleasure of work, and many middle-class workers struggled with the fact that they could no longer "choose" their own labor, thereby fracturing their own abilities in making "their own choices."[21] What developed in the middle class was a pervasive "fear of falling," and there were "horror stories" of middle-class workers losing both their social status and material markers that were hallmarks of middle-class life. As Morris Dickstein notes, those who believed that America was "a land of progress and opportunity in which everyone could become middle class," struggled greatly as the "Depression . . . undermined the central myths and beliefs on which the system was founded."[22]

Overall, American popular culture generally tried to celebrate the norms of middle-class life, especially in terms of consumption and leisure, as well as narratives of characters and regular people "discovering" or "rediscovering" themselves. In one sense, the proliferation of self-help books from the decade illustrate that work norms were no longer the only sphere for identity, and that the tenets of the Puritan ethic—the value of thrift and discipline—were not the only keys to one's measure of success. In Walter B. Pitkin's *Life Begins at Forty*, for example, the author reassures middle-aged (and likely middle-class Americans) that the best years of their lives were ahead of them and that advances in technology would permit them to experience shorter working hours and increased leisure time. In her *Orchids on Your Budget*, Marjorie Hillis reminded her female readers that the Depression had made everyone poor, and there was no need to compare oneself or her family to "the Joneses" in the way one had in the 1920s. Yet despite her proclamations for embracing the reality of the Depression, Hillis still promoted the need for women to keep up their appearances through the purchase of makeup and clothing to maintain their femininity in the contemporary world. Joanna Scutts argues these self-help manuals "rarely concerned themselves with anything as mundane as budgets but promised instead that a reader could vault over the raging river with the help of mantras and magical thinking."[23]

Politically, a good portion of the New Deal was concerned with the restoration of middle-class work, both in terms of providing employment but also reinforcing long-standing views of middle-class work ethics. One of the most consistent ways in which New Deal programs reinforced middle-class work and social norms was through their respective approaches toward both hiring and training women. Drawing on a longer tradition of middle-class maternalistic reformers who held "fear that ethnic, racial, and class deviations from Anglo-American, middle-class maternal norms imperiled the cultural and ideological reproduction of a distinctively American citizenry," reformers helped construct models of the welfare state that equated social uplift through women's adoption of Americanized, middle-class norms of motherhood.[24] These positions of middle-class, white, and Anglo-American norming continued into many aspects of the WPA (but generally not the programs of Federal One), as the WPA refused to hire women who had access to the wage of a male "breadwinner." The organization also "routed most successful female applicants to jobs in sewing, canning, and school lunch preparation" while the CCC and the Household Service Demonstration Project trained women in both the "wifely arts" and as "domestic servants."[25]

These programs aligned with the Roosevelt administration's increased emphasis on promoting consumerist spending for workers. As Lawrence Glickman shows, the Roosevelt administration's promotion of consumer spending was hardly a new impulse in government policy as many Progressive politicians promoted such models, while Labor leaders had long promoted the adoption of living wages for workers of all backgrounds.[26] The central piece of New Deal legislation designed to encourage consumption was the NRA of 1933. The NRA tried to enable consumers to spend out of the Depression through a series of codes of competition that raised wages and allowed companies to establish minimum pricing of goods. While the NRA may have permitted the cartelization of major industries, it spawned a recognition in placing power with the consumer in programs like the AAA and its promotion of fair farm produce prices and other subprograms encouraged grass-roots movements for consumer organizations and cooperatives.[27] Additionally, many within the administration began to subscribe to Keynesian economic theory, especially after the Roosevelt Recession of 1937–38, whereafter "pump-priming moved to an entirely new level, with government spending to expand mass consumption becoming the assumed route out of depression toward new economic growth."[28] But many of these programs promoted a model of consumer spending that was predicated, again, on middle-class norms—especially in terms of domestic appliances and tools that were considered the mark of bourgeois status. Moreover, while the 1930s cemented this view of the importance of the consumer as an engine of economic growth, there remained real questions over the extent to which the Roosevelt administration enacted protections for those consumers.[29]

But the government's most "heavy-handed endorsement" of the domestic, middle-class sphere was its promotion of and intervention in the American housing market through two acts. First was the Home Owners' Loan Act of 1933, which bailed out the bankrupt mortgage system with far easier refinancing terms for both banks and investors. Second was the National Housing Act of 1934 that encouraged private investment in home construction by extending federalized loan insurance over primarily middle-class mortgages.[30] While these moves did prop-up the middle-class homeowners, banks, and construction companies invested in the project, other New Deal programs aimed at more urban, public housing projects were not as well-developed. Further, the Federal Housing Authority began to implement far more extensive loans and redevelopment programs to middle-class, white Americans for the purchasing of single-family homes in redlined neighborhoods that, along with post–World War II policies like the GI Bill, contributed to the de facto (and often de jure) segregation of many Black Americans in major cities.

Toward the end of the decade, middle-class Americans began to reembrace reactionary views of labor and consumption. As the Lynds detail in *Middletown in Transition*, many members of the middle class in Muncie, Indiana, voiced initial support for Roosevelt's New Deal policies when he first came to office, but by 1936, many middle-class residents had readopted their long-standing views that progressive programs reeked of socialism and endangered the stability of middle-class life. Middle-class residents understood that the "community is moving uneasily from its old world of 'charity' to a new and feared world of frank recognition of continuing community responsibility for the unable." Yet a considerable portion of that community—especially the "business class"—"is coming out of the depression in a mood of anxious resentment toward those on relief . . . and is prepared to give no quarter to, those whose morale has been broken by long unemployment and the humiliation of relief."[31] Moreover, the Lynds conclude that traditions in "optimism, growth, making money" that had marked the city prior to the onset of the Depression, were coming back in greater force in the later 1930s. People considered the Depression "just a bad bump in the road"—an occurrence that might "spoil things temporarily." The Lynds observe: "In a culture built on money, the experience of better homes, better cars, winter vacations in Florida, and better educated children dies hard; and while some people's hopes, especially among the working class, have been mashed out permanently by the depression, the influential business group who determine the wavelength of Middletown's articulate hopes are today busily broadcasting the good news that everything is all right again."[32]

This sense that "everything is all right again," combined with the various reaffirmations of middle-class work promoted by American culture and much of the New Deal, informs the FTP productions of *Ah, Wilderness!* and *To the Ladies.* On the one hand, these plays align with the broader confirmation of middle-class work and social norms, and certainly many audiences would have been more than content with seeing those values reflected in those productions. However, both plays contain critiques to the same societal and labor norms of the middle class, especially when considering how middle-class patrons were veering toward older models of work and charity and how issues of consumption still registered with audiences.

Ah, Wilderness!

When Flanagan received permission from George Bernard Shaw and Eugene O'Neill for the FTP to stage their plays for minimal compensation, it was a huge coup for her program. O'Neill himself saw the staging of his plays as the source of real potential for playwrights around the world; in his press release announcing his agreement with the FTP, he declared, "The WPA units can present important plays before audiences that never before have seen an actual stage production. The possibilities in this respect are thrilling . . . these units are translating into action the fact that the government has an obligation to give a reasonable amount of encouragement and assistance to cultural undertakings."[33] And over the course of its run, the FTP staged fourteen different O'Neill plays—ranging from *The Iceman Cometh* to *Emperor Jones* to *The Hairy Ape.* However, the O'Neill play most often selected for performance on the federal stage was not one of his modernist dramas but the comedy *Ah, Wilderness!* The play was often described by critics as a simple and nostalgic view of small-town life at the turn of the twentieth century, and in several respects, the play promotes a vision of middle-class work and life that is incredibly conventional. Indeed, part of the play's popularity can be connected to its portrayal of the angst-ridden teenager Richard who eventually disavows leftist politics.

And yet the play's reputation as nostalgic, family-friendly fare (for O'Neill at least), ignores the more problematic elements of the play. In this section, I examine the background of O'Neill's comedy and chart his own rationale for writing the play, as well as its broad reception nationally—especially how those in conservative circles embraced the text. But I also note how FTP performances of the play may have also promoted a complicated view of professionalization and, more importantly, the fallacy that work alone can cure what "ails" a suffering workforce.

Ah, Wilderness! centers on the Millers, an upper-middle-class family living in an unnamed Connecticut town in 1906 (based on Waterbury where O'Neill grew up). The play focuses on the relationship between Nat, the patriarch of the family; his brother-in-law Sid, who struggles with alcoholism; and Richard, the sixteen-year-old son of the Millers. As the play begins, the Miller family is busily preparing for their July 4 activities—and Nat kindly listens to Richard's thoughts on poetry and politics. Nat and Sid are planning to head to a civic club's holiday picnic—which causes Essie Miller and Lilly, Sid's girlfriend, some concern given Sid's drinking. Richard then attempts to sleep with his girlfriend, Muriel, but is rejected by her. Richard is then told by a friend of his older brother about a bar on the outskirts of town that might help satisfy his urges. As Richard heads to the bar, Nat and Sid return from the picnic drunk, and the family becomes amused by Sid's drunken singing.

While at the bar, Richard encounters a prostitute named Belle who tries to get Richard to purchase some services from her. A traveling salesman appears at the bar, and he, Belle, and the bartender begin to toy with Richard, until the bartender throws a drunk Richard out for trying to fight both him and the salesman. Back at the Miller residence, the family is reminiscing about previous holidays and singing songs when Sid reappears after having passed out from too much alcohol. He begins to dramatically apologize to Lilly for his actions, bemoaning the fact that he is not worthy of her love.

Essie and Nat contemplate Richard's punishment while Sid attempts to allay their concerns over him. Nat declares that he will punish Richard by not sending him to Yale (and then forcing Richard to apologize and repent). After Nat returns to work at the newspaper, Richard comes downstairs and learns that his girlfriend, Muriel, wants to see him. After a spirited debate, they reconcile, and Richard returns home to face his father. Nat lectures Richard on the error of his actions and then "punishes" Richard by telling him he will not be going to Yale—to which Richard accepts happily as he wants to marry Muriel. Backtracking, Nat declares his son's punishment will be to go to Yale and the play ends with the Millers happy that their son will be able to take care of himself.

O'Neill's play was quite popular on the FTP stage, being staged eleven times in 1937 and 1938.[34] The popularity of the play can be, in part, explained by O'Neill's status as a preeminent playwright, but also by, as Leslie White notes, how his comedy was the "amusing, entertaining, and sentimental story of an average small-town family, which touted homespun values and evoked a bygone era when life was simpler and problems were easily solved with massive doses of love and understanding."[35] This reading of O'Neill's play is reflected in the reader reports for *Ah, Wilderness!*, and the reviewers vacillate between seeing the potential of the play on the FTP stage, while also being puzzled by O'Neill's drastic shift in style and tone in this play compared to his other work. In a lengthy memo detailing the original New York production, the author of said memo frequently repeats the words *Homey* and *tender*—often underlining those phrases so that any reader is *sure* to get their message.[36] In another anonymous report, a writer notes that while there is a "good deal of Marxian philosophy . . . inferred by his remarks about salvaging the downtrodden working masses," it is only to show the effect of such leftist literature on O'Neill's "sensitive youth." The writer ends this memo by noting that the play "closes without once offending the delicate sensibilities of anyone" remaining "a composite tender and charming picture of sweetness and light" but "hardly a step forward in the growth of the drama."[37] A final reviewer, while recommending the play, summarized *Ah, Wilderness!* as "definitely a reaction against a reaction." The reviewer posits that not only is the play a drastic departure from O'Neill's earlier work, but it is also problematically devoid of any social context: "a romantic reaction against the post-war prowling into the nature of small-town life as well. The small-town folk are not seen realistically, but sentimentally through the haze of memory. O'Neill gives a picture of the American of 1906 with all the quaint trappings of the age as a background for his story of the sufferings of adolescence. . . . Of the tremendous intellectual and social forces at work during the period there is only the slightest hint."[38]

This reading of the play as politically neutral and family friendly was echoed in the press and internal coverage of the FTP productions. One critic, commenting on the New Orleans production, notes that there is a "human appeal in the play, such a time defying quality that we love it, not because of the presentment of manners and clothes, but because of the emotions which it evokes."[39] The director of the Des Moines, Iowa, production reported a generally positive response to O'Neill's work, one in which he and the actors played up certain aspects of O'Neill's play and downplayed others. He noted that "comedy relief in the script was played up to get the most value from it and any objectionable material or situations (swearing, etc.) were toned down so as not to make the production offensive to anyone who might object to these elements." In particular, the director noted that he advised his actors in the bar scene to play their characters to stereotypical levels in order to "give these unpleasant and sordid characters a slight touch of unreal artificiality," thereby taking any "vulgar sting" from the scene, and ensuring the play was "enjoyably received by the audience" in Des Moines.[40] In the same play report, there is a clipping from the *American Citizen*, a publication of the National Italian-American Civic League, in which a Catholic priest urges his parishioners to attend the play.[41] But perhaps the most telling responses were audience surveys from the Los Angeles production of the play. One commentator, referencing the play's film adaptation, noted that there should be plays performed that "as far as possible have not been screened" as it is "hard to compete with them." Another reviewer noted that the play appealed to a specific crowd: "I have never seen a gathering of so many old people which proves to me that the interest of the older people is still with the spoken drama." The older crowd's enthusiasm for "spoken drama," which suggests a rejection of more than contemporary dramatic fare, is echoed by another audience member who wanted the FTP to stage "similar plays, comedies, and family plays" but no "deep dramas or problem plays."[42]

Based on the reception of the play, audiences certainly seemed to have embraced the text in part due to what they saw as its embedded nostalgia. Indeed, part of his rationale for writing *Ah, Wilderness!* was a sentimental turn O'Neill experienced. In the summer of 1931, O'Neill revisited his childhood home in New London, Connecticut—the same home that was the basis of *Long Day's Journey into Night*—and began to reflect on both the nature of adolescence and his own upbringing. For whatever reasons, O'Neill's reflections turned nostalgic, and he began to write the play after taking a break from *Days without End*, completing the script within a month. By 1932, O'Neill had lost his father, mother, and brothers, and he had been divorced twice and was beginning his turn toward the isolation and health problems that would last nearly two decades. So it seems the writing of the play aligned with a brief period of contentment in his life. Scholars read the play as O'Neill partially romanticizing a vision of his childhood that he would have liked, but despite the nostalgic tone of the play, there remains a rather looming sense of darkness with the characters. In fact, as James Fisher shows, O'Neill's original plan was to write a sequel to *Ah, Wilderness!* that would have featured Sid fully recovered from his alcoholism, but an older Richard having returned from World War I a broken, bitter man.[43]

Aside from being the most atypical play O'Neill ever wrote, *Ah, Wilderness!* might be the playwright's most conservative play in terms of themes, as well as reception as the Broadway productions, touring productions, and film adaptation promoted some conservative readings. While the original play was confounding to critics upon its premiere, it was incredibly popular with audiences. Much of its popularity can be attributed to the casting of George Cohan in the initial Broadway production. Long associated with sentimental, patriotic performances, Cohan's career had suffered post–World War I as Broadway moved toward embracing more European-influenced plays—including the works of O'Neill. As I detail in Chapter 1, Cohan became a vocal proponent of "theater as entertainment" in the 1930s, condemning the offensive material he saw in many plays of the 1930s. In addition, his reputation as a political and social conservative preceded him onstage, adding to a star persona that cultivated more reactionary views. Cohan also toured with the play for a time, and while some managers grew concerned over how Cohan was ad-libbing and generally going off script to add a more folksy element to his performance, his "Norman Rockwell" approach to pacing and delivery resonated with audiences who wanted to see, in their minds, real Americans onstage.[44] In addition, the casting of Will Rogers in the touring production of the play in the western states (Cohan toured with the touring production in eastern states) added an additional layer of comfort to the reception of the play nationally. Rogers had cultivated a cross-class, cross-cultural persona in American theater and film since his days on the vaudeville circuit, and while Rogers's politics often leaned toward the left, he often maintained a more neutral political persona publicly and was a considerable draw on both stage and screen. The casting of both men signaled to audiences the relative political safety of the play—and its reputation transferred to FTP audiences.

The 1935 film adaptation of the play, directed by Clarence Brown and starring Lionel Barrymore and a young Mickey Rooney, also signaled a more conservative reception among audiences. It was produced by MGM at a time when that studio was embracing family-friendly art and conservative politics. While MGM gained a reputation in the pre-Hayes Hollywood world for promoting more risqué films, once Louis B. Mayer assumed more control of the studio after the death of Leo Thayer in 1936, he began to promote more family-friendly films, and generally adopted a far more conservative ethos in the production and marketing of MGM films. Mayer's own conservativism was well-known in the industry. While Mayer did initially support the Roosevelt administration in the early days of the New Deal, the studio became far more politically opposed to leftist politics by the middle 1930s, going so far as to help film a series of anti–Upton Sinclair short films to air in their California-based theaters during the former writer's failed End Poverty in California campaign for governor in 1936.[45] While *Ah, Wilderness!* would premiere one year before Mayer took more direct control of the company, it certainly aligns with the ideological shift of the studio that would embrace in the following years. The film did so well at the box office, it inspired MGM to bring back most of the cast for *A Family Affair* (George B. Seitz, 1937), which would be the first of sixteen Andy Hardy films made during the 1930s and 1940s.[46]

A good portion of this positive reception among conservative circles of the play lay with its content, which generally promotes a stable vision of middle-class life. One way is how the play treats Richard's interest in leftist politics as a childish fad, which certainly would have been appealing for national and regional audiences leery of leftist rhetoric in 1930s politics, as well as the FTP's more radical productions. In Act 1, Richard proclaims his political allegiances by condemning capitalist America in a rant influenced by his reading of leftist literature. He declares, "I don't believe in this silly celebrating the Fourth of July—all this lying about liberty—when there is no liberty."[47] He continues by sarcastically commenting on American society, evoking the socialist rhetoric of the early 1900s (the historical setting of the play), as well as the communist language of the mid-1930s:

> The land of the free and the home of the brave! Home of the slave is what they ought to call it—the wage slave ground under the heel of the capitalist class, starving, crying for bread for his children, and all he gets is a stone. The Fourth of July is a farce![48]

Richard's embrace of leftist ideals also parallels the criticism leveled against middle-class intellectuals from many affiliated with the Communist Party, such as O'Neill's friends Michael Gold and Genevieve Taggard. Gold was blunt about his rejection of the intellectual class, preferring to promote writers who wrote about the authentic experiences of working-class life. Yet O'Neill was, by the 1930s, beginning to voice concerns over communism in the United States and thus portrays Richard's political stance as nothing more than a passing fad.[49] Just as the closing number of *O Say Can You Sing* reminded audiences that interest in "the red" was only temporary, the FTP performances of *Ah, Wilderness!*, with Richard's recommitment to his family, his girlfriend, and college would have suggested to its audiences that even the most boisterous of middle-class radicals would eventually reembrace the norms of middle-class life.

The key tenet of middle-class life that the Millers promote is a middle-class view of working, especially that of professionalization. There is, for starters, a clear-line of gendered labor in the play: the Miller family is divided between the male professionalized workers (Nat and Sid as reporters) and female nonprofessionalized workers (Essie and Lilly as domestic workers). And while the action of the play primarily takes place in the Miller residence and the labor we do see onstage is prescribed women's work like cooking and nurturing the family, the characters place greater emphasis on the needs of the male professional workers, specifically Sid's struggles with employment and Nat's desire to head to the office even when the family has to deal with Richard. Nat bemoans, "Damn it, I'd ought to be back at the office putting in some good licks! I've got a whole pile of things that have got to get done today!"[50] This gendered view of middle-class work and professionalization also extends to Richard's education, as Essie notes: "You mark my words, that boy's going to turn out to be a great lawyer, or great doctor, or a great writer."[51] As such, Nat's rationale for jokingly suggesting that Richard's punishment for his transgressions would be to not attend Yale is that his son would be so horrified at this loss of professionalization that therein would be the punishment onto itself. Yet Richard—deeply in love with his girlfriend—is ecstatic when his father suggests Yale is not in his future, as he reasons to Muriel, "Perhaps I needn't go to Yale. Perhaps Pa will give me a job."[52] Richard's emphasis on "job" suggests that he is not thinking of a potential career, but more of a lower-position that will simply offer him a salary—a position that both horrifies his girlfriend and his father—who changes Richard's punishment to going to Yale. The "punishment" functions as comedy, but it is Richard's reembrace of the need for professionalization that alleviates the fears of his parents as the play reaffirms the norms of middle-class work.

While Richard may be positioned to readopt the tenets of middle-class life, I think it is fair to read the play as challenging some other aspects of middle-class life—especially in terms of the socioeconomic climate of the era. Certainly, the play presents Richard's interest in Marxism not as a calling, but as something more akin to a hobby or fad—even if he may believe in the righteousness and legitimacy of his cause. And while O'Neill himself may have started to doubt the plausibility of communism, he nevertheless saw the damage that capitalism placed on social classes of all types—especially the middle class itself. In some respects, we can read the play as forecasting O'Neill's condemnation of the socioeconomic climate at the start of World War II. O'Neill saw the middle class, "the small businessman, shop keeper, whiter collar worker, professional man, small farmer, etc.," being destroyed by the dual forces of "Big Business and Unionized Labor." Richard's eventual disavowing of his Marxist interests can also be read as an acknowledgment of the growing concern of leftist sociologists of the 1930s that the middle class's reembrace of capitalist impulses—especially concerning work and consumerism—was disavowing the very real dangers that capitalism had inflicted on middle-class stability during the Depression.

The play also presents some problematic views of class politics and charity in relationship to O'Neill's other work as well as within the context of the New Deal. In part, the play's portrayal of lower-class labor seems to align with a more middle-class view of the permanence of lower-class life—a sentiment seen in *The Iceman Cometh*. Such a perspective is not unusual in discussions of O'Neill's work, as scholars have long noted the playwright's doubts about the benefits of charity to the poor. As John Patrick Diggins argues, O'Neill illustrates his complicated view about the nature of charity and reform in *The Iceman Cometh* when drunken characters "shape up and don clean clothes in order to exit the tavern—only to scurry right back in the next scene."[53] Despite his sympathetic portrayals of the patrons of the Last Chance Saloon, O'Neill presents figures who cannot see their own realities and do not seem capable of changing their circumstances. Unlike his communist playwright peers, O'Neill "could see no revolutionary potential in the working class."[54] This view of the working class as self-destructive is represented in *Ah, Wilderness!* through an interaction between Richard and Belle, the prostitute he encounters at a bar. Richard attempts to convince Belle to change her life: "Only you oughtn't to lead this kind of life. It isn't right—for a nice girl like you. Why don't you reform?" He even gives her five dollars out of a sense of pity. Belle angrily rejects Richard's money, as she interprets an ideological motivation behind his gift. She says, "Nix on that line of talk—Can it. You hear! You can do a lot with me for five dollars—but you can't reform me. See!"[55] Richard naively, perhaps condescendingly, believes he can reform Belle, but, at the same time, Belle refuses to listen to Richard's pleas and then proceeds to berate his morals and his poetry.

Yet while the play mirrors O'Neill's skepticism of the working class, *Ah, Wilderness!* is equally critical of the rationales of the middle classes toward charity and, by extension, distorted readings of the relationship between work and the New Deal. Richard's interactions with Belle parallel the Lynd's criticism of the white-collar class in their work *Middletown in Transition*. In their critique of the business class of the United States, the Lynds found that while the middle classes were initially supportive of Roosevelt's programs, their enthusiasm quickly waned as older attitudes about work and relief began to reappear in their rhetoric. Increasingly, the Lynds and their researchers found that the middle class was "coming out of the depression in a mood of anxious resentment toward those on relief."[56] In certain respects, Richard's interactions with Belle illustrate the Lynds' criticism. Richard's plea that Belle does not need to work as a prostitute and his offer of some money reflects long-standing views over charity and the concept of work relief. There is both an overtone of social reformer rhetoric in Richard's exchange with Belle and the expectation that a small payment, or figurative dole, will help resolve Belle's social and economic plight. When Belle screams that his payment will not reform her, she is not just alluding to how unwilling she is to change her ways, but also to how ineffective such a small amount will be in helping her out of her situation. In a sense, Richard's "dole" toward

Belle and his own frustration that she will not accept his payment parallels this middle-class view of social charity.

This approach of older models of reform and charity toward social problems is also reflected in how the Miller family addresses the alcoholism of Sid. Drawing on newer reform movements, the play seems to suggest that the Millers believe that the cure for Sid's disease is simply more work. While *Ah, Wilderness!* does not engage in as lengthy an interrogation of alcoholic reform and charity movements as *The Iceman Cometh*, the characters certainly voice frustration toward Sid's drinking, especially his girlfriend, and the play also suggests that Sid may have been exposed to older forms of moral reform. At his most intoxicated after a holiday picnic, Sid entertains the Miller family by wandering offstage and singing an old Salvation Army hymn, "By the Sweet By and By." But the play also aligns with the rise of newer reform organizations like Alcoholics Anonymous. Founded in 1935, the group promoted a religious approach to combating alcoholism, one that preached self-discipline and appealed to many middle-class audiences. As Eoin F. Cannon shows, this culminated with the publication at the end of the decade with what is colloquially termed *The Big Book*, which showcased stories of many professional, executive, and skilled workers who detailed the disintegration of their labor stability due to alcoholism. *The Big Book* detailed stories of "long strings of second chances, gradually sullied reputations, charitable interventions by friends and family,"[57] and the downfalls of middle-class people who went from "country-club comfort to back-alley destitution."[58] These narratives promote the idea that the meaningful work of recovery is not simply about improving oneself, but "redeeming career failure and returning to work," thus illustrating for readers a path to "reconstruct middle-class senses of self."[59] And while *The Big Book* comes into existence only in 1939, Sid serves as a model example of the middle-class struggles and stories so often repeated in the literature—especially in terms of his continual employment struggles. After his latest drunken outburst, Nat confesses to Essie that Sid confided to him—"after he'd got enough Dutch courage in him"—that he had been fired from his new post working for the Waterbury paper, a job that we learn that Nat had procured for his brother-in-law.[60]

Yet like Richard's own misplaced approach to the "dole" he provides Belle, Nat's work solution to the struggles of his brother-in-law is also problematic. Evoking the language of social reformers, both religious and secular, Nat preaches a need for Sid to gain self-reliance—but there is no indication that employment will alleviate his suffering. As he expresses his rationale for giving Sid work, Nat reasons that there will have to be personal reform on Sid's behalf: "I knew something was wrong when he came back home. Well, I'll find a place for him on my paper again, of course. He always was the best news-getter this town ever had, though you can't always print what he brought in. But I'll tell him he's got to stop this damn nonsense."[61] But the play provides us no indication that will happen. The person who knows him best, his girlfriend Lilly, laments at the beginning of the play that no matter how often she implores Sid to change, his drinking, gambling, and philandering continues unabated.[62] Writing about *The Iceman Cometh*, Cannon argues that at the end of that play, the "real suffering involved in both alcoholism and economic depression made promises of redemption and serenity especially alluring" but "no sooner has the new salvation won its converts than it self-destructs by its own self-deception." In short, no matter what conversion is offered to the suffering, reform is unsustainable.[63]

Work as portrayed in *Ah, Wilderness!* functions as a cure-all for the tribulations of the middle class. And while that holds the power to provide temporary alleviation from serious struggles, it cannot fully alleviate those issues. And unlike Richard, who will reembrace the tenets of middle-class life and work, there is no guarantee that another member of the middle class, the alcoholic Sid, can be reformed through labor. In a sense, the play comments on the nature of work-relief itself. While good-intentioned, it cannot make up for the broader issues facing those who face social and economic deprivation. And the views of the middle class, which align with such approaches to work-relief, as well as work on the whole, are not helping those on the dole.

To the Ladies

One of the other avenues via which the Roosevelt administration actively sought to promote middle-class work norms was through the medium of radio. After Roosevelt's reelection in 1936, the federal government—drawing on the institutional framework of the Federal Radio Education Committee—developed the Office of Education, as well as the Radio Division within the FTP. In her work, Joy Hayes argues that New Dealers saw to capitalize on the connections between commercial advertising and education with these radio programs: "Advertising and publicity gained a foothold in everyday life in the 1920s and 1930s with the growth of chain stores, corporate-controlled media, and broadcast advertising. Rather than seeing a contradiction between propaganda, education and advertising, these New Deal officials identified a kinship between them." Working with commercial networks, New Deal radio workers developed "commercial genres including variety shows, detective stories, audience participation shows, and the historical pageant . . . program popularized by DuPont's Cavalcade of America (1935–1953)."[64]

The federal government also produced a series of "domestic drama" radio programs like *Wings for the Martins* and *Pleasantdale Folks* to promote the Social Security Act. One of the central aims of the programs "was to convince women to embrace their dependence on male breadwinners as the best means of achieving economic security."[65] Another key theme in these domestic radio dramas was the "internal" threat of women to domestic stability. In *One Man's Family*, one of the central characters is Fanny Barbour—a devoted wife, mother, and grandmother, who frequently decries the "modern" women of the 1930s who have neglected their families and are "responsible" for 90 percent of divorces. But "in the familial discourse of *One Man's Family*, all women have the potential to corrupt and compromise the traditional family home and thus the moral strength of America. As the woman in the Barbour family with the most authority, then, Fanny must be carefully policed and contained."[66] Structurally, the show rebukes Fanny's independence and demonstrates the "menacing potential" of her freedom. But Hayes also argues that the self-conscious assertions of patriarchal power in the show—such as characters saying, "You know Mother, I think you'd have made a rather imposing Matriarch but for the fact that Dad's so definitely head of the house"—undermined male authority. Within the homes of the radio dramas, "female prerogatives could not be so easily contained."[67]

Within this context, *To the Ladies*, Marc Connelly and George Kaufman's popular Broadway comedy, straddles the line between endorsing the New Deal ethos toward middle-class values and women in the workplace and undermining those standards. Through the play's illustration of work values, gender, consumerism, and domesticity, the FTP productions of *To the Ladies* suggest a push-back against larger New Deal conservatism, especially in terms of WPA hiring practices.

To the Ladies centers on a recently married suburban New Jersey couple, Elise and Leonard Beebe. At the beginning of the play, the couple prepares for the visit of Leonard's boss and his wife, Mr. and Mrs. Kinkaid. Leonard is a clerk at Mr. Kinkaid's piano factory, and Leonard's invite is a not-too-subtle attempt to sway his boss for an open middle-management position. While Leonard frets, Elise carefully prepares their home for the visit. We learn that Leonard is a bit financially reckless, having spent a considerable amount of money purchasing a share of a grapefruit farm in Florida (which will turn out to be a fraud) and buying a Kinkaid piano on credit to impress his boss. When the Kinkaids finally arrive, Mr. Kinkaid and Leonard struggle to engage in conversation while Mrs. Kinkaid and Elise become fast friends. But then two truckmen come to collect the piano due to Leonard's lack of payment. While Leonard attempts to find money to pay his creditors, Mr. Kinkaid pays Leonard's balance due—angrily declaring that it is hardly the look for an employee of his to be in debt. Elise then pleads to both Mr. Kinkaid and his wife about their situation and to not judge Leonard for his bad investments. She tells them that she and Leonard are just a poor couple just looking for their chance, and her appeals sway Mrs. Kinkaid to nudge her husband into inviting Leonard to a formal banquet.

At the banquet, there are a series of vacuous speeches from a senator, Mr. Kinkaid himself, and a vice president detailing the company's struggles with a strike. But just before Leonard is to give his speech, Chester, his friend and office rival, gives his speech—which is the exact same speech Leonard planned to give. As her husband clams up, Elise steps forward and after claiming that her husband has laryngitis, gives an impromptu speech that encourages the assembled to be like Mr. Kinkaid and earns her loud applause.

The play's final act takes place in the space outside Mr. Kinkaid's private office where Leonard is working as Mr. Kinkaid's assistant. Leonard has his own secretary—whom he talks down to quite frequently—and his promotion has made him unpopular at the office. On an afternoon when Elise is coming to go to lunch with Leonard, two of his coworkers angrily condemn Elise's speech as overrated and charge that Leonard is not only less of a man but also undeserving of his promotion as he did not pen the speech as Elise claimed at the banquet. Mr. Kinkaid overhears this and immediately demotes Leonard to his old position. But Elise and Mrs. Kinkaid urge him to reconsider as they point out that all husbands who work in business have wives who assist them—including Mrs. Kinkaid who reminds her husband of various ideas she has had. Trying to save face, Mr. Kinkaid promotes Leonard to his old position, and as the play ends, Mrs. Kinkaid and Elise savor their victory and plan to discuss other ideas for the company at their weekly lunch.

To the Ladies was originally commissioned by producer George C. Tyler as a vehicle for Helen Hayes. While the initial plot of the play was easy for Connelly and Kaufman to develop, the writing of the play itself was more complicated. Their general idea was to "satirize big business in as many ways as came to mind," but they wanted to write the play not from the perspective of an executive but of an ordinary white-collar employee.[68] Originally, the pair had Leonard become so exacerbated with the pretentiousness of management that he would pull himself out of the running for a promotion and remain a clerk for the piano company, but Tyler wanted a final act that had Leonard becoming a success with the help of Elise.[69] A modest hit that ran for 128 performances, the show soon went on the road, but Tyler was confused by audience responses to the play. They did not respond to the satire of the play since "so strong was their identification with the Beebes in the struggle to secure Leonard's promotion," and they often did not laugh at the banquet scene which rang too close to audiences' own insecurities. As Malcolm Goldstein asserts, it was perhaps "not satiric enough for a robust run in New York and too much so for the road."[70] The *New York Times* was certainly praiseworthy in its review, in which the writer extolled the virtues of the latest offering from Connelly and Kaufman. The play was "guilefully and humorously tweaked," and climaxes with its takedown of "that astounding institution, the American banquet," and its terrible cliché, the smug and pompous "after-dinner speech."[71] Of course, such praise from the *Times* is tempered by the fact that the writer of this piece was Alexander Woollcott, a founding member—along with Connelly and Kaufman—of the Algonquin Round Table, a group that was rather well known to have engaged in logrolling of one another's works.[72] With its modest success, Kaufman and Connelly did sell the rights to the play to Paramount, which released a film version in 1922 (which is now considered a lost film).

When the play was discussed for inclusion in the FTP catalog, readers found the play to be staid and outdated. One reader felt the play was simply like "all the other of Kaufman's works" with a very basic plot with a "simple fellow is given the job of creating sympathy." The reader feels that the play succeeds in presenting Leonard as a sympathetic figure as he "believes in all the ads about getting rich quick" as "would any fellow" who is susceptible to such rhetoric.[73] Another reviewer, Henry Bennett, found the play rather behind the times as its "theme, a young man's advancement in business, is no longer fashionable" and that a great many of the play's references to "prohibition or vaudeville" are dated. Bennett argues that the play could "be brought-up-to-date in its topical references; it would then have a good deal of appeal for audiences who don't insist on the very latest in comedy styles."[74] However, one reader went so far as to reject a revival of the play by the FTP, noting that while there is good comedy in it, "much of the dialogue is dated and localized" (to New Jersey) and that the "entire part of Chester would have to be rewritten to bring it up to date." The reviewer complains that since Chester is attracted to vaudeville and mentions a lot of vaudeville theaters, this would be "confusing to most auditors" since "the death of vaudeville is of common knowledge." Moreover, "names of personages now dead are also used." While rejecting the play for FTP production, the reviewer concludes that "if these changes would be made, then the reader reasons it could be a pleasant comedy."[75]

Despite the apprehensions of readers, the play was performed by the FTP four times, three of which were staged in California.[76] The interest in the Golden State possibly stems from both the state's 1930s politics and the reputation of the play itself. A conservative stronghold in the 1930s, the WPA and the FTP (as well as the New Deal overall) were frequently targeted by more conservative newspapers in places like Los Angeles beginning in 1935. And given the complicated politics of California in the Depression era, it stands to reason that any play without an overt political agenda would be privileged by the FTP units of the state.[77] As WPA Southern California director Colonel Connelly told Hallie Flanagan, the FTP units in the state should stage anything that would keep us "out of the papers."[78] Of course, this did not prevent accusations of political subversion from being lobbed at individual productions and performers, even within the units themselves. Amy Brady details the complicated production of *The Sun Rises in the East*, produced by the experimental branch of the Los Angeles Unit, the Southwest Theatre Unit. As new director Alexander Leftwich became suspicious over the amount of time spent on developing the play, he reported several Southwest Theatre Unit actors to Congress for subversive activity.[79] Brady also shows how *The Sun Rises in the East*—which was also unique in that it was set in the southwestern United States when most plays produced by the California units lacked any regionalism (including, it should be noted, *To the Ladies*)[80]—not only portrayed the working conditions for Latinx workers but also suggested that "the Depression-era American Dream was little more than a myth perpetuated by ideological conservatism."[81] As such, just as it appears likely that the Chicago Negro Unit of the FTP staged *Mississippi Rainbow* to counter criticism of controversial works, the Southern California units may have staged *To the Ladies* to temper press criticism of the program.

While California's complicated political context certainly was a factor in staging a play that many thought a bit outdated, Kaufman's public persona may have contributed to the play's production in California. Both Connelly and Kaufman publicly maintained leftist politics—Kaufman himself appears to have supported Eugene Debs and socialist candidate Norman Thomas in 1932 and was generally in favor of Roosevelt—and both had several of their works performed by the FTP.[82] However, by 1937, Kaufman himself was no longer simply a playwright but an incredibly wealthy "celebrity director and producer," having won a Pulitzer Prize in 1936 for the success of *You Can't Take It with You* and was no longer writing opinion pieces for the *Nation* but appearing in photospreads in *Life* magazine.[83] Additionally in 1937, Kaufman would collaborate with Moss Hart for the satirical musical entitled *I'd Rather Be Right*. The musical featured George Cohan as a singing, dancing FDR who struggles to balance the national budget while helping a young couple get married. While critics at the time found Cohan's portrayal of Roosevelt to be charming, Garret Eisler finds the musical to be hypercritical of New Deal tax policies and is primarily concerned with class identification.[84] And within their anti–New Deal, anti-Roosevelt play, both Moss and Kaufman offer several pointed critiques directly at the FTP. In Act 1, Roosevelt is approached by a dirty-looking man and a dozen attractive women. The man claims to be "Federal Theatre Unit No. 864" and asks Roosevelt if he and his troupe can "give a show here?"[85] When the president protests, the man says whenever there is a gathering of more than three people, the actors must give a show. When the man says he found FTP actors in his bathroom, Roosevelt asks if they were taking a bath and the director responds, "No, my wife was in the tub, and they were giving a performance of *She Stoops to Conquer*."[86]

Given its production context, it is no surprise that the reception of FTP performances of *To the Ladies* suggests audiences sometimes regarded them as simply entertainment. In the director's report for the San Diego production, the director reported that audiences' reactions to the play were "far beyond our expectation" and "newspaper reviews were flattering," and also noted that the city "consequently demands . . . CLEAN drama with an accent on contemporary American home life."[87] In reviews of the Los Angeles production of the play, the focus tended to be on the star power and attractiveness of the woman playing Elise. The *Los Angeles Times* noted that Christine McIntyre "is a welcome new member of the Federal forces, being beautiful, clever, and possessed of a nice singing voice."[88] The reviewer for the *Herald & Express* also praises the work of McIntyre, who is "a brunette after the style of Olivia De Havilland," speaks with "an engaging Southern drawl," and was "the first hopeful that the Federal Theatre has got behind with . . . springs of the stereotyped Hollywood ballyhoo."[89] One audience member dismissed the play as "very good for light comedy but froth is so unsatisfactory" and wished for something more serious: "I approve this sort of play for an occasional evening's entertainment—but I would prefer a steadier diet of something with a backbone."[90] Meanwhile, a reporter for a print review from the *San Bernardino Sun Telegram* suggests that some audience members detected a more political aspect of *To the Ladies*. As the unnamed reviewer notes, the amusing play is engaging, in part, because of it "showing the ladies in control of the situation."[91] Moreover, two other audience reviews suggest audiences parsing out more political content than other readers and producers saw. An audience member in San Diego noted *To the Ladies* as "presenting a satire on modernism," while a Los Angeles audience member voiced their discontentment with the narrative of the play: "The story of the benevolent capitalist is a fairy tale in these times."[92]

As the unnamed audience member suggests, the idea for many Depression-era audiences that Leonard's boss would be willing to assist his worker seems offensive given the contextual evidence that the benevolent businessman was simply mythological. When workers from a collection agency come to take away the couple's piano, Mr. Kinkaid, Leonard's boss, pays off the debt. However, Kinkaid decries his employee's spending habits. He declares, "Well—I'll admit I'm a little prejudiced, but I don't like to see any of our young men in debt. It indicates bad management. Especially a married man. . . . He should think of his family—his future."[93] In his admonition, Kinkaid echoes the Lynds' critique of the white middle class, when they detail how the business class was unchanging in its outlook toward other workers, often seeing them as, in essence, from the proverbial "wrong side of the tracks." Like the subjects of *Middletown*, as well as proponents of male-centered work, Kinkaid cannot quell his own hostility to giving aid to those he feels cannot help themselves.

Kinkaid's condemnation illustrates how the play navigates a far more complicated view of work: that of gendered middle-class labor of the Depression era. The first few decades of the twentieth century saw an increase in the rise of women's employment outside of the home, especially single women in the clerical and sales industries as those fields grew. Many employers saw women's social training—that they were nurturers and caregivers—as vital to these more service-tailored jobs (plus the fact that single women could be offered lower pay). Yet employment through the onset of the Depression was more problematic for many married women for several reasons: not only did the then standard workweek discourage many women from working, but many firms simply refused to hire married women for jobs.[94] In addition, the rise of consumerism and domestic technology had reinforced the position that a middle-class woman's sphere was at home. Advertisers promoted to women that there was pleasure to be had in domestic labor and that using modern appliances "could minimize the monotony and allow more pleasurable time with children and husbands, thus integrating mother's love with mother's work." Advertisements featured "illustrations of happy housewives reading to their children, going to the theater with their husbands, and otherwise 'working' with their families while appliances sit in the basement doing the drudgery."[95] Of course, as Stephanie Coontz shows, this conflux of technology and consumption only expanded the expectations of domestic duty, as the 1920s saw a significant increase in the amount of time married women spent on domestic labor despite the supposed elimination of many arduous tasks. In addition, there was a rise in the rates of married women working outside of the home as, in part, an extension of the demands placed on them to maintain the home. The emphasis on consumerism had "produced a new cultural rationale for the employment of married women: an ideology stressing the importance of home as a center of consumption and a higher standard of living."[96]

The onset of the Depression complicated norms of middle-class women's work, especially for married women. As men lost their jobs or were forced into pay cuts, women sought employment to make-up for lost wages. Yet despite the necessity of labor-seeking for these women, public views of such employment plummeted, and this had real-world ramifications. Many business practices discouraged the hiring of women and mandated that married women would be first in line for any job cutbacks, while twenty-six states passed laws outright denying married women the right to work.[97] And in many respects, the various programs of the New Deal did little to alleviate these issues. While the programs of Federal One did provide many white-collar women workers employment, most programs for both married and unmarried women were situated in domestic or traditionally feminine fields that only served to reinforce gendered views of women's work.

Given the social reinforcement of gender work norms during the era, one could argue the comedy of the play is born from an inversion of that dynamic. However, there is serious skepticism about this dynamic embedded in the play itself. For starters, the masculine space of professional work is hardly as stable as the male characters in the play would promote. *To the Ladies* clearly shows that Elise and Mrs. Kinkaid are the driving forces behind the success of their husbands, but the male characters in the play operate as if they are in total control of their workspace. When it is discovered that Elise concocted his speech at the banquet, Leonard is derided by his coworkers, and Mr. Kinkaid cannot comprehend how or why Leonard would permit his wife to take control of his "space." This complete lack of awareness about the impact women have on the business space is further illustrated by Leonard attempting to purge women from the office. At the beginning of Act 3, he dictates a letter to his secretary, Miss Fletcher, about the deficiencies of the female workers in the company: "Mr. Toohey now has twelve girls in the mailing department, but believes with me that men not only could do the work better, but much more quickly than women. . . . As you know, we believe that as a general rule women are not so capable as men in business."[98] Even though Miss Fletcher, Elise, and Mrs. Kinkaid are shown to be integral to the success of the business, the men outwardly view the women in the workplace as expendable and inferior to other men. And given the unequal levels of unemployment for women during the Depression, this fact certainly would have resonated with segments of the FTP audience differently than in the play's original 1920s context.

Just as the play is skeptical about the stability of the male workplace, *To the Ladies* also casts doubt on the model of the male breadwinner though its portrayal of Leonard and his problematic consumerism. Leonard purchases items he can barely afford and, in particular, is susceptible to the suggestion of advertising—such as when he reads about a speechmaking book that promises to "electrify one and all by your eloquence, fairly swinging them off their feet by the magic of your words."[99] Reflecting shifts in advertising of the era, Leonard believes that all aspects of his life from the professional to the domestic can be solved through the acquisition of consumer products, and Depression audiences would have also been very familiar with newer models of advertising that emphasized the solution to the domestic melodrama—such as hunger, body odor, lethargy—was solved by characters in ads purchasing Lifebuoy Soap or Ovaltine.[100] In this manner, the play functions similarly to the critique of advertising and advice columns present in the more satirical work of Nathanael West: by borrowing the generic conventions of advice columns and the ads Leonard consumes, the play can critique the continued influence of such genres on the middle-class workers taken with their promises of economic security through consumption. Leonard also demonstrates an interest in the "sport" of real estate that mirrors the rhetoric of the investment rage of the 1920s. To his wife's consternation, Leonard announces that he has invested in a Florida grapefruit farm he bought, sight unseen, that will, he claims, bring in "$350 a week" after a four-year investment.[101] Like many investors in real estate and the stock market during the 1920s, Leonard adopts a sport mentality toward investing, hedging his bets on the principle that he and his wife will eventually reap the rewards of his speculation. Leonard's character traits—while humorous in its original 1920s context—seem far more tragic given the economic struggles of the 1930s. Indeed, in the 1930s, his investment in a grapefruit farm would have reminded audiences of real estate and agriculture busts in places like Florida in the late 1920s.

Equally problematic for the Beebes is that much of Leonard's consumption is done on credit—especially his purchase of the piano—and debt was a driving fear for both the middle class and many workers on relief. The mass extension of credit to middle-class households and workers in the 1920s contributed to the economic instability of the 1930s, and certainly audiences would have also been keenly aware of the extension of credit for the purchasing of stocks in the 1920s as well. Moreover, many audience members would have been aware of the continued issues for those struggling with credit bills. As Viki Howard shows, one of the worst-hit industries were retail and department stores, which struggled not only with sales but also with the problem of bad debt losses from customers unable to pay their bills. While most stores had charge account customers, many stores, especially in rural areas or small towns, still used book credit accounts, and these smaller stores often had to "pull payments out of their cash-strapped customers one dollar at a time."[102] This specter of credit also resonated with many WPA workers, who were denied credit or punished by retailers for being on the dole. Retailers routinely denied credit to customers employed by the WPA, while knowledge of any employment through the New Deal was enough to sink a customer's credit.[103] It certainly stands to reason that Leonard nearly having his piano repossessed would have resonated with many performers and audience members, especially those of the middle class where financial and purchasing stability was an expected norm.

This questioning of the gender work norms in the FTP productions of *To the Ladies* also aligns with the screwball comedy genre in film. Long associated with the Great Depression, screwball filmmakers produced films that reflected the financial and social unrest of the era, often ridiculing high-society life while affording audiences a reprieve from the Depression. Moreover, these films, by combining comedy of manners and physical comedy, permit a space for a "battle of the sexes" dynamic. On the one hand, this was a way, as Andrew Sarris argues, to show covert references to sex while navigating the standards imposed by the Production Code.[104] But more to our purposes, the screwball genre afforded women relative independence, especially in contrast to their male counterparts who were framed as childlike or, at times, desexualized—a trait, Olympia Kiriakou sees, in the repeated character of the male absent-minded professor in such films as *Bringing Up Baby* (Howard Hawks, 1938), *Ball of Fire* (Howard Hawks, 1941), or *The Lady Eve* (Preston Sturges, 1941).[105] Heather Gilmour argues these comedies, while affirming of feminism, are more about the problematizing of masculinity: "The strength of their female protagonists has the inevitable effect of challenging the masculinity of their counterparts: men in romantic comedies are repeatedly depicted as neurotically out of control—and behind this loss of control is their female costar."[106] Moreover, she argues that romantic comedies represent an inversion of conventional norms—men are feminized, women are masculinized—and that 1930s romantic comedies are even more radical as "traditional binaries of gender are not simply inverted but reinvented and transposed to the point where the binaries are dissolved. It is not just that men act like women or women like men, but then men act like other men . . . or like women, and then act like themselves again" (see Figure 3.2).[107]

Whether the films are about problematizing masculinity or promoting feminist agency, one can read *To the Ladies* in the context of the 1930s as subverting gender norms publicly and privately. In one sense, the success of the women here harkens back to the New Woman ethos of the play and its original 1920s context. The New Woman was characterized by her shift from the private sphere into the public by becoming a wage earner and participating in activities that had long been constructed as male.[108] While certain audiences may have again read the FTP productions of *To the Ladies* as reactionary, the presence of so much gender inversion in screwball comedies of the era suggests that we can read the play as more radical. The key moment of the play is the banquet scene where Elise can outdo her husband and every other male speaker. Not only is Elise succeeding in the public, masculine space of business, but she also completely undermines the bland performative nature of these generic speeches, especially the one Leonard planned to give. She accuses the businessmen of being "so busy looking for . . . a machine that will attend to business for them" and "that they're either too bored or too busy or too tired to attend to life." She then upholds Mr. Kinkaid as an ideal businessman whose approaches to business are "just as efficient"

Figure 3.2 The banquet scene from the San Diego production of *To the Ladies*. Standing to the right is Jackson Perkins as Elise as she gives her speech; seated with glasses is Paul Nordstrom as a rather submissive and tense Leonard. *(FTP LC. Retrieved from https://www.loc.gov/item/musftpphotoprints.200223472/.)*

as new approaches to work. She concludes by noting, "Now why don't you follow his example? Go in for business and go in for it just as much as you want to. But for God's sake do try to be a little bit human."[109] Elise undermines the supposed stability of this business rhetoric in two ways: first, even though she has no professional training, she delivers a fantastic speech by simply parodying the generic conventions of other speeches she has heard; second, she is able to present a stronger performance because she ignores the rhetorical and performative conventions that hamper the competing speeches. While the men are afraid to deviate from their rote scripts, she delivers a speech that is simply more effective—undermining the masculine space.

For the male characters of the play, there is no greater fear or personal failing than being emasculated. And of course, the play shows them being emasculated by their wives. And in the context of the FTP, the play critiques the male as breadwinner model so embedded in the New Deal as the men of the play are hardly capable of holding down their labor. For a program like the FTP, which along with other Federal One programs was far more liberal about hiring women for projects, to stage a play featuring a woman who outsmarts and outworks her husband and his employers was a political statement. Not only do the productions suggest that men can be ineffective at work, but they also note that agencies like the FTP could provide women more power than they would receive in traditional work settings.

By the end of the decade in mainstream American culture, there was a palpable reembrace of the virtues of middle-class life, but even before 1940, a range of government and cultural events aimed at reinvigorating the work of those who identified as middle class. And outwardly, the FTP productions of *Ah, Wilderness!* and *To the Ladies* follow that pattern with narratives of caring, diligent middle-class people in the former and a comic fantasy of women running the show in the latter. But as I have shown here, both texts problematize the promotion of middle-class work values by skeptically illustrating middle-class views of charity work (and to an extent work relief), the gendered labor situation, and the promotion of consumption. These subversive performances served to remind their audiences of the inequality of middle-class work and the lingering issues facing a population who believed the good times were back again.

Comedies of Chance

W hile his *A Moral Entertainment* was on the FTP stage, one of Richard Maibaum's less successful plays was getting a second life in Hollywood. In 1935, *Sweet Mystery of Life*, written by Maibaum, Michael Wallace, and George Haight, had closed after a poor run but was optioned by Warner Brothers to serve as the basis for the latest installment of their popular Golddiggers film series—*Golddiggers of 1937*. After their show closes in Atlantic City, two performers, Genevieve (Glenda Farrell) and Norma (Joan Blondell), decide that the only way to find financial stability is to begin "gold digging." After spying some insurance salesmen on a train, Norma convinces a salesman named Ross to give her a job as a stenographer at his insurance company. Meanwhile, Genevieve lands a role in a financially troubled new Broadway show. She convinces the producers to take out an insurance policy on the head of one of her suitors named Hobart—a man so sick that Genevieve assures the producers that he's near death. Of course, Hobart is healthier than expected, and the producers convince Genevieve to try to "weaken" Hobart's health to collect the insurance money.

Golddiggers of 1937 ends like many musicals of the era with the "security" of marriage (Genevieve and Hobart marry, as do Norma and Ross), but also illustrates some cultural apprehension over the notion of security and chance. While the characters in *Golddiggers of 1937* eventually find security through their risky schemes, two of the show's investors have lost the money for the new production speculating in the stock market, and Genevieve and her producer friends gamble the finance of their production on the health of Hobart. And like *A Moral Entertainment*, several of the characters just reason there is more to be gained in finding more traditional work rather than dealing with the risk and uncertainty of the theatrical job market.

This chapter shows the complicated cultural and political debate over chance in the 1930s, its connection to work and labor, and how these issues manifest in two popular plays that feature characters who engage in risky speculation that would not be out of place in *Golddiggers of 1937*: George Kelly's *The Show-Off* and John C. Brownell's *Mississippi Rainbow*. *The Show-Off* struggles to place itself in the context of Keynesian and New Deal constructs of chance, wherein characters embrace both the concepts of arduous work while acknowledging that security might be better provided through a partial embrace of chance. *Mississippi Rainbow* reveals a history of racial imbalance toward the concept of risk, while also promoting chance as an avenue for Black Americans when government work or American society was not providing it to them.

Chance, Culture, and Government

Before delving into the debates over chance in the 1930s, I want to pause and first detail how I am defining chance as a concept, and at the risk of oversimplification, I want to adopt a broad definition. To this end, I am following what Jackson Lears outlines as the components of the American culture of chance and its various forms—especially those that relate to or are positioned in opposition to labor such as gambling or speculation.

In short, the range of beliefs in chance and risk and its associated actions—especially gambling and speculation—have long been decried by moralist thinkers and framed as antithetical to the nature of work and self-reliance.[1] As Lears writes, broadly summarizing the historical condemnations against gambling and speculation, "Life became, for many Puritans, a constant struggle for control of the inner self and the outer environment, not through magical ritual but through technical mastery. There was no room for divination—and none for its near relation gambling—on this Puritan quest."[2] The best example of this is the Puritan work ethic's emphasis on diligent labor and frugality as not only the mark of good work but also as a sign of divine providence on the worker.

But such "Yankee" attitudes toward labor were complicated as there became a blurring between control impulses and chance. Lears notes that "the defenders of diligence have never entirely vanquished the devotees of chance" and especially in "flush times, it has not always been easy to distinguish gambling from speculation or investment, and even Horatio Alger knew that luck was as important as pluck in achieving success."[3] In her analysis of nineteenth-century gambling and speculation, Anna Fabian shows how the

American economy embraced a kind of "speculative ethic" by the time of the Panic of 1893. These new gamblers, who profited from stock and commodities exchanges, presented themselves as moral, rational citizens in a culture that was beginning to reject some elements of the more communal, republican ethos of the founding of the republic.[4] This was especially true in a quasi-rejection of Protestant ethic values by the turn of the century, which "reflected a greater tolerance for risk taking, a corresponding decline in the valuation of steady labor and prudent saving, and a more pervasively isolating individualism than ever."[5] This blurring between gambling and speculation produced a mythos of risk-taking that bore some resemblance to the Protestant ethic. Risk takers seek success not just for monetary gain, but also for "luck conceived as the personal possession of power as *mana* here takes on religious significance as a sign of external favor." "Gamblers," Gerda Reith argues, "want simply to *know* their status,"[6] as "winning in games of chance is taken as confirmation that the player is favored by destiny."[7] The impulse of chance and gambling also manifested itself in the performance of chance. Reith argues that "games of chance and those of skill are united in their common disregard of financial gain. In neither one is money the primary motive for gambling, rather it is the aspiration to be a 'dice thrower': the demonstration of character and courage and the consequent affirmation of the self that makes the play meaningful." The emphasis on risking all in games of chance becomes a performative measure to show the player is one with the game.[8] To fully engage in risk—and in many ways speculation—meant to fully engage in the potential for a dangerous loss: to only gamble for small gains meant one was not fully engaged in the sport.

Yet there remained the impulse to separate the legitimacy of certain forms of work of chance—specifically speculation—from illegitimate forms like gambling. In this respect, the rhetoric of many moralists, government reformers, and policymakers helped cement this dynamic. While the ideological debate over speculative risk and gambling never really eased from public discourse, arguments over the two binaries were often most acute during economic downturns. And what began to cement within those discourses was an (unaware or self-aware) move of businesspeople and investors to ignore their own engaging in speculation and promote traditional work values. Commentators and businessmen would decry idleness and speculation, and as Daniel Rodgers notes, would stick "to the canon" of "hard work, self-control, and dogged persistence" despite "the speculative booms that so conspicuously dotted economic life" such as "the financial adventurism and ardent pursuit of the main chance" that dominated the aura of the Gilded Age for instance.[9] During the recession of the late 1860s and the Depression of 1873–78, the refrain from conservative commentators seemingly blamed everything on overspending, overconsuming, and rampant speculation, and the "remedy" was rather predictable: "a return to the hard-pan of work and frugality."[10] At a macro level, this discourse would often inform reform policy to the point where speculative practices would contribute to panics or downturns, but institutions would blame outlier speculators and what reforms were put in place were often cosmetic.

While academics and economists were beginning to downplay the role of speculation as the root cause of economic downturns in the early twentieth century,[11] that certainly did not reflect both the root causes of the Depression in both reality and in the public imagination—especially after the stock market crashes of 1929. The move of financial houses and banks, especially the National City Bank under the guidance of Charles Mitchell, to promote stocks to the widespread public and to promote buying on the margins—especially poor-quality stocks promoted by pools of large-scale investors to neophyte investors—had drastically problematized the stock exchange. Moreover, in the 1920s, investing and speculation had become a national pastime akin to sport, as technological advances like Trans-Lux's "movie ticker" allowed crowds at retail brokerages to "see" real-time stock prices on a brightly lit facsimile screen, while the proliferation of radio permitted stock reports to be delivered to a wide swath of the American public. Reinforced by how-to manuals on stocks that flooded the market during the 1920s—as well as advice columnists and fortune tellers—these narratives promoted to investors a new paradigm of financial success predicated on "getting into the numbers" and embracing the chance of the market itself.[12]

Regulating the "rulers of the exchange of mankind's goods" and enacting "an end to speculation with other people's money," as Roosevelt noted in his first inaugural address, was clearly an aim of New Deal legislation in various forms.[13] But this impulse was mitigated by the complicated ideological makeup of the New Deal wherein public security was balanced by a desire to encourage "accepted" risk to the American public or, "given sudden urgency to the task of reducing economic chance without pretending to eliminate it."[14] Some of this can be traced to the writings of John Maynard Keyes, who, in his treatise *The General Theory of Employment, Interest, and Money*, argued that the challenge for governments was balancing consumer and investor protection while encouraging the risk of investment, albeit investing that was for the greater society rather than just simply the investors themselves. Arguing for the increased involvement of government spending into the economy, Keynes defended such an approach as to encourage "the individual enterpriser" to enter "action" of a system where typically "the odds [are] loaded against him." So rigged is the current game of investment that "the players as a whole will lose" and may "deal all the cards" unless they possess "expectational skill or unusual good fortune." But "if effective demand is adequate, average skill and average good fortune will be enough."[15] And much of New Deal legislation—especially within the programs of the First New Deal—reflects this balancing of regulation and government oversight with the encouragement of financial risk into the market for investors. The most overt example of the mitigation of risk were the various reforms enacted to regulate the stocks and investment practices that had facilitated much of the economic calamity of the 1930s, namely, the Securities Act of 1933 and the Securities and Exchange Act of 1934. These acts remolded the marketing of securities, requiring the registrations of proposed offerings and documentation about projected performances, as well as bans on insider trading and market manipulations.

This intersection between risk protection while navigating a system of risk is best exemplified by the most-lasting piece of New Deal legislation: the Social Security Act. In contrast to many European models of social insurance for the aged and disabled which provided categorical relief or established universal pension systems, the Social Security Act was a complex and exemption-riddled program based on individualized contributions that were contingent on participation in the insecure labor market. While there was generous aid for family welfare, medical aid, and old-age benefits, most of the act functioned as a "myriad of private contracts," and without supplemental tax funds, it relied primarily on the employee and their employer to self-finance the program.[16] Roosevelt resisted any attempt to merge public relief with the social insurance system, and he was convinced that public unemployment systems were antithetical to his administration's aims and the basis for failures of similar programs in Britain and Germany. The model of commercial insurance "so pervaded the air in 1930s America . . . that the New Dealers could not escape it."[17] And that model of commercial insurance was predicated on the individual seeking, procuring, and maintaining employment in an unstable marketplace to gain access to many programs designed to enact a level of security to that individual.

This manifestation for security against risk manifested broadly in American popular culture of the era.[18] Like the promotion of middle-class norms through consumption, advertising of the 1930s played on the personal fears over security of Americans through a range of campaigns. The Hartford Insurance Company warned that modern life was "affected by the monsters of disaster" that were "ready and waiting to wipe out savings of years," while Johnson & Johnson questioned how safe and clean bandages of competitors were. Commenting on the patterns of such advertisements, Lawrence Levine asserts that "if security was in fact more difficult to obtain in the real world, the world of ads was not one of unremitting fantasy; it mirrored and—intensified" the social concern that "security was within reach if only individuals took the proper initiative."[19] Meanwhile for many Americans, the proper initiative was engaging in leisurely risk with the hopes of landing a financial windfall. Local community lotteries like numbers games flourished especially in impoverished communities, while Nevada became the first state to legalize gambling in 1934. Bank Nights, the brainchild of a Fox movie theater manager, encouraged patrons to enter their names next to a number in a book in the lobby, and then if their number was drawn, they won a cash prize.[20] And in fan magazines, readers read articles about models and actors that focused on the celebrities "being discovered" or their "lucky breaks," narratives that strongly equated the measure of success with the cruelty of chance.

But the best example of this cultural interrogation with chance and security were screwball comedies, many of which had nuanced views of luck. One of the most popular screwball comedies of the era was *My Man Godfrey* (Gregory La Cava, 1936) starring William Powell and Carole Lombard. The story centers on Parke Godfrey, an unemployed businessperson, who is asked by the socialite Cornelia Bullock to become the butler of her family's estate. The film's climax is when the patriarch of the Bullock family announces that his business is failing, and he is facing legal action after having attempted to recoup his business losses using stockholders' money. However, Godfrey announces to the assembled family that he has "sold short" on the stocks of Bullock's company, and he, having also pawned Cornelia's necklace, has reacquired Bullock's stock and has enough money left over to purchase his own nightclub. In one sense, Godfrey's character is praised by the film for having the skill to engage in "smart" business practices and having the foresight to manipulate the market to protect his community. His benevolence is contrasted by the poor risk management of the Bullock patriarch, who not only has errored in the management of his company but also has used the risk capital of his investors to try to ensure the security of his family and company. While Godfrey engages in more accepted risk, the fact that he was down on his luck at the beginning of the film suggests a message that poverty and deprivation can happen to anyone (just as it happens to the Bullock family). But the narrative also reaffirms that desire and hope for audiences that a benevolent force would appear in their lives to restore their senses of happiness and safety.

For a great many texts of the Depression era, especially comedies, chance and security function in a dualistic dance where one must engage in some form of chance, risk, or speculation to obtain some measure of security. And often, the embrace of risk that is most promoted by the text aligns with long-standing "good" risk-taking practices seen in capitalist ideology. And in the context of the broader New Deal, with social and business reform programs that sought to navigate risk and security for Americans, these plays attempt to do the same, both promoting the need for embracing social or private insurance while deftly challenging the limitations of such programs.

The Show-Off

In 1947, Edward Maisel penned a reflection on the works of George Kelly for *Theatre Arts* entitled "The Theatre of George Kelly." In the piece, Maisel struggles with what he sees as Kelly's deep-rooted misogyny in the construction of his women characters as well as the Philadelphia playwright's overt moralism. But he also sees Kelly's men as representative of socioeconomic angst: "The basic anomaly of all Kelly's work belongs to our age: how to assimilate the transcendent concept of vocation now that its religious and social guarantees have disappeared. . . . But more serious, with industrialism—the society founded on the machine—came man's estrangement from the end results of his labor, his personal alienation from whatever role he was compelled to play in the dehumanized complex of social forces." This sense of alienation is also manifested, Maisel feels, in a generalized lack of control: "More and more, existence has taken on the aspect of a giant pinball machine in which lives are sent spinning and caroming at the successive pulls upon the plunger of vast impersonal forces: wars, unemployment cycles, stock market curves, economic laws of supply and demand."[21] Maisy argues that one of the "only true approximations of a hero" that Kelly creates is *The Show-Off*'s "irresponsible braggart, Aubrey Piper," whose charismatic triumph is "a series of coincidences, lucky breaks and accidents" which never make Piper question his "unswerving fidelity" to his "unregenerate way."[22]

Maisy's analysis does illustrate a couple key points about Kelly's (arguably) most popular play. Its central character lucks into success in ways he does not understand and is a product of a society wherein people are increasingly unable to control their fates. That sense of the powerlessness of people is something that Kelly claims was part of his motivation to write the play and might also explain why—despite reviewers and audiences being enamored of its blowhard main character—it found an audience during the Depression on the FTP stage. But Aubrey Piper's luck and, as we shall see, his embrace of risk serves as a reminder to audiences about the danger of unmitigated chance, especially in contrast to the labor and security afforded to his family-in-law, the Fishers. In the FTP productions of *The Show-Off*, there is a delicate balancing between the promotion of work and the advocacy for the security of the New Deal, and a tepid promotion of risk at the opportune moment: while Piper may succeed through his embrace of chance, it serves as a warning that such successes are rare.

Originally conceived as a vaudeville sketch entitled "Poor Aubrey," *The Show-Off* is set in the living room of a lower-middle-class home in North Philadelphia, where Mr. and Mrs. Fisher have three adult-aged children; Clara; Joe, an inventor; and idealistic Amy. Amy is engaged to Aubrey Piper—a braggart who works as a clerk for the Pennsylvania Railroad. Despite the warnings of her parents that Piper cannot take care of her, Amy declares that she is an independent woman and will marry Piper. Six months later, Amy bemoans to her mother that she and Piper cannot find suitable housing on his salary and need to stay at the Fisher home, while Clara reveals that Piper has been borrowing extensively from her husband, Frank, to purchase a car. Piper enters onstage with a bandage around his head and reveals that he has had a traffic accident. Not only did he wreck his car, but he managed to also hit a police officer. By chance, his brother-in-law, Frank, witnessed the entire incident from a streetcar and proceeded to post the $1,000 bond to release Piper from jail. Meanwhile, Mr. Fisher has a stroke at his job and dies.

Mrs. Fisher receives an insurance claim check for $1,000 on the death of her husband from an insurance agent who also leaves some brochures for Piper about an accident and death policy (which he cannot afford). When Piper returns home, he proceeds to engage in a series of lies about his accident and his relationship with Mr. Fisher and claims that he owns the Fisher home. The culmination of the play centers on Joe, who announces that he has sold his antirust formula to a steel company for $100,000. Given that she distrusts her son-in-law, Mrs. Fisher suggests to Joe that he keep news of his windfall a secret—but then Joe shocks her by revealing that it was Piper who suggested Joe experiment with his formula in the first place. Even more shocking, Joe reveals that it was Aubrey Piper who happened to, through his bluster, convince the steel company into giving Joe a more-lucrative payment. As the play concludes, Mrs. Fisher is resigned to the fact that her daughter is still in love with Piper, who, despite his successes, is hoping to invest in a suspicious-sounding copper mine in the West.

Kelly's play was a smash hit when it premiered on Broadway in 1924, playing for 571 performances before closing in March 1925. *The Show-Off* was also a mainstay of Hollywood during the era, including a 1926 silent version from Paramount featuring Ford Sterling as Aubrey Piper and Louise Brooks as Clara (which Paramount remade in 1930 under the title *Men Are Like That*). MGM would produce *The Show-Off* in 1934 based on a screenplay written by Herman J. Mankiewicz that stars a young Spencer Tracy as Piper. Deviating from the play, the 1934 version portrays Piper far more sympathetically as the film opens with him saving a man from drowning. However, Piper still spends lavishly and recklessly on gifts for his girlfriend and is also fired from his railroad clerk post for making an unauthorized offer on a piece of land. While the film ends in much the same manner as the play, Tracy's Piper hits more rock bottom by working as a sandwich board promoter before his big break. And while there would be another film adaptation with Red Skelton in 1946, the 1934 version suggests a change in how much of the public saw Piper. The film premiered just a year after a 1933 revival of *The Show-Off* on Broadway. In his review of the production, Brooks Atkinson noted that while the play was still "amusing" in spite of "the undoubted fact that times, especially since 1924, have changed." Indeed, the reviewer notes the performance, while good, was not "greeted with the same degree of hilarious rapture" as previous productions on account of three factors: "Depression, politics, prohibition."[23]

For Depression audiences, Piper becomes something of a reckless yet tragic figure as seen in his embrace of boosterish, 1920s views of work and consumerism. The Fishers represent a range of older models of laboring—a fact best personified by Joe Fisher, who as he discusses his invention that could make him wealthy still notes that he has already begun work on a new project and that he is "not going to stop working."[24] In contrast to the Fishers, Piper demonstrates little work ethic but happily pontificates on the value of work. His ideology is informed by an advice columnist's essay that he reads in a magazine, borrowing language familiar to those columns that promoted more middle-class values of labor: "He said, 'I would say, to that innumerable host of young men, standing on threshold of life, uncertain, and mayhap, dismayed—as they contemplate the stress of modern industrial competition, 'Rome was not built in a day.' Those were his very words, I wouldn't kid you, and I think the old boy's got it right, if you ask me."[25] Like Leonard in *To the Ladies*, Piper is allured by the call of consumerism: not only does he buy expensive clothes, but he searches for a luxury home in Philadelphia, and much to Mrs. Fisher's chagrin, heads to an automobile show to buy a car to celebrate his anniversary. Additionally, to afford these status symbols, Piper buys nearly everything on credit, noting "that there are least fifteen first-class establishments right here in this city that will furnish a man's house . . . and give him the rest of his life to pay for it."[26] While consumerism was certainly not extinct the in the 1930s, as I discussed in my previous chapter, Piper's ultra-reckless approach to purchasing places him more in-line with the previous decade. Since it is clear he has no ability to pay for any of the items he purchases and lives beyond his means, Depression audiences would have forecast economic calamity awaiting Piper.

And while there is certainly an added element of recklessness in Depression-era Piper, many of the then contemporary texts also portray him in something of a more sympathetic light. In part, these views of Piper can be traced to Kelly himself, who wanted to portray the trials and tribulations of a young couple who cannot financially support themselves. Foster Hirsch asserts that the play is representative of Kelly's satirical eye as he not only critiques some aspect of each of the main characters in the play, presenting his "paternalistic disapproval" of their attitudes and actions, but also presents the play through "a precarious mixture of genres and viewpoints."[27] Kelly claimed that part of his rationale for writing the play was born out of an interest in the "problem of marriage among the young and poor."[28] In an interview in 1924, Kelly explained what he felt was some of the embedded tragedy within *The Show-Off*:

> I was constantly hearing about a young girl in the same social set as *The Show-Off*, who was planning to return to the parental roof because she was tired of trying to make twenty-five dollars a week do the work of one hundred dollars. When the first glamour of love and marriage vanished, those poor innocents had nothing to sustain them. Devoid of intellectuality, wisdom, humor, struggling to keep their attic homes going, the mediocrity of their existence seemed appalling to me. That's what prompted me to write a play about them.[29]

Despite the reputation of the play as something antiquated by the 1920s, *The Show-Off* was still produced seven times by the FTP.[30] I want to focus on productions of two subagencies. First, the Yiddish Unit, specifically in Chelsea, Massachusetts, under the auspices of the Boston FTP, that hired veterans of the Yiddish stage to perform Yiddish language productions. Led by Benson Inge, a former drama critic for the *New York World Telegram*, the Yiddish Unit was designed to stage plays for Jewish American communities throughout the United States.[31] Just as Flanagan advocated for the FTP itself to cast off the vestiges of older forms of theater, Inge advocated for the Jewish American unit to abandon the "ancient" relics of the Yiddish stage and embrace, new, more progressive fare and plays that were more "universal" in their subject matter—in other words, plays that were not strictly "Yiddish" in nature. As such, Inge commissioned a series of more mainstream plays to be translated into Yiddish, including *The Show-Off*, for production by his subunit.[32] Why *The Show-Off* was selected remains a bit of a mystery, but in many respects, the play ties in with much of the rest of the performance history of the Yiddish Unit, in which complex portrayals of various themes, including work, were common. Detailing the structure of many Yiddish productions, Joel Schechter argues that many plays both portrayed difficult working conditions and celebrated Yiddish-speaking Jews who wanted to work. For example, the vaudeville-style sketch revue *We Live and Laugh* deals with a variety of characters in various fields, such as miners and doctors, and at times focuses on the ludicrousness of working. One such scene features a provincial theater troupe that sings about "hardship, about declining numbers in their band, and then fall to the ground, faint or near death" to convince passersby for money to keep on performing. However, the play also features Jewish characters "accepting jobs as seamstresses, minyan-maker, modern cantor, and courtroom musician." Schechter argues that the play serves as a metaphor for the FTP itself, as the characters accept the jobs they are offered, just as actors took the work of the New Deal program. He says, "Their jobs are to portray characters with jobs, jobs they dislike, jobs that bore them."[33]

Whether the work was something that provided the workers agency or alienated the workers, the emphasis on work can also be seen in *The Show-Off*—especially with the Fisher family (an element still very imbued to the original playscript and productions). The most prominent characters promoting work are Mr. and Mrs. Fisher, who continually condemn Piper's work habits while praising the work ethic of their children—especially Mrs. Fisher, who lauds Joe's work as an inventor. But the audience reaction to the Yiddish Unit's Chelsea production suggests they viewed Piper as not necessarily the antithesis of work. As the director for the production noted, "The audience reaction to Aubrey Piper, the mother, the young daughter and particularly the working man provoked a great deal of laughter and sympathetic understanding."[34]

Second, the Harlem Negro Unit (HNU), one of the units charged with hiring Black workers, used *The Show-Off* to tailor Aubrey Piper's character to Harlem and address more transgressive politics of the era. In the HNU production, Piper refers to himself as the "kid from Corona," a reference that certainly resonated with then audiences due to the Corona neighborhood of Queens being a place of both growing Black middle-class influence and a hotbed of discussion over the role of gentrification as that area was connected to various projects associated with the 1939 World's Fair expansion.[35] In addition, Macki Braconi shows that one of the changes to the HNU script was changing Piper's place of employment from the Pennsylvania Railroad to Standard Oil—he still brags about his status in the company—so as to expose and ensconce the racialized workspaces of both organizations. Black Americans were long familiar with Jim Crow segregation on the railroad—both as passengers and employees—but Standard Oil of New Jersey was one of the few organizations where Black workers could move into management or executive positions, and therefore, it was more realistic that Piper would obtain work in a white-collar position there.[36] Perhaps the most significant revision that the HNU did was to morph Piper from a boosterish, hedonistic "worker" to a bragging, dandyish character who espouses socialist rhetoric. In this portrayal, Piper embodies blackface minstrelsy's Zip Coon character and presents a portrayal of modern Black masculinity that deviates from popular conceptions of Black men as sexual predators and being lazy and idle.[37]

In adapting Kelly's play for its stage, the HNU also tweaked Piper's character to more overtly address the racial and economic politics of the 1930s. The HNU Piper carries many of the same arrogant and reckless behaviors but is one who, rather than engage in proclamations about hedonistic labor, espouses pseudo-Marxist rhetoric, frequently commenting on and discuss-

Figure 4.1 A scene from the Harlem production of *The Show-Off* featuring Amy and Aubrey (*standing*), while Joe, tinkering with engine parts, casts a skeptical eye toward his brother-in-law from the chair. *(FTP LC. Retrieved from https://www.loc.gov /item/musftpnegatives.12320247/.)*

ing the intersection of socialism and capital labor—dialogues that further alienate the Fisher family from their daughter's beau (Mrs. Fisher grows so frustrated with Piper's prattling that she tells him "he didn't know the meanin' of the word Socialism.")[38] But unlike the original production, in which Piper seems keenly unaware of a great deal of how the capitalist space operates, the HNU production affords Piper some legitimate views in the intersection between race and class issues, as Piper feels that racial discrimination holds him back at work and has dissuaded investors from his invention—the formula to prevent rusting that Joe Fisher has developed (true, Piper in this version does take credit for things he had no development in, playing up the braggart aspect of his character). In this way, Piper's eventual complicity was "both transgressive—in that African American workers subverted the racial and class status quo (and stood to gain in these transactions)—and simultaneously rendered less threatening on the grounds that his success paradoxically shored up nationalistic ideals of capitalism," Brackoni argues (see Figure 4.1).[39]

No matter which version of the play was performed, a consistent element in the FTP productions of *The Show-Off* is the presentation of risk and insurance as there are competing visions between Mrs. Fisher and Piper over how to engage with both ideas. By showing Mrs. Fisher receiving an insurance payment after the death of her husband, the play promotes the necessity of insurance to mitigate risk; at the same time, the play's discussion of risk and insurance can be read as an explicit endorsement of New Deal programs like Social Security that provided a measure of protection to Americans. While in mourning, Mrs. Fisher signs for the check from Rogers, and their exchange would have spoken very directly to Depression era audiences:

> ROGERS: That's money we like to pay, Mrs. Fisher, and money we don't like to pay.
> MRS. FISHER: No things are never very pleasant when this kind of money is bein' paid.
> ROGERS: Well, at least, it doesn't make things any less pleasant, Mrs. Fisher.
> MRS. FISHER: No, I'm sure I don't know what a lot of folks 'ud do without it.
> ROGERS: Pretty hard to make a good many of them see it that way, Mrs. Fisher.
> MRS. FISHER: Yes, I guess we don't think much about trouble when we're not havin' it.
> ROGERS: Lot of people think they're never going to have trouble.
> MRS. FISHER: They're very foolish.
> ROGERS: Very foolish indeed.[40]

There is a rather clear tone of moral indignation over the failure of people to protect themselves from risk, but the conversation between Mrs. Fisher and Rogers also seems to be an overt argument for and defense of various security programs of the New Deal. Even allowing for the fact that Mrs. Fisher is taking a check from a private insurer, the play's dialogue emphasizes the insurance in this scene, and it is not difficult to see the implied connection between private insurance and social insurance (and given the overt debates about the passage of Social Security and general awareness of the program's more capitalistic nature, I suspect audiences would have seen such a connection). Adding to this promotion of New Deal programs is a line after the insurance exchange between Mrs. Fisher and Clara. When her daughter asks what she plans to do with the money, Mrs. Fisher responds: "Why, I think I'll just put it into a bank somewhere; everything is paid. And then I'll have something in my old days."[41] For audiences familiar with the failure of banks in previous years, this act of Mrs. Fisher may have been concerning but given large banking reforms of the New Deal and acts like the Federal Deposit Insurance Corporation may have alleviated fears for Americans about that industry. Moreover, Mrs. Fisher's reasoning that she'll have something in her old days seems like a clear endorsement of Social Security.

But while the play promotes insurance, *The Show-Off* also illustrates some of the anxieties over the nature of insurance through Piper's interactions with risk, especially the details of his car "accident" which overlap with rampant fraud as well as a growing sense of the social limitations of insurance. In his description of the car accident—which is problematic in that the term *accident* implies no causality—Piper, who is clearly at fault and is operating a borrowed car without a license and no insurance, accuses those he has injured of faking their injuries, aligning his perspective with the growing rates of insurance fraud. As Ken Dornstein details, there was an extensive underground network of accident racketeers in Jewish enclaves of New York that operated like other organized crime groups. Figures like the Laulicht brothers blurred the lines between criminal and legitimate business, creating an accident mill that processed "illegitimate claims" and manufactured "flops illegally when supply slackened." In a two-year run, the Laulicht brothers "netted . . . tens of thousands, maybe more than one or two hundred thousand dollars, from flops and false claims" through their network of doctors and lawyers under their operation's umbrella.[42] Similarly, a 1937 report in the *Nation* suggests a widespread network of injury fakers working in conjunction with "the shyster lawyer and the unprincipled doctor" to bilk thousands and thousands of dollars from insurance companies. The reporter also mentions that among the "other astonishing frauds [that] have been uncovered" is for a "flopper" to "take advantage of an earlier injury which left permanent effects," then threaten a lawsuit until a cash settlement was offered.[43] While not as overtly criminal as these cases, Piper claims that he is the victim of fraudulence as, in his interpretation of the accident, the police officer ran into his car or "was jaywalking—trying to beat me to the crossing, after giving me the right of way."[44] When he is not claiming that the police were not able to find him at fault so they "tried to cover themselves up as gracefully as possible by trumping up a charge against me of driving an automobile without a license,"[45] Piper also performs the victim of an accident by wearing a bandage over his head while, at the same time, condemning the struck police officer for being performative: "He was faking a broken arm around there when I left—but it's a wonder to me the poor straw ride wasn't signed on the dotted line; for he ran head on right into me."[46]

We can laugh at Piper's blatant lies as an audience, but his recklessness without insurance makes his interest in buying a policy even more problematic.[47] Piper's interest in insurance aligns with a growing public apprehension over the very nature of insurance—both private and social—that such programs do not discourage the embrace of moral hazards or risky behaviors that violate the spirit or statutory laws of these programs. Outlining this social concern over how security attracts risk, Jason Puskar observes, "Auto insurance may make an owner more willing to park in a high-crime area; liability insurance may make a business owner more careless of the safety of patrons and employees," and such concerns are often applied by reactionaries to public insurance programs "so unemployment insurance encourages idleness, insurance for dependent children encourages pregnancy, and Medicare and Medicaid encourage patients to overconsume health care."[48] What increasingly became the prevailing view of insurers in the first decades of the twentieth century was a moralization of risk that allowed "insurers to disown the kinds of conduct it inadvertently promoted, by consigning those unwanted effects back to a traditionally private sphere."[49] Even before the New Deal, foes of social insurance often claimed that public insurance would result in moral decay—and even Isaac Rubinow acknowledged the potential for demoralization of the working class through the promotion of insurance.[50] While Mrs. Fisher's view of insurance promotes socialized, public insurance, Piper's interest in insurance aligns with conservative apprehension over the moral decay and the increased risk the expansion of insurance might entail.

Yet despite his embrace of risk, Piper is the driving force in securing financial security for the Fisher family. And in doing so, we see the play align with two movements that embraced "acceptable" risk: the long-standing endorsement of business practices operating as risk and the promotion of mitigated risk within the rhetoric and policies of the New Deal. First, Piper blunders into giving Joe an idea for improving his metal refinement formula. One of Joe's startling reveals to his mother is that Piper accidentally gave Joe an innovative approach to his work: "[Piper] said—that it was a combination of chemical elements to be added to the metal in its molten state, instead of applied externally as they had been doin'. And I landed on it. . . . That was exactly wh't I'd been doin'—applying the solution externally—in a mixture of paint. But the next day, I tried adding parts of it to the molten state of the metal, and it did the trick. Of course, he didn't know what he was sayin' when he said it."[51] While his error in rehashing the metal process to Joe is by chance, it is Piper's general bluster and adoption of the "risk-taking" businessperson that secures a larger payment for Joe's invention—and positions the play as endorsing some aspect of measured risk. As Piper explains his approach to the negotiation with the steel company:

Why—I simply told them that your father was dead—and that I was acting in the capacity of business advisor to you: and that, if this discovery of yours was as important as you had led me to believe it was, they were simply taking advantage your youth by offering you fifty thousand dollars for it. And that I refused to allow you to negotiate further—unless they doubled the advance, market it at their expense, and one half the net—sign on the dotted-line.[52]

There is, of course, the risk that the management of the company would reject Piper's demands—and one can certainly argue that Piper is engaging in another dangerous game of chance here—but his gamble pays off. Piper has become the risk-taking businessperson by emulating the language of the magazine columnists he has read, and the managers of the company have responded to his "accepted" daring. And while Piper concludes the play by positing a desire to acquire a piece of a shady mining deal, he has achieved his financial windfall by engaging in the accepted risk that has long been promoted as the tolerable action for Americans. In a sense, it is tempting to classify Piper as a confidence artist that I might discuss in Chapter 5, as he bluffs through the negotiation as Chris Stringer might in *Help Yourself*. But there are two key caveats here: first, Piper is not shown to audiences as in control of his performance as a con artist might be. Indeed, throughout the play, we see his incompetence on full display, and there is a line between bluster without skill and determined swindling. But I think for our purposes, it is more accurate to read Piper as a gambling risk-taker, who is willing to chance driving without insurance or a license and willing to risk his brother-in-law's advance by brashly demanding the company double it.

To my mind, *The Show-Off* serves a litany of purposes for many of its audiences. Certainly, we can see the conflict between Piper's lackadaisical view of working and his family-in-law's embrace of traditional work norms. But *The Show-Off* is also about the struggles over embracing and managing risk that would have resonated with many Depression audiences. Within the context of the Social Security Act, the play functions as a government-sponsored endorsement of the need for federalized social insurance as the Pipers benefit from their adoption of insurance. Yet the play also speaks to growing apprehension over the very nature of social insurance itself: Aubrey Piper at every turn of the play engages in reckless and risky behavior that not only likely reminded audiences of the hedonistic 1920s but also spoke to the growing social resentment of insurance as encouraging risky behaviors. Yet the final puzzle piece of *The Show-Off* is how the play—following the tenets of many leaders of the Roosevelt administration—endorses the sort of risk that falls in line with "accepted" risk long promoted by business leaders and cultural conservatives. While the play promotes a sense of security through managed risk, even in the context of the Depression, the conclusion still suggests an embrace of risk at the right moment may be the only way to further secure, well, security.

Mississippi Rainbow

As I mention in Chapter 1, the Chicago Negro Unit (CNU) was where Richard Wright felt that the potential of the theater was undermined by performers only interested in stereotypical fare. But in several respects, Wright held a narrow view of the potential of performance as suggested by what Kate Dossett calls "black performance communities."[53] Dossett argues that many Black-produced and acted plays of the FTP produced performance communities that, although temporary, had "a long-lasting impact on how Black Americans imagined the performance of theatre manuscripts. Shared experiences of performances past produced communities capable of coming together again to imagine, create, and sometimes resist new performance possibilities."[54] Referencing the CNU's refusal to perform one of Paul Green's works, Dossett sees actors who understood "the latent intertexts produced when Black men appeared in chains before whites" having been "well practiced in imagining the absent potential in theatre."[55] Analyzing the same unit's presentation of the living newspaper *Stevedore*, Dossett asserts: "The performance community that developed around *Stevedore* helped imagine into existence a society in which black women and men talk back to and confront white power in front of black and white spectators alike. It helped created the circumstances that allowed Pickens, a black critic, to tell his black readers how white spectators performed in front of black actors and audiences. That he was able to watch white spectators cheering black actors playing characters who defied white supremacy suggests this was a theatre capable of producing social transformation."[56]

After staging *A Hymn to the Rising Sun*, the CNU presented a play whose author, like Wright, voiced frustration with the unit and wrote extensively about his problematic relationship with the production. *Mississippi Rainbow*, written by the white playwright John C. Brownell, is a story of a Black man who avoids work, preferring to think about his "big idea," and, in the process, earns the ire of everyone in his town. Staged eleven times by various Negro Units across the country, the play was popular with audiences but also problematic—especially given it was written by a white playwright.[57] Brownell himself found the Chicago production of his play of particular interest as most of his collected papers at Yale University are of correspondence between him and members of the CNU like Shirley Graham and Theodore Ward. And while Brownell felt the play progressive, it certainly raises a range of issues in terms of representation. But for many in the Black community of Chicago, the play demonstrates a rejection of white norms of labor that were often imposed on Black communities during the era. *Mississippi Rainbow* shows that minority communities can use privileged speculation to counter the dominance of racial economic hierarchy.

Mississippi Rainbow centers on the Washingtons, a Black family living in 1920s or 1930s Mississippi. Henry has been without work for two years after having lost his job working for a riverboat company. His wife, Carrie, and son, Charlie, are working odd jobs to support the family, including laundering for the head of the riverboat company, Mr. Covington. Instead of working or finding a job, Henry spends his days by the riverbank, "using his brain" to think of his big idea—a notion on whose details he is vague. While Henry's family is fairly supportive of his plan, his approach to work earns him some vocal critics—namely Reverend Tatum, the local minister who desires Carrie, and Angie, Henry's sister-in-law, who spends the play demeaning him at every opportunity. Henry reveals to Tatum that he was inspired to take this approach by a tattered advice book he found while working on the riverboat. That book encouraged him to keep on smiling and dreaming of his big idea, and eventually, it would come to fruition. Henry then begins to try to convince his friend Flatfoot to pull his life savings from the bank and invest in Henry's idea.

Angie reveals that Charlie and his girlfriend, Lucy, are expecting a child and that she (Angie) and her husband, Jake, a bootlegging gambler, are going to give the couple a thousand dollars to start a new life. Henry says that as the father, he should be gifting his son money, at which point Carrie loses her patience and orders her husband to act like a man and find some work. Henry feels betrayed by his wife and heads out into a raging storm. The next morning, Henry is missing, and after a search, Jake and Charlie return with only Henry's hat. Meanwhile Jake informs Angie that he gambled away the money they were going to give the young couple. Carrie and Angie seek the council of a voodoo priestess who declares that Henry has drowned, and the family holds a funeral to Henry's memory.

Carrie is forlorn and resigned to the fact that not only is Henry not coming back but also that she must use the collateral of their home to give her son some money to start a new life. Suddenly, Henry appears in the house wearing fine clothes, proclaiming that his "big idea" has come to fruition. Having borrowed money from Flatfoot, Henry has claimed riverside land that is coveted by the riverboat company, and Henry's former employer is willing to pay a substantial amount of money for the land. Henry's family is certainly skeptical of his claims—and then Mr. Covington arrives. However, Covington tries to make a less substantial offer for the land and then tries to assert that Henry's loan from Flatfoot was taken out under false pretenses and that the claim to the land invalid. But the Washingtons refuse to budge, especially Carrie, who lambastes Covington's counterclaims as ridiculous because her husband was able to outsmart the owner at his own game. Covington relents and agrees to pay $10,000 for the land. Henry doles out money to Flatfoot, Angie, and his son and, as he declares plans for his "next big idea," pulls out a cigar, and all the characters rush to light it for him.

In several respects, *Mississippi Rainbow* aligns with some larger problems with the FTP Negro Units, especially in terms of play selection. While the works of Black playwrights were adopted and performed by the various Negro Units across the country, there was an institutional embrace of the work of white playwrights, especially Eugene O'Neill, Paul Green, and Ridgely Torrence. Despite growing concerns about the representations of Blackness in these plays both from commentators and from many of the actors themselves, the heads of the FTP often relied on "folk dramas, melodramas and dramas of social realism" whose differences in genre "were transcended by white playwrights whose 'uses' of the black body had much in common, both with each other and with the commercial theatre. No less than Broadway, the Federal Theatre offered many opportunities and multiplicity of forms through which white Americans might enact racial mastery."[58] Moreover, as Lauren Rebecca Sklaroff argues, several members of the Play Policy Bureau (PPB), which oversaw play selection for the program after 1937, declared that they would not select plays for the Negro Unit that were "too militant" or "unproducible" and would avoid staging plays that eschewed racial stereotypes. But while care was taken to stage plays with "the least problematic depiction of race relations,"[59] many times reviewers for the PPB "related their own assumptions on what constituted 'authentic' black life," as even realist portrayals of lynching in certain plays were critiqued by reviewers as passé, thereby denying the persistence of racial violence.[60] And while members of the PPB attempted to eschew those stereotypes, they often staged or planned productions that drew the ire of the NAACP for the racial caricatures embedded in the plays.[61]

The readers who endorsed *Mississippi Rainbow* for production by the FTP reflect this criticism of the PPB's view of Blackness as many find the play harmless and/or an authentic view of Black life. One reviewer found the play to be "a keen insight into the negro mind,"[62] while another, Samuel Krieter, found the play to be "well-written" about a typical group of "Mississippi negroes done in their best characteristic dialect," while further noting that it "would appeal to any type of audience."[63] Alfred B. Kuttner recommended the play due to its "joyous, ebullient quality in the telling" and, reading the play as nonpolitical, found *Mississippi Rainbow* to be a "welcome variation from the somewhat too self-conscious tragic quality which weighs down so many pictures of negro life."[64] But perhaps the most loaded endorsement of the play comes from C. C. Lawrence, who opined that the play was "a good example of Negro Theater," and found "nothing offensive to anyone" in the text. He further noted that the playwright "does not over emphasize dialect or degrade to hold interest" and found the play rather universal and representative of Black theater: "Many commentators will say 'This is not a Negro Drama, it could happen anywhere.' Yet it is Negro Drama at its greatest height, for I personally have come in contact with several persons who had acquired Henry's philosophy. Yes, all groups have the same problems only in a different environment and manner. Henry is a type that can be found among any people or in any place, country, or climate."[65]

Claims of knowing the makeup of Black theater and what were authentic representations aside, the selection of *Mississippi Rainbow* also aligns with the tendency of the PPB to select plays about Black life written by white playwrights. Born in Vermont in 1877, John C. Brownell spent time touring on the vaudeville circuit in the 1910s before working in the film industry, appearing in some comic films and working as scenario editor for Universal Pictures. At some point in 1928, Brownell had lost his job in Hollywood and began to write more work for the stage. What inspired him to write the play, originally entitled *Nothing But Trouble*, is unclear, but he was likely inspired by the success of *Showboat* and *Porgy*, plays written by whites, set in the South, but also prominently featuring Black actors. The play did not garner Brownell much support from Broadway. As an agent for the Richard J. Madden company advised Brownell in a letter about the "colored play": "For God's sake lay off it. This town has been flooded with them for the past twelve months. . . . The only man that I know that can write an interesting and salable play on colored people is Carl Van Vechten and even he does not dare do it so what chance has poor white trash?"[66] After a regional premiere, Brownell changed the play's name to *Brain Sweat*, and it was gaining interest from places like Cleveland, where the play was garnering some positive feedback from theater operators who found the play "took" with the theater's "regular following . . . from the university, the artist crowd . . . those a little weary of the commercial theatre and definitely the intellectuals of the town."[67] *Brain Sweat* then premiered on Broadway in April 1935 but closed after five performances.[68] After the failure of *Brain Sweat* on the Broadway stage, Brownell began tweaking his play into *Mississippi Rainbow*. Brownell initially was not interested in having his work produced by the FTP, but Susan Glaspell eventually convinced Brownell to permit the program to produce the play.[69] In addition, there was a great deal of overlap between the *Brain Sweat* Broadway production and the FTP.[70]

Brownell's correspondence suggests a man who both advocated for Black theater workers and harbored mainstream white supremacist views. At times, Brownell shows a knowledge and appreciation for Black theater. In several letters, Brownell seems to take a sincere interest in the careers of both Shirley Graham and Theodore Ward—whose work he promotes to both Susan Glaspell and the Samuel French Company.[71] In a letter to George Kondolf, Brownell laments that the late Bert Williams could not have appeared in *Mississippi Rainbow* while believing that Paul Robeson would be perfect in the role of Henry Washington.[72] But at other points, Brownell's correspondence reveals attitudes that speak to a less enlightened view of racial politics. In a letter response to Ward, who was inquiring for general advice about playwrighting, Brownell suggests to Ward that the only measure for financial success in theater is to "write for white tastes and interests."[73] Brownell is even more racially condescending in a letter to Shirley Graham. Complaining about the lack of interest in the play from the Black community in Chicago and some tepid press reviews, Brownell bemoans the lack of interest in *Mississippi Rainbow* as indicative of broad racial attitudes about art and Blackness and notes he will not write another play for "the race":

> If your race will not give their support to a clean play written out of a sincere regard for your race what is the use of writing another? Russell Wooding told me long ago that negroes would not support a play written for them. I didn't believe it. I believe it now. From outside information I learn that inty nine [sic] percent of the patrons at the Princess are white folks. It is therefore apparent that the race doesn't give a hoot about it—isn't interested. . . . Because it was clean, devoid of propaganda and racial problems they [Samuel French] believed negro schools and colleges would welcome it. They haven't. . . . Write another?? Not me![74]

Graham, for her part, did not take kindly to Brownell's accusations. Noting that perhaps he was given erroneous information about play attendance and that her theater was invested in the long-term success of *Mississippi Rainbow*, Graham lambasted Brownell by asserting that she did not "feel responsible for what the members of my race do, and certainly I feel no responsibility for what the Negroes in Chicago do."[75]

Brownell's concerns about audiences and reception were somewhat accurate. The play, at least initially, was drawing close to 90 percent white audiences to the Princess Theater, and in the white press, reception to the play was generally lukewarm.[76] *Chicago Daily Tribune* reviewer Charles Collins wrote a review in which he unfavorably compared the play as a "wan Negro version of *The Show-Off*" and a work "rankly written for amusement purposes, [that] carries no burden of folk-play seriousness or sociological theme. The author's pattern appears to have been found among the minor cabin comedies of Irish drama, and his story telling begins with a situation that is vaguely reminiscent of *June and the Paycock*—a shiftless, babbling husband, a patient hard-working wife and eccentric boon companion . . . one suspects that the author has seen *Porgy* several times too often."[77] A reviewer for the *Chicago Daily News* found the play to be "of no significance nor importance, whatsoever, to the Negro race, which the Federal theatre should be encouraging along the line of its great theatrical potentialities" and could have easily been written about "poor whites and played by white actors." The reviewer also notes that "In many ways the play is a pale. . . . Negro edition of *The Show-Off*, since its central character is a trifling and irritating butt who, in the end, emerges as the savior of all."[78]

There was also a complicated reaction from Black Chicago toward the play. While initially there was a tepid reception to *Mississippi Rainbow*, there were some positive responses. Some of this was born from the advocacy of Graham, who was actively engaging Black community groups to become more involved with the CNU. In a letter she wrote to various Black civic organizations, Graham promotes *Mississippi Rainbow* by drawing on the shared Black experience of "age-old wisdom, blazing-suns and tropic colors which has been distilled and purified by the years of suffering and pain and privation," out of which "have come songs," and tears dried from laughter. She then presents a nostalgic view of the South, aiming at memories of the Great Migration of the 1910s by asking potential patrons to recall that "wide, muddy river turning all crimson gold beneath the bow of promise? Doesn't it mean something to you?" She also provides potential audiences a sense of ownership and stakes in the performance: "This is your play, presented at your theatre."[79] And some Black Chicagoans approved. Claude A. Barnett, the editor of the Chicago-based Associated Negro Press, opens a letter to Brownell asking for a referral for his client Etta Morten by asserting that: "*Mississippi Rainbow* is truly remarkable in its lifelike portrayal of Negro idiom and dialect. It seems almost impossible that a Vermonter could have grasped the racial expression of so many of us so completely, without considerable exposure to Negro life."[80] Even the *Chicago Defender*, which condemned the CNU for not taking aesthetic risks, had some positive press of the play.[81] In an interview for the paper, visiting Langston Hughes praised the CNU's work, noting that the Chicago production was far superior to "the same drama played by New York artists."[82] One reader of the paper also praised the play as well, noting that while it was not "entirely free from criticism," it was "without that offensive tinge we always find in plays written by white authors" and that all "should avail" themselves of "the opportunity to see a play in which your Race does not exit at the little end of the horn."[83]

But the biggest defender of the play was Theodore Ward, who appeared as Flatfoot in the Chicago production and would later have his play, *Big White Fog* produced by the CNU. Noting the intersection between Richard Wright and Ward's politics, Julie Burrell notes Ward's work rejects "middle-class uplift ideology dominant at the time, propounded by 'black elites.'" While characters of Ward's can achieve various versions of success, they "ultimately cannot defeat the crushing intersection of racist and economic oppression."[84] Pointing to the structural racism in American capitalism, Ward's play "exposes how Chicago and the urban North—often called 'up South' by African Americans—was as shaped by Jim Crow economics as the South." In turn, Ward believes the idea that high-achieving members of the race—whether in terms of education or those who engage in "capital accumulation"—will escape the oppression of racism through their ascension into the bourgeoisie is laughable: "The Depression has shown that . . . almost religious belief in the power of capitalism to lift up the race is ultimately untenable."[85] We can see traces of these political views from Ward in a letter to Brownell. Ward reasons that it is the conclusion of the play and its subversion of racialized roles that affected the initial bottom-line:

> I don't suppose you will readily appreciate the fact but, in allowing Henry to triumph as you do, you have violated a pretty serious American Theatre tradition. It just isn't the thing to do, in fact, I doubt if you can find a single precedent—the Negro just doesn't get the best of the white man in anything. Your audiences laugh; they really enjoy the show, but once they leave the theatre the old folkways immediately begin to reassert themselves. I think this was the thing that irked some of your critics here though I doubt if they were aware of it.

In the same letter, Ward points to a growing Black audience for the play—he asserts that "no other downtown play has ever drawn so largely from the Southside"—but bemoans the fact that many educators seem to have rejected the play for what Ward calls their "ignorance" and a belief that "the Negroes in your play are too close to the soil to be representative." Despite this criticism, Ward believes that Brownell had, on a certain level, offered a blueprint for how Black writers, like himself, should engage with their audiences: "But I am convinced that the present lack of Negro contributions in the field [theater] is due to the folly of Negro writers of the past, and indeed largely of today, who, in their desire to eat, have striven too hard to square their ideals with the demands of their white public."[86]

One of the difficulties with this play is how, to certain audiences, it outwardly reinforces stereotypical and nostalgic views of Blackness in 1930s America. The play seems to be influenced by romantic views of the southern Black experience seen in texts like *Showboat* and *Porgy*, nineteenth- and twentieth-century views of the region, and stereotyped views of Black labor. The fact that Henry's inspiration to engage in his "big idea" comes from the advice in tattered booklet on his former riverboat certainly could have reinforced the racist view of Black maleness and work ethic as infantile and lazy. But Black audience members may have found some nuance in the portrayal of labor in the play. Dream books, as Ann Fabian shows, were popular texts that sought to provide a system to the world and, "more important, the means of ordering and acting on the chaos."[87] These books evaluated the dreams of the reader for purposes of the reader to apply their lessons to financial gain (or perhaps more accurately for the author of said dream book to sell his product). These books promoted the idea that dreams did not belong to a private universe, but to the public sphere where they "offered every man access to the plans of the gods, but like all divination, meaning rested on correct interpretation." If a dream failed to accurately sense the future, the fault did not lie with the system espoused by the dream book, but with the interpreter themselves.[88] By the late nineteenth century, the publishers of dream books began to print books with fictional Black authors, all of whom had "interpreted plantation life for fellow slaves" and had knowledge of dreams and expertise "derived from slave communities or exotic knowledge increasingly lost to city dwellers."[89] While these books and pamphlets could serve various needs for various audiences—Fabian notes that they were trivial souvenirs or parlor entertainment for the white middle class—their existence points toward a larger cultural point. While things like insurance companies and other social controls helped diminish folk beliefs, there was still an interest in folk or mystical belief in the United States and the "presence of these seers, however gestural, is evidence of the African American hand in northern popular culture and of the survival of folk beliefs."[90] But the agents of interpretation—especially poor Black Americans—were never able to manipulate the economy. And while Henry's book also bears some similarities to self-help books of the era like Napoleon Hill's *Think and Grow Rich*, the vagaries of the advice presented to Henry and his general lack of agency, align with the racial economic politics of dream books.

Moreover, some of the most vocal critics of Henry's own work ethic—namely, Reverend Tatum—are presented as less-than-noble characters. Tatum often evokes language that parallels the asceticism of work found in Protestant norms of labor. He condemns Henry early on in the play by saying, "De good book say you gotta work six days a week but de only one in dis house dat works six days a week is yoh good wife—an' yoh son. . . . You ought to be ashamed of yoself!"[91] However, the play showcases Tatum as somewhat morally duplicitous as he proposed marriage to Carrie before her marriage, and the play implies he is still desires her. Skeptical views of ministers or portrayals of ministers as duplicitous were prevalent in Black culture from at least the time of Reconstruction and became even more prominent during the 1920s and 1930s: "The substantial anger blacks felt at the hypocrisy and dishonesty of the 'respectable' world around them was projected onto the figure of the black minister, whose lofty pretensions were constantly pictured as being undermined by his compulsive lust for chicken, liquor, money, and women."[92] Sensational stories about "wayward ministers and their transgressive behavior" were often found in Black newspapers of the 1920s and 1930s, while the famous comedic performer Bert Williams's "famous sketch of Elder Eatmore lampooned the Elder not only for having a voracious appetite but also—playing with stereotypes prevalent in white minstrelsy and vaudeville—for stealing chickens, excessive drinking, and gambling."[93] And one of the most prominent examples from the decade prior to the 1930s is Paul Robeson's minister character in Oscar Micheaux's *Body and Soul* (1925), in which the director "challenges the authority of the minister . . . and implies the congregation's complicity in his abuse of authority" by portraying a minister who revels in drunkenness, womanizing, and thievery.[94]

While Reverend Tatum condemns Henry's perceived lack of work ethic on spiritual grounds, his sister-in-law Angie lambastes Henry for his inability to provide for his family. But Angie's condemnations of Henry's embrace of chance are complicated by the fact that Angie has benefited from other risky ventures into informal economies as her husband Jake earns his living through bootlegging and gambling. While participants in such economic structures were de facto cultural heroes in many Black communities, and she herself has benefited from the work of chance, Angie is skeptical of an overreliance on speculative forms of labor. This skepticism is driven, in part, by the fact that her husband may not be as successful a gambler as he suggests:

> JAKE: What's a lil' money lak a thousan' berries? Wid de luck Ah'm playin' in Ah'll have dat much back in a week.
> ANGIE: You will if you let dose dice loose.
> JAKE: De money dat bought dat sparkler on you hand, beautiful, Ah I wins wid dose dice. Dey *rolls* for me.
> ANGIE: *Sometimes* dey does.[95]

Angie's tempered embrace of her husband's gambling labor continues in Act 2, when Henry begins to sell Jake on his "big idea," tempting the gambler with a note that Henry will be "a mighty 'potant man . . . soon when Ah gits a lil' help." Upon hearing her husband's interest in what is to her, and to the audience at this stage as well, a dangerous investment, Angie responds to both Jake and Henry forcefully: "Keep yoh hands off dat bankroll, Mr. Gambler. Jake ain't gwine to put no money in no wildcat scheme if dat's what you aimin' at. Our money—an' notice Ah said our money—is gwine where 'twill do some good."[96] And when her husband loses the thousand dollars in the middle of Act 2, Angie's rage at her husband's risk is fully founded.

But Jake's gambling losses are not just a sign of the dangers of chance labor. His failure signals a conflict with the spirituality of chance, a sign for him that he is not favored by God or fate. Decompressing after his losses and Henry's disappearance, Jake uses passive voice when describing the action of his losses—as if there is some divine power at work, one that he had never witnessed before: "Gawd, Angie, Ah nevah saw money fade away so quick. Ah lose it in seven passes." He then blames Henry's disappearance for his gambling losses, deflecting his own risk and attributing it to external causes: "Well, after we fin' Henry's hat on the de bank, Ah got the heebie-jeebies. If it hadn't ben foh *him* doin' what he did Ah'd have dat money now."[97] In contrast, Henry openly evokes a sense of divine grace to his embrace of risk and chance. When explaining his decision to not throw himself into the river after his row with Carrie, Henry details a spiritual reaffirmation of his embrace of speculation:

> Den Ah hears 'nother voice—clear—lake a bell. Ah raise up mah head an' listen, 'cause it seem lak it come from de sky. It say "Don't you do dis terr'ble thing, Henry Washington—only a mis'ble coward gonna do 'way wid hisself an' you ain't no coward," de voice say. "Yoh has got to live—so you kin bring happiness an'prosperity to you fam'ly wid yoh project." . . . De voice say—"no mattah if nobody b'lieves in yoh—b'lieve in youself an' yoh gwine to win!" Ah tears off mah hat! Ah throws it on de groun' an Ah lif' up mah head an' say—"thank yoh, Lawd—Ah'm gwine to go on lak yoh tell me."[98]

Both Jake and Henry seek some sort of divine intervention into their embrace of risk and gambling, but based on what the play shows us, it is Henry who—at least in this instance—can claim divine intervention in the success of his gamble. And in one sense, by contrasting the Black ethos of chance—gambling—to the white vision of it—speculation—it is certainly not a stretch to read Henry's success as something of an endorsement of white norms of speculative work.

The play also presents a nuanced view of risk and security through Henry's attempts to persuade his friend Flatfoot to invest in his big idea. Flatfoot voices skepticism over Henry's plan, in part, because of an emotional and intellectual attachment to the nest egg the insurance company paid him after the death of his wife. For him, not only is the money a reminder of the tragic loss of her life, but also, he reasons that he only has his nest egg because of her chance death—and that is enough measured risk for him: "Ah jes' cain't Henry. It's all Ah got. Why, if del ole woman hadn't died Ah wouldn' have dat. Ah'd of let de premums lapse."[99] Moreover, Flatfoot sees his money as safe in a bank: responding to Henry's query of "Wouldn't you lake to see dat thousan' dollahs grown into two—three—four—wouldn' yuh?" Flatfoot says "Sho Ah would, but she's *safe* now—safe in de *bank* an'growin' slow but *sure*."[100] And like the Fisher family in *The Show-Off* voicing their anger at the recklessness of Aubrey Piper's daring, Flatfoot also condemns his friend's request for becoming a partner in his plan by decrying the very real chance and lack of security Henry's big idea represents: "I—I'd lak to make dat money, Henry, but—but—sumpien maght go *wrong*."[101]

Yet despite these real reservations, the play also demonstrates a racialized component to Flatfoot's view of insurance, investment, and speculation that illustrates white control of Black economic power and labor. Given Black Americans' long-standing distrust of white banking institutions that continued into the Depression era, the play aligns with these skeptical views of the stability of the banking system as both a buttress against risk and of an institution that values Black perspectives.[102] Flatfoot's view of Henry's speculation seems partly informed by the advice of a banker that parallels the rhetoric of white banking standards that were espoused by reformers and media critics of the Black work ethic: "Mr. Burnham in de bank he say 'Mr. Mobly—you leave dat money here wid me 'til you cain't work no mo'. You jus' fohgit 'bout it,' he say, ''til de time come when nobody wants yoh 'roun' wid no money in yoh pants."[103] Moreover, Flatfoot also reveals a distinct lack of agency for himself as he has ceded control of his security to Mr. Burnham the banker, and the banker evokes racist paternalistic rhetoric straight out of many white newspaper accounts of the inability of Black Americans to control their finances. For Henry, Flatfoot's faith in the bank—both in terms of the certainty of his continued financial success and that Mr. Burnham has his best interests at heart—are laughable. In part, Henry sees the financial security promised his friend to be a pyric victory as he will only see any financial support from his work once years of toil have destroyed Flatfoot's body and soul: "Ah'm sorry foh yuh. You jes' go on breakin' yoh back 'til de time come when you cain't enjoy nuffen—'til you is so ole an' crippled up dat yoh ready for de grave. Den dat money will give you a nice funeral!"[104] He further decries his friend's thinking by pointing out the racial components of the banker's perspective that ties their interactions to the larger racial politics of speculation. After Flatfoot asks Henry if it "would be all raght wid you if Ah talk wid Mr. Burnham in de bank about it?" Henry responds: "No! No! Don' do dat! What's *he* know 'bout what *Ah* know? Ah'm jes' a poor nigger to him what ain't earned a cent in two years"[105] (see Figure 4.2).

Henry's embrace of speculation functions as both a critique of white speculative work and as a model for Black co-option of such practices to gain a measure of economic security. While it is tempting to read Henry's assessment of white labor practices as simplistic, I think the play allows Henry to signify the discourse of white work culture, such as in his assessment of the "work" of the heroes of the Gilded Age, the robber barons. He says, "John D. Rock'feller or Peepont Mogun, dey puff on they cigars an' think—keepin'

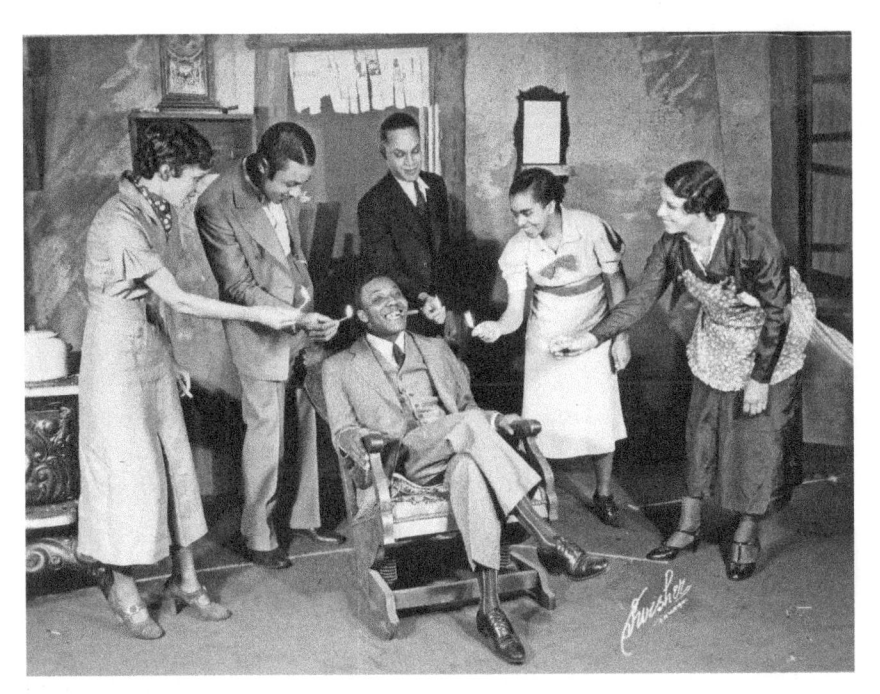

Figure 4.2 Henry's triumph at the conclusion of the play as seen in the CNU's *Mississippi Rainbow. (Box 570, FTP LC.)*

dey minds wide open."[106] As Henry describes them, the major figures of American capitalism "don't do nuthin' but think" and when the opportunity arises, they 'hop' on it and "make big money."[107] In Act 2, Henry pontificates on how Robber Barons like Rockefeller became so wealthy: by simply seizing on an opportunity via their brain sweat; citing the story of a man named Hurley in Memphis who had no education:

> But he's got a brain! He kin think! Lak John D. Rock'feller or Peepont Morgan he don't do nuthin' but think. What happen? First thing you know he own another house. Why? How he get it? . . . He keep his ears open an' his eyes peel foh opp'tunity. He look lak he's half asleep, walkin' 'roun' smokin' his big black cigar, but he' aint. No sah—not Mistah Hurley. He see a project—a sure fiah chance to big money dat ev'body else ovahlook. What he do, den? He hop on it.[108]

But the play also illustrates these business tactics as effective. Indeed, Henry's speculative claim emulates the same tactic we can presume the riverboat company has used in the past, for Covington uses unscrupulous speculation tactics to try to undercut Henry's claim, noting that the riverboat company "may not need that land for twenty years" and that the land is otherwise worthless.[109] Despite Covington's pressure, Henry refuses to waver from his demand of a $10,000 payment for the rights to the land. Henry's stance infuriates Covington, who has already successfully convinced Henry's friend he will lose his money because Henry secured it under false pretenses. But Henry, Carrie, and Lucy do not succumb to Covington's demands, in part, because of Henry's example. His speculative work has created a space in which he and his family can challenge white work norms. As Carrie demands that Covington pay up and agree to the land transfer, she declares that his tactics are feeble as Henry has countered white economic power by utilizing standards of white economic norms. She tells Covington, "Yoh'd a sit tight in yoh office 'til mah husban' come crawlin' to yoh. Yoh ben tryin' to pull yoh own fat out'n de fiah cause he got up too early in de mawnin' foh yuh. Now yoh's gwine to do some fancy crawlin' Mistah Slave Drivah, 'cause yoh's flat's a pancake."[110]

The success of the Washingtons in *Mississippi Rainbow* parallels that of Aubrey Piper in *The Show-Off*, especially the HNU's production of that play. Reflecting on that production, Braconi, while acknowledging the problematic elements of the play—including some accusations of the HNU's Piper as a bulwark of the minstrel tradition in some aspects and the lack of realism with the loans given between characters toward one another—still locates the play as beckoning to an alternative path for Black Americans by "proposing that oppression could be vanquished if blacks gained greater agency in the corporate system. The HNU's production of *The Show-Off* called into question the traditional power dynamics of white hegemony and emphasized blacks' fraught relationship with capitalism while simultaneously delivering a subtle counter mimicry of middle-class values and ambitions."[111] The Negro Unit productions of Brownell's play tease the idea that economic oppression could be undermined if certain approaches of white norms of speculation be adopted by Black Americans.

Writing about *Golddiggers of 1937*, Michael Szalay asserts that the final number of the film, "All's Fair in Love and War," is partially about the interchangeability of characters as Joan Blondell and Glenda Farrell become, at times, indistinguishable from one another, availing themselves of both "autonomy and security." More than any other grouping of plays I discuss in this project, the productions of both *The Show-Off* and *Mississippi Rainbow* seem to reflect the most nuanced of positioning within the New Deal. The two plays here present endorsements of New Deal views on security and chance but also challenge the philosophical underpinnings of both concepts: security is lauded through the promotion of insurance in *The Show-Off*, while it is ultimately reckless risk that secures the Fishers' security; in turn,

Mississippi Rainbow presents insurance as inadequate while praising capitalist speculation (and condemning leisurely chance). These productions are also problematic in several ways, especially in the case of the Negro Unit productions of white playwrights. But these plays suggest that perhaps the only true guarantee of security was by embracing chance—and that might not be a guarantee in the slightest.

Con Artist Comedies

By the beginning of the 1930s, professional wrestling in the United States had evolved and morphed from two generally divergent lines: the first was authentic, amateur wrestling that was held in stadiums across the United States; the second was far less legitimate in nature, born out of the sideshow and carnival circuit in which wrestlers would be "challenged" by local strongmen in exhibitions with all entertainers in on the facade. Eventually, when promoters and the wrestlers themselves realized that less authentic, acrobatic moves and holds were less taxing (relatively) on the body and far more popular with audiences, professional wrestling began to embrace a more theatrical element. Crowds filled arenas to watch, as Ronald Barthes observed, a mythological melodrama and morality play. And more importantly, "The public is completely uninterested in knowing whether the contest is rigged or not, and rightly so; it abandons itself to the primary virtue of the spectacle, this is to abolish all motives and all consequences: what matters is not what it thinks but what it sees."[1]

Professional wrestling was and remains a confidence scheme at its heart: not only have the words associated with the con filtered their way into the language of wrestling—matches can be "works," fans who buy too readily into stories are "marks"—but also that wrestling, like the con, sells its audience on an idea and seeks profit from that belief. As Susan Maurer explains in her analysis of wrestling, professional wrestlers relish their participation as members of an elaborate confidence game, selling audiences their roles, personas, and the narratives in the environment.[2] And while many wrestling narratives focus on the 1980s as the "death of kayfabe"—the illusion maintained by wrestlers, promoters, and fans that what happened in the ring was real—many audiences of the Depression era often were keenly aware that what they were witnessing was not "real."[3] As a fan told the legendary sportswriter Grantland Rice in 1931: "As far as I know the shows are honest. But even if they're not I get a big kick out of them, for they are full of action and all the outward signs of hostile competition. It is either honest competition or fine acting and in either case, I get a real show."[4]

And like their professional wrestling brethren, confidence artists—defined as any person who defrauds or outwits another person or group by gaining their confidence—were hardly unusual in the FTP.[5] There are shades of the con artist in *The Torch-Bearers*' Mrs. Pampinelli, *The Show-Off*'s Aubrey Piper, and several of the actors in *A Moral Entertainment*, and in *Room Service*, most of Gordon Miller's acting troupe resorts to swindling in order to just get by. And one of John C. Brownell's other plays produced by the program was *The Nut Farm*, about an aspiring film director named Willie Barton who outwits a shady film producer by taking control of the project through swindling. But in this chapter, I focus on two of the more popular con artist comedies: Lynn Root and Harry Clork's *The Milky Way* and Paul Vulpius's *Help Yourself*, plays that deal with, respectively, a boxing promotor and milkman who engage in a series of staged boxing matches and the story of a young man who pretends to work in a bank without having a job at the bank. These plays present complicated views of confidence artists that draw on long cultural traditions of the confidence artist in the United States, as well as addressing fields—boxing and banking—rife with fraud and scandal. They also portray growing concerns over the importance of media and advertising in American society as well as the reactionary movements gaining traction in the country at the end of the decade. But they also serve to provide audiences' spaces to delight in the mythological counterswindling of institutions onstage and to remind the same audiences that legitimate, dangerous confidence schemes still threaten the security of all Americans.

The Confidence Artist and Society

While much of New Deal legislation was concerned with the promotion of work, another impetus for various reforms passed under the auspices of the Roosevelt administration was the elimination of deceptive, fraudulent business practices. While these reforms did not "absolve buyers from the duty to keep a sharp lookout" in their purchases and investments, the Roosevelt administration's embrace of *caveat venditor*—"Let the seller also beware"— signaled a shift in both political discourse and national policy. While there were reforms in fields like food production and advertising, perhaps the most prominent reforms occurred in the securities and banking industries.[6] And the banking system had engaged in a number of deceptive practices: investment banks underpriced shares and reserved placements for corporate insiders and favored clients when underwriting initial public stock offerings; and in addition to "based remuneration policies that encouraged stretching of the truth, they [banks] trimmed the firms' losses on poorly performing stocks in their portfolios by instructing sales personnel to push those securities on retail customers."[7] In legislation like the Securities Act of 1933, the Securities and Exchange Act of 1934, the 1938 Maloney Act, and the 1940 Investment Companies Act, the federal government banned insider trading, market manipulations, and deceptions in public offerings, and established the Securities Exchange Commission to oversee trading and investment practices of public companies and generally sought to protect the American public from fraudulent practices.[8]

However, one of the struggles for New Deal antifraud legislation, as well as postwar reforms, were long-standing historical views toward hucksterism that still maintained power in the American psyche. Despite the shifts away from the premises of caveat emptor in American law and governance, many sectors of American society "retained contempt for the sucker and grudging admiration for those who took advantage of them."[9] This also manifested in American linguistic practices of the mid-century, which "communicated a disfavored status for those taken in by bait and switch advertising or investment scams." Edward J. Balleisen notes that even when commentators attempted to educate consumers and investors about the need for reasoned skepticism over too-good-to-be-true claims, these commentators often relied on rather unflattering monikers like *mark*, *egg*, *chump*, or *pigeon* to place a good deal of blame of the suckerism of the investors on consumers themselves.[10] Moreover, Balleisen asserts, attempts at reform were often countered by the frequent billing of the "picaresque confidence man" in popular culture, as texts generally repeated the message that "those preyed on by financial bilkers had only their own greed to blame."[11] This conflict between condemning fraud and condoning swindling underscores the long and complicated cultural history of the confidence artist in American society. And in this section, I briefly provide an overview of this history that will set the stage for the popularity of the con artist plays of the FTP.

While the term *confidence man* likely did not appear in print until 1849 with New York coverage of the case of William Thompson, both fascination with and contempt toward the art of the confidence scheme was long embedded in American culture and society. Various Native American and African folkloric traditions feature trickster figures who exist to deceive or challenge heroic or gullible figures in stories, while duplicitous figures show-up in a range of Anglican texts that existed before the colonial settlement of the

United States. But to be certain, the dominant discourse that existed in American culture from the colonial period to present day has condemned the work of the confidence scheme as antithetical to traditional values of labor. For many, the confidence scheme bore none of the hallmarks of craft, diligence in labor, and frugality, instead relying on duplicity, fraud, deception, and contempt for noble labor. Like the dominant views of the work ethic, much of this contempt can be drawn from the views of Puritans with commentators like Cotton Mather who derided the general dishonesty of the swindle and its purveyors as immoral actors. This Puritan contempt grew from the "loathing for the hypocrite who cloaked his sinfulness with the appearance of virtue." Moreover, Puritan thinkers also believed that those who acted hypocritically were victims "of a confidence game play by Satan, the Prince of Liars." "So crafty was the demonic confidence man," claimed some Puritan intellectuals, "that he could actually counterfeit the Spirit's saving operations in the exact order of their appearance, and thus lure men into thinking they were saved."[12] Detailing the rise of pre–Civil War handbooks aimed at young men (and women) entering the developing city space, in which people did not know one another in the same way they did in smaller communities, Karen Halttunen details other growing concerns over the rise of confidence artists in the religious and genteel communities. These groups feared the capacity of certain confidence artists to move toward demagoguery as they had no fixed principles and inspired fanatical loyalty among their adherents; in turn, in the minds of many moralists like Henry Ward Beecher, speculation, like gambling, produced nothing of benefit, encouraged an aversion to industry, and defrauded all those around the risk taker.[13] By the mid-nineteenth century, this growing fear over the major social forces transforming America—"a high rate of geographical mobility and particularly of migration to the city, the decline of social deference . . . and in general a replacement of traditional hierarchical social relationships"—had manifested into a growing fear over the confidence artist and a shaping of that figure in much of American society as a villain to be feared.[14]

This demonization of the confidence artist in American society was not necessarily represented in much of the literary texts of the pre- and post–Civil War eras. While there were nefarious confidence artists represented in American fiction and theater,[15] the years surrounding the Civil War saw the confidence artist become a covert cultural hero, occupying "a central place in our popular mythology."[16] For Gary Lindberg, the appeal of the confidence artist in American culture is, in part, predicated on two key situations. First, the con artist "*makes* belief" as "everyone around him believes in some larger promise." Whether the con man is a professional criminal, a booster, a gamesman, or a healer, the appeal of the con for marks (as well as readers of con artist narratives) is the creation of an idea that they can hold on to, even if the idea is without substance. Second, Lindberg argues that the con artist suggests that "the boundaries [of the social structure] are already fluid, [and] that there is ample space between society's official rules and its actual tolerances."[17] The appearance of confidence artists in the mid-nineteenth century imposes "order of comedy upon the chaos of these cultural fears, temporarily resolving them for the reader. . . . In the humorous successes and failures of the confidence man, the reader perceives a fictional model of boom and bust, one that allows him to reconcile antithetical attitudes of hope and fear, confidence and suspicion, and optimism and pessimism." For William Lenz, these narratives allowed readers to participate imaginatively in humorous confidence games and "envision the worst image of Americans within the safe confines of comic fiction and to discharge the anxieties this image creates."[18] For Lindberg and Lenz, the importance of the con artist in American culture is not only how the figure provides a safe space for readers to work through their respective contemporary problems but also how the character promotes its own mythology and meaning.

Whether the confidence artist was a figure of derision or a hero, aspects of "swindling" began to be readily embraced by American society—especially concerning the notion of appearance. While the first half of the nineteenth century saw middle-class Americans believe that the "key to success was character formation" born of "industry, sobriety, and frugality," the later nineteenth century saw this formula morph to "a demand not for ascetic self-discipline, but for the arts of social manipulation."[19] While the main character of 106 of Horatio Alger's *Ragged Dick* novels did not abandon the character ethic aligned with the Protestant synthesis of religious and secular callings, he nevertheless relies on three qualities that were "new to American success ideology: aggressiveness, charm, and the arts of the confidence man."[20] And whereas advice manuals for young men of the pre–Civil War period had warned against the perils of the confidence man to manipulate and defraud those new to the city space, post–Civil War self-help manuals had removed the "evil" confidence man from the equation while still warning against overindulging in vices. Moreover, these manuals espoused a performative success that bore several hallmarks with the confidence game. Readers who worked in business fields were advised to "keep up appearances" that business was good and prosperous—even if the reality was far from true.

These traits were often repeated by confidence artists themselves who further noted the intersection between performance, labor, and the confidence scheme. Even a short con—one consisting of a narrow window and potentially one shill, such as the shell game or three-card monte—requires rather significant honing and performative skill with sleight of hand and cooperation with other con artists.[21] Additionally, as David Maurer says, many confidence artists find they must be versed in "business and financial matters, have a glib knowledge of society gossip, and enough of an acquaintance with art, literature, and music to give an illusion of culture." As such, many con artists work by reading "ten to a dozen newspapers daily" to keep up to date on news.[22] The narrator of a *Collier's* exposé on a mine scam argues the perfect con is like a play complete with preparation and acting. The narrator writes, "A perfect con game is made up of five or six consecutive and closely knit parts, stages or acts, absolutely like a play in a theatre. Each must be put forward and carefully worked out or acted out in proper sequence, or there is no game."[23] The unnamed swindler details how much staging is needed to convince his marks to agree to invest in his fraudulent company. To fully convince a mark of a mining con, the author argues that a swindler must procure an actual piece of land that is the mine "or what purports to be a mine," form a company, issue stock certificates, and prepare the literature and letters. Additionally, a con man must take care to make sure that the promises of his correspondence and literature must be so ambiguous as to not legally guarantee the mark anything.[24] For the mining scam, the con artist had to get an "engineer" to issue a false report on the mine's reputability, while constructing work buildings and installing antiquated machinery near the mine to make it seem as if work is in progress.[25]

For the actual con artists themselves, there is little or no difference between their labor and the work of "the self-made man" that is praised in American rhetoric. As the famous 1940s con man Yellow Kid Weil argues, discussions of the con ignore the unethical practices of the mark. While most marks are "supposedly honest and respectable," Weil notes that moralists ignore the fact that marks are completely entranced with the "opportunity to get rich quick."[26] When the mark turns the con man into the police, he is upheld as a hero, but society conveniently forgets that he is a "would-be fleecer" who has been outsmarted by a swindler.[27] Critiquing this double standard, Weil concludes that it is not simply the con man who is dishonest but everyone has "larceny in their hearts."[28] As Weil was aware, American history is littered with swindles perpetuated by both criminals and reputable businessmen. Many of the key panics and financial crises of American history have been, at least in part, precipitated by widespread swindling in the banking industry or speculative markets.. Moreover, many of the most celebrated figures in American business were de facto con men, such as the Robber Barons engaged in a war of one-upmanship with one another.[29] In his analysis of nineteenth-century finance, Stephen Mihm asserts that conning and finance are "to a certain extent," interlocked as "the story of one is the story of the other." He argues that it is a testament to the mythology of the work ethic that it has persisted in American society when dishonest swindling has been rampant throughout history. Noting the preponderance of counterfeiting in nineteenth-century America, Mihm argues this history does not resemble Weber's spirit of capitalism, as finance and conning do not bear the attributes of "plodding, methodical, gradual pursuit of wealth." Instead, Mihm argues, the true American financial ethos "captures the get-rich-quick scheme, the confidence game, and the mania for speculation" that not only obsessed antebellum America but also continues to grip American society into the present day.[30]

While the con artists in nineteenth-century culture were emblematic of an optimistic country, the confidence artists that appear in American culture after 1920, like Jay Gatsby, Miss Lonelyhearts, and Elmer Gantry, are "painful victims betrayed by a vision of the new country that retains only the power to delude rather than to fulfill."[31] Lenz argues that the confidence artists in William Faulkner's *The Hamlet* are less "conscious" confidence artists than emblems of "the impersonal forces that are systematically destroying" the nation or nostalgic devices "signaling the end of the new country, of humorless horse swaps, and of a coherently ordered nineteenth-century world, and [with] the advent of modern America, of humorless business deals and of an increasingly disordered twentieth century."[32] Increasingly confidence artists are unable to control their own destinies, becoming characters whose primary purpose is to reveal the helplessness of the main protagonist as victim, or to act as symbols of universal disorder. As each confidence artist character appears, they become less representative of a specific, cultural or literary convention and more a revelation of the ubiquity of the traits of confidence schemes in the twentieth century.[33]

At the same time, there exist several confidence artist narratives that feature their con artist characters being reformed and reacclimated into "acceptable" circumstances by other characters or social forces. While this is far from a comprehensive list, there are several prominent comic films of the screwball genre that feature confidence artists being "reformed" through the process of marriage, thereby acquiescing to social norms. Featuring Carole Lombard, *Nothing Sacred* (William Wellman, 1937) focuses on a woman from a small Vermont town who is reported to be dying of radium poisoning and is invited by a New York City reporter (played by Frederic March) to come to the city to live out her last days while he reports on her condition. But Lombard's character knows she is fine and the two must maintain the illusion of her illness to prevent any public outrage. When doctors discover that Lombard's character is not really dying, the newspapermen and city officials decide it is better to maintain the illusion, and she and the reporter eventually marry and sail to the tropics on honeymoon.[34] In Preston Sturges's *The Lady Eve* (1941), Barbara Stanwyck plays Jean Harrington, a woman who comes from a family of confidence artists, all of whom are attempting to swindle Charles Pike (Henry Fonda), the heir to a brewing fortune.

After Pike becomes wise to Jean's identity, Jean then adopts the persona of a rich European countess who convinces Pike to marry her, and after a series of complications, including Jean admitting her past to him, the couple reconcile, leading to an implied marriage. And while both films appear after the imposition of the Hays Code in Hollywood, even some pre-Code films centered on confidence artists generally acquiescing to social norms or being punished for their actions. Take for instance two of James Cagney's pre-Code films. In the tragi-comedy *Blonde Crazy* (Roy Del Ruth, 1931), Cagney plays a bellhop who engages in several side hustles, including running a craps game, selling bootleg alcohol, and blackmailing various hotel patrons. After one particularly powerful score, he and a chambermaid abscond to another city where they themselves are swindled by a more experienced confidence artist, and after a series of schemes to recoup their losses, Cagney's character is sent to prison. Even in the far more light-hearted *Hard to Handle* (Mervyn Leroy, 1933), Cagney's character—a con man who engages in a series of swindles—ultimately embraces capitalist norms of advertising and promotion to untangle his own troubles with the law.

Given the context of their production, the con artist plays of the FTP align with this complicated sense of confidence artists and swindling present in the United States during the Depression era. To be certain, the plays I examine in the rest of the chapter parallel older views of the confidence artist as a quasi-heroic character who audiences identify with and root for. But the plays also reinforce—as the plays of chance do—the need for security. Like many screwball comedies, the plays reinforce the need for integration into the capitalist space. Yet like other confidence artist tales, these plays illustrate the transgressive space between "noble labor" and swindling, showing several intersections where the two supposedly antithetical forms overlap. The confidence artists of *The Milky Way* and *Help Yourself* are certainly victims of social forces beyond their control, but at the same time, comment on the hollowness of the American Dream and warn against the integration of fraud in all aspects of American society.

The Milky Way

The history of boxing has long been aligned with accusations of fraud and fixed fights dating back to at least the 1890s.[35] Having attracted the interest of racketeers and gamblers as the sport grew in popularity in the 1920s and 1930s, "a slickly engineered fix could be worth millions" to those who pulled off the fixed bout.[36] And like other confidence schemes, a successful boxing fix requires the skill to give the appearance that everything is on the up-and-up. In his autobiography, the boxer Jake LaMotta, the inspiration for the film *Raging Bull*, explains that the most important aspect of throwing a fight was selling it in the ring. Recounting his infamous thrown fight with Billy Fox in 1947, LaMotta explains a successful fixed fight must, like other cons, be predicated on a near-flawless performance:

> I'll also tell you something else about throwing a fight. The guy you're throwing to has to be at least moderately good. . . . I thought the air from my punches was affecting him, but we made it to the fourth round. By then if there was anybody in the Garden who didn't know what was happening he must have been dead drunk. There were yells and boos all over the place. Dan Parker, the *Mirror* guy, said the next day that my performance was so bad he was surprised the actors Equity didn't picket the joint.[37]

While LaMotta's performance may not have been convincing, the extent to which a staged boxing match could fool an audience was clearly on the minds of Lynn Root and Harry Clork when they cowrote their comedy *The Milky Way*. Centering on a milkman who is at the center of a boxing promoter's scheme to stage boxing matches to protect the image of his client, the play was also the basis for a major Hollywood film adaptation that preceded the FTP productions. And based on its performance history within the program, the FTP staged *The Milky Way*, in part, to connect to the film, drawing on the intertextuality of star Harold Lloyd. But while the film concludes with employment and a restoration of middle-class work norms, the play reveals tension over the nature of work, contemporary media, and the stability of the American dream and suggests that there is something liberatory for audiences to actively participate in the narrative of a confidence scheme.

The play opens with Speed McFarland, the world's middle-weight champion, attempting to work out with his trainer, Spider, after a night out on the town. McFarland is sporting a black eye and is struggling to remember how he acquired it. His manager, Gabby Sloan, enters and frustratingly points to headlines in the morning newspapers of McFarland being knocked out in a street fight. McFarland vaguely recalls getting into a scuffle with another man over a cigarette girl he was trying to pick up, when Burleigh Sullivan, a meek-looking milkman, knocks on the door of the apartment, inquiring as to how the champion is doing. Sullivan explains that there was a row over his sister Mae, the cigarette girl, and while attempting to intervene, the two men, Spider and McFarland, punched each other out—or that is Sullivan's recollection. Moreover, Sullivan has been credited with knocking out McFarland in news reports, and Sullivan hasn't exactly dissuaded the narrative. During another scuffle, Spider attempts to punch Sullivan—who has a proclivity for ducking punches learned from being bullied as a kid—and accidentally knocks out McFarland again. As McFarland struggles to awaken, a group of reporters come into the apartment and take photos of Sullivan standing over the knocked-out cold champion. Desperate to manage the public relations disaster, Sloan concocts a plan: he will stage a series of boxing matches across the country to make it appear that Sullivan is in fact a legitimate, undiscovered boxer.

Act 2 of the play focuses on the preparation for Sullivan's first bout in the ring, and the machinations the characters engage in to convince him that his fights are legitimate. While everyone else—including his sister, Mae—are operating the confidence scheme, Sullivan himself is unaware the fights are fixed, and his fame keeps growing as he's involved in staged fights in Pittsburgh, Chicago, and Milwaukee. Sloan then concocts a plan for Sullivan and McFarland to square-off for the middleweight championship in New York City, wherein Sloan's pals can bet heavily on McFarland to win the title in a legitimate fight.

In the fight itself, Sullivan accidentally catches his rival on the chin, knocking McFarland unconscious. As Sullivan is declared the new champion, Sloan, furious at Sullivan for having wrecked his plans, chases the milkman around the ring as the crowd erupts at the scene before them. In the play's final scene, the characters—aside from Sullivan and his sister—sit around McFarland's apartment bemoaning their situation. When Mae and Sullivan arrive to check in on McFarland, the brother and sister reveal they've shared a joint bank account, but Mae discovered prior to the fight that her brother withdrew a great amount of cash. Sullivan reveals that he bet on himself prior to the fight believing he would win, and he cashed in. The characters rejoice until they hear that Sullivan has already spent the money: investing in dogs that will, like St. Bernards, carry small barrels of milk. Sullivan also reveals he has purchased the dairy where he worked previously and wants to employ all his friends from the confidence scheme. As the play concludes, Gabby Sloan begins to call his reporter friends to promote his new venture with Sullivan.

Prior to penning the play, Root and Clork had been actors, and both would later find steady work writing various screenplays in Hollywood and other plays for Broadway.[38] The play was originally penned by Root under the pseudonym Leonard Scott and the working title *The Cheese Champion*; according to his own handwritten notes on a copy of *The Cheese Champion*, Root developed the non de plume to get honest feedback about his play from his friends, and eventually one of his friends, the actor Bob Glecker, put Root in touch with Harry Clork.[39] The revised play premiered on Broadway in 1934 and ran for sixty-three performances at the Cort Theatre before it was considered for production by the FTP. Many FTP reviewers saw the play's potential but found it inconsequential. Koby Kohn saw the play as a "clean story" that made it "suitable for any part of country. If cast and directed correctly, will prove a winner as proved by its Broadway production, but the play is not necessarily Broadway at all. Shows the inside workings of the fight game sarcastically and practically but not offensively" and could be shown before "adolescents as well as adults of both sexes."[40] One reviewer noted that the play bore a resemblance to the plays *Three Men on a Horse*, *Personal Appearance*, and *June Moon* but was not quite up to par with those works.[41] However, for them, *The Milky Way* was "a riot right now and will continue to be successful for another year or so. In five years from now this sort of farce based on a freak theme and carried through by wise cracks will be passe."[42] Gus Weinberg found the play's "situations are a little far-fetched but I will recommend it for the CCC camps. I think the boys there will enjoy seeing it."[43] In his report, Arthur Bond found the play—potentially because of the play's subject matter—as "wisecracking commercial farce especially appealing to a man's audience." Bond argued that, in his mind, the play did "not do so well in New York," but the film version "has gone over well" and his recommendation would be to stage the play in the CCC camps "before the picture" presumably to give those younger audiences an unbiased view of a live production without the comparison to the film version.[44]

Performed nine times by the FTP in 1938, the reception of the play was that of a trivial or disappointing text.[45] An audience member in Portland believed that "regular audiences, accustomed to serious theatre, were apathetic to this show" and some "individuals were critical of our doing a 'trivial' show, and contrasted the bill unfavorably with *Prologue to Glory, One Third a Nation*, etc."[46] Meanwhile, an unnamed reviewer for the *San Diego Union* noted in his or her 1938 review that the play's authors had written a text that, while humorous and representative of the boxing world, was simply entertainment. The reviewer notes, "We are ready to believe the funniest possible stories about the fighting ring promoters, champions and their trainers, but Lynn Root and Harry Clork have written a three act play that . . . is merely something to be enjoyed."[47] And to one reviewer from the *Los Angeles Evening News*, the film was far superior to any stage production. The reviewer writes, "At best, the Lynn Root and Harry Clork comedy, which made a choice film vehicle for Harold Lloyd, would seem pretty flat in any stage production."[48]

As evidenced by some reader reports and reviews, *The Milky Way* of the FTP was dwarfed by the RKO film version featuring Harold Lloyd. Released in 1936 to relatively strong reviews, the film featured the silent comedy star in the role of Burleigh Sullivan as well as the character actor Adolphe Menjou as the manager Gabby Sloan.[49] Like many silent film stars, Lloyd had struggled with the transition to the sound era of cinema, often voicing frustration that the more hyper-talking comedies popular with audiences in the

1930s did not permit him the opportunity to showcase his physical comedy skills that he had demonstrated in his popular 1920s pictures. Working with Leo McCarey, who developed several screwball comedies, Lloyd was able to be part of a production that balanced dialogue and slapstick. While the film performed moderately well at the box office, reviewers were generally positive toward the film and Lloyd's performance. Otis Ferguson of the *New Republic*, for instance, praised the film even if the final act was a letdown for him and, in a later piece, found that Lloyd's film was far more contemporary in nature than was the work of Chaplin.[50]

While the scope of Lloyd's film was on the mind of reviewers and play readers, it also appears that the FTP was trying to intersect with the film's relative popularity, especially in terms of having their Burleigh Sullivans connect to Lloyd's take on the character. While both the play and the film present Sullivan as a touch problematic, the film is more overt in presenting Sullivan as a sympathetic figure and connective to audiences. The film's first scene centers on a Sunflower Dairy meeting led by the demanding company president, who praises various other milkmen but lambastes Sullivan as an inferior. Moreover, Sullivan himself is clearly also derided by his fellow workers as they dump ink into his paper cup of water. The film further positions Sullivan as a sympathetic figure by having him interact with Agnes, his horse (who, understandably, is just mentioned in the play), and by showing the initial confrontation develop between Sullivan, Spider, and McFarland outside of Mae's club. Spider and McFarland are shown to be visibly harassing Mae, and Sullivan's intervention is more clearly justified. In particular, the Los Angeles production of the play appears to have been directly influenced by Lloyd's attire in the film as the production designers dressed the actor portraying Sullivan in loose, sleeveless T-shirts that emphasized the actor's lack of muscle mass and, as evidenced by Figures 5.1 and 5.2, they also had the actor wear black-rimmed glasses that are evocative of Lloyd's iconic eyewear.

In addition, another intersection between play and film was the text's generally proconsumer and probusiness narrative—both of which contrasted with the general press coverage of the FTP's work as inherently anticapitalist. While there are confidence artist themes rather clearly in both texts, for the most part consumerist and capitalist structures are not the focus of the play's satire (however, both media and advertising are critiqued by *The Milky Way*). Perhaps even more so than *Help Yourself*, the variations of *A Milky Way* reinforce the status quo in terms of capitalist consumer drive as Sullivan's ultimate usage of his bet winnings is to both reinvest that money into buying dogs for a marketing scheme and to provide jobs for his friends at the dairy he purchases. Of course, that presentation is, as in *Help Yourself*, complicated by how Sullivan is able to get the capital through both

Figure 5.1 Gabby Sloan (Adolphe Menjou) steps in between Burleigh Sullivan (Harold Lloyd) and Spider Schultz (Lionel Stander) in Paramount Pictures' 1936 film version of *The Milky Way*. *(Paramount Pictures.)*

participating in a confidence scheme and through illicit gambling. Nevertheless, whatever the process, the film version of *The Milky Way* was also produced by a major film studio and was, as Adam Reilly details, associated with a major advertising campaign. Dairies across the United States saw a great deal of promotional tie-ins with the film, and given its broader comedic content, an opportunity to reach out to younger audience members. Borden subsidiaries in nearly three dozen cities included a cutout of Harold Lloyd straddling the top of a milk bottle with their daily deliveries, featuring the tagline "Here's your Borden's milk, the Milky Way to health." Children were then prompted by the cutout to head to their local theater to receive a more elaborate cutout of Lloyd, his horse from the film, and a milk wagon handed out by a real milkman in the lobby.[51]

In a similar vein, the FTP productions were attempting to connect to the more politically neutral star persona of Lloyd, who stood in contrast to his silent comedy rival Charlie Chaplin, who had released the highly politicized *Modern Times* in 1936. Indeed, the long-standing view of Lloyd's work in his characters and narratives is about the need for conformity and belonging, whether that his slapstick is consumed by the Hollywood classical cinema or that his films convey a bourgeois sense of a desire to conform and belong. "While Chaplin's 'Everyman of the slums' distilled the essence of immigrant

Figure 5.2 Photo of Peter Brocco, whose attire borrows heavily from Harold Lloyd, as Sullivan in the Los Angeles production of *The Milky Way*. *(Box 1040, FTP LC. Retrieved from https://www.loc.gov/item/musftpphotoprints.200223105/.)*

pride as well as the pathos of separation, Harold's glasses reflected back the hopes and fears of an overwhelmingly middle class, profoundly bourgeois audience," writes Alan Bilton, continuing that Lloyd "seeks acceptance into the material world of a good job, a swell place, nice things, with a pretty girlfriend as the final seal of approval, a young man's reward for a sufficiently high income, well-developed personality and social conformity."[52] And while Chaplin's films, especially *Modern Times*, were far more pragmatic and politically complicated than being simply Marxist propaganda, Lloyd's own star persona veered far more toward the political center in the public's imagination and drawing on that connection makes a great deal of sense for the FTP.

However, Lloyd's films do convey a more complicated relationship to the demands of middle-class life and are not simply texts that reaffirm or affirm bourgeois values. Alan Bilton deftly argues that while Lloyd's films and characters do outwardly reinforce middle-class norms, his characters are so determined to adhere to these norms that they both disguise themselves in inauthentic roles or are consumed by a fear of failure and being unable to maintain these roles. Drawing on the actor's personal history of how he would disguise himself to sneak through studio security[53] and Hal Roach's oft-quoted claim that Harold was not a comedian per se, but instead a talented actor playing one, Bilton finds the themes of impersonation and disguise throughout Lloyd's work.[54] Whether it is pretending to be his boss in *Safety Last* (Fred Newmeyer / Sam Taylor, 1923) or engaging in a role he is ill-fitted to pull off like a football hero in *The Freshman* (Fred Newmeyer / Sam Taylor, 1925), the plots in his films feature Lloyd as frequently engaged in impersonation and impression.[55] Moreover, Bilton argues that Lloyd's films demonstrate a tension within the performances therein of "publicly prescribed" personas in conflict with the internalized fear of failure or of being caught and ridiculed. He writes, "Hence the fact that embarrassment plays such a strong part in his films; it is precisely because Harold is so concerned with how he is seen by others, of performing for their benefit by impersonating an exaggerated version of normality, that he is terrified of exposure, of the discovery of his own inadequacy." Comparing the camera work and aesthetics of Lloyd's films to those of Buster Keaton, Bilton alludes to a similar need for the maintenance of illusion and deception (albeit in terms of film aesthetics): "Perhaps surprisingly, illusion and deception—camera tricks, the deliberate fooling of the audience, the sense that things are rarely as they appear—play as large a role in Lloyd's work as it does in Keaton's; if all the world is a social stage for Harold, then his real fear becomes not just fluffing his lines but crossing that third wall that means being excluded from the world of appearances forever."[56]

In many respects, Lloyd's persona in his other films—a middle-class figure concerned with his performative appearances that is willing to go to great deceptive lengths to mask his inadequacies—aligns near perfectly with *The Milky Way*. However, unlike most of Lloyd's other films, the main character is presented not as middle-class but as working class. And both texts present nuanced views of working—or a lack of working. To be certain, Sullivan does achieve perhaps the most clear-cut reinforcement of bourgeois society by becoming a business owner at the conclusion of the play, but his path to achieving that is problematized by his process of both engaging in a large-scale confidence scheme and illicit gambling. In an overlap with the comedies of chance, Sullivan also endangers the security of his and his sister's financial security by withdrawing their savings to bet on himself. But like the comedies of chance, Sullivan's risk pays off financially as it becomes a clear parallel to the celebration of promoted risk in business. But aside from engaging in gambling or engaging (somewhat passively) in a confidence scheme, Sullivan is rarely shown engaging in any work. This is more pronounced in the stage versions where Sullivan's labor only occurs offstage and the only descriptions we get of his duties as a milkman are in passing reference. In the play, Sullivan never bemoans his leaving of the dairy during his engagement with the confidence scheme; in fact, the film version demonstrates the struggles that Sullivan encounters at the dairy with his fellow milkmen who bully and humiliate Sullivan at every turn—as if his decision to go along with the confidence scheme is justified.

Moreover, the other characters in the play espouse perspectives that signal a strong distrust of traditional norms of working, and the realm of professional boxing becomes a stand-in for the struggles of capitalism. At various points, the characters bemoan the economic conditions that repress them—and for them, the only real recourse is engaging in the confidence scheme. After learning that Sloan is planning a championship bout between her brother and McFarland, Mae voices her concern over her brother potentially getting hurt as well as how she foresaw the whole scheme as a chance for seeing beyond the scope of his labor: "I thought, with a few dollars in his pocket, he might realize there was something in the world beside a milk route. I stood for the crookedness because it seemed like a start."[57] If Mae sees the confidence scheme as an opportunity to move beyond the confines of her and her brother's work drudgery, then those involved in the boxing space see the same. Perhaps the most interesting figure is Gabby Sloan himself, who, as the manager of McFarland and Sullivan, stands in as a repressive capitalist as well as a reckless businessman. In convincing McFarland to fight Sullivan, he evokes language that is both demeaning and threatening to the boxer. As he is convincing Sullivan to commit to the final fight, he parallels his condemning of McFarland but also reveals that at least for him, this is also his chance to escape the drudgery of the fight game:

> That's it—happiness and happiness means thinking of others, those who have worked for us, lived for us, built unselfishly for our future. I've lain on my bed at night, thinking, planning, scheming. Not for myself, Burleigh, for you. I've staked everything I have in this world on this fight. Not only money—that doesn't matter to me—it's my hopes, my ambitions. You're not going to tread on those, are you?[58]

There is something disingenuous to Sloan's argument here—he is certainly not an egalitarian figure—but manipulation aside, it is Sloan's view that this fight could enable him to find a measure of security through his gambling winnings. Even if the scheme could potentially destroy the professional boxing careers of all involved, Sloan and his fellow con artists embrace the capitalist embrace of risk.

And to find a way out of their working lives, the characters in *The Milky Way* must perpetuate a confidence scheme on a national scale. But what problematizes this is their swindle is predicated on a boxer who is hardly believable as a prizefighter and leads us to questioning the plausibility of the confidence scheme's success. While Sloan does labor in "dragging the village idiot" across the country for "eight weeks,"[59] Sloan does not seem to give Sullivan any coaching for interactions with the press, leaving the former milkman woefully unprepared for his role. When a reporter asks Sullivan if he is the relative of the famous boxer John L. Sullivan, Sullivan responds that he has never heard of the man, which makes Sloan claim that the milkman is just joking, exclaiming, "That's a good one! Quote that—'The contender, with a sardonic smile and a twinkle in his eye.' . . . He'll clown like that with you all day."[60] Moreover, Sullivan's in-ring performances are even weaker. During his first fight, Sullivan begins the bout with his bathrobe on. Later, in his fight with McFarland, Sullivan needs to be "boosted into the ring" like a child because he has trouble with the ropes and becomes entangled in them. And his boxing style consists of incredibly awkward jabs and ducking of punches.

For the confidence scheme to work in *The Milky Way*, Gabby Sloan and his shills require some rather easy marks, and Sloan can manipulate one group in particular: the media. Throughout the play, Sloan actively guides newspaper and radio reporters to promoting Sullivan's matches as legitimate, and the performances suggest a growing skepticism over the increasing role of media in the promotion of confidence narratives. Part of that grew from the knowledge of the "corrupt press corps" that managers of stock pools had relied on to both "disseminate news favorable to their trades" and manipulate "prices directly through wash or matched sales—transactions in which they arranged to have confederates purchase shares to create the appearance of intensifying demand and increasing prices."[61] By the 1930s, newspapers—as well as other forms of media—were increasingly committed to presenting news objectively and without the appearance of political bias. While some of that shift was due to the rise of more professional journalistic standards, scholars argue that much of the objectivity was born out of commercial interests. Newspapers and other media sought to pull in as wide an audience as possible and began to morph their coverage. Accordingly, there were new revenue streams from commercial interests like department stores and other retailers whose advertising dollars fueled newspaper budgets and encouraged more neutral coverage of events. At the same time, while aspects of media coverage were heading toward objectivity, other media was becoming far more partisan and subjective. Certainly, politicians had become adept at manipulating media to promote their own personas, as evidenced by such figures as Huey Long, Charles Coughlin, and even Roosevelt himself, but also media companies were active in developing propaganda to send to audiences, best evidenced by the development of highly politicized newsreels to target Upton Sinclair's 1934 California gubernatorial campaign.

In this context, it is helpful to read the media in *The Milky Way* as eager to both objectively report on the actions of Sullivan but also participate in the mythology being presented to them. In one of my favorite moments of the play, Anne details to McFarland one of the bouts of Sullivan's that took place in my adopted hometown of Milwaukee: the headline reads, "Gabby Sloan's Middleweight sensation outsmarts Kelly" and the report notes that "Sullivan's a natural. A born fighter. Cheered as he leaves the stadium." The press coverage is so over the top that a disgusted Anne retorts, "I knew it was a funny town, but this is the first time it got me hysterical."[62] There is no questioning of the fights themselves as the reporters only report the fights. The same is true for the radio broadcast of the final match between Sullivan and McFarland where the radio commentators—despite observing that Sullivan struggles to climb through the ring ropes, is wearing a bathrobe to the ring, and forgets to take off his glasses as the bell rings—are unable to apply any editorial commentary to what they see, merely objectively relaying to their audiences what they witness in the ring.

The Milky Way is also critical of another form of confidence scheme presented to Americans—the continued rise of mass advertising in the Depression era. Roland Marchand outlines a growing hostility toward advertising practices from both outside the industry as well as within advertising spheres. In 1931, the first issue of the magazine *Ballyhoo* premiered; a humor publication, *Ballyhoo* featured parody advertisements of products like "Blisterine" and satirized many of the conventions of advertising in the early 1930s. While many in the advertising industry loved the referential humor of the magazine (and would eventually tailor ads to run in the magazine in *Ballyhoo*'s style), several advertising executives worried about the growing hostility toward conventions of adverting. There were increasing calls for grassroots pro-consumer organizations throughout the United States, including the founding of the Consumers Research organization in 1932, as well as advocacy for the Roosevelt administration to extend its powers to regulate advertisers. As early as 1932, Marchand writes, the industry journal *Advertising and Selling* began to warn readers that pseudoscientific ad campaigns like one run by Scott Tissue that claimed the "dire results of using the allegedly arsenic-laden brands of toilet paper sold by competitors" were an open invitation for government regulation.[63] In addition, there was a rift among advertisers themselves as many lambasted their colleagues who were resorting to over-the-top, ludicrous, vulgar copy or scare tactics to attract customers. For these advertisers, the new impulse of hysterical advertising in the early to mid-1930s was born out of not more reasoned approaches to advertising but the tactics of patent medicine con artists of the nineteenth century. And the play presents a diegetic ad that really aligns with this growing hostility and conflict in advertising. Right before the staging of the fight, Root and Clork have an advertisement read during the radio coverage of Sullivan and McFarland's bout. The ad features a "Doctor Emmaneul Pussfeather, physical director of the Llama Institute of Gallipolis, Ohio," who provides "weekly talks on 'Clean bodies make clean bodies.'" The "doctor" pitches a rather nefarious-sounding medical product for presumably halitosis or a breathing issue and urges listeners to purchase the product: "So go to your local druggist tonight. He will gladly give you a bottle in either the dollar, twenty-five cent or ten-cent sample size. Remember, you too, can have the charm and grace that comes with perfect breathing."[64] This parody of a radio commercial is mocking not merely the conventions of such advertisements but the very structure of the copy, which plays to the vagaries of commercial promises. The character of Dr. Pussfeather seems to not only align with the reputation of advertising as nefarious but also connect it to its medicine show roots. In turn, the Llama Institute of Gallipolis, Ohio, reads as both a comic play on the words themselves and a critique of vague-sounding institutes that harbor no real accreditation.

Given the play's critique of media and advertising as at least partially bearing hallmarks of con schemes, or at the very least worthy of skepticism, it is reasonable to read the play as finding the boxing audiences equally culpable in the success of Sloan and Sullivan's confidence game. The play gives us no indication from the radio or newspaper reports or from the audience reactions outlined in the text itself that the boxing fans who watch Sullivan's matches are aware that the bouts are staged. Even during the fight between Sullivan and McFarland, which lasts only a few moments, the audience only gasps at the conclusion of the bout and is "left in a daze" over the sudden ending.[65] While the final bout ends accidentally, we have never been given any indication that audiences were ever skeptical about the nature of Sullivan's matches. And given the meek milkman who forgets to take off his glasses is now the middleweight champion of the world, could we not expect some reaction from audiences like what Jake La Motta heard from the angry Madison Square Garden crowd?

However, there is a broader implication of Sullivan's performances and of the audience's acceptance of them. *The Milky Way* shows a con perpetrated on institutions. The con artists of the play symbolically subvert the power structures of the era. The complicit audience of Sullivan's fights read his bouts not only as a triumph over adversity but also as a counter-con of the boxing establishment. After having been treated to a litany of fixed matches, the audiences within the play are celebrating their own complicity in a con that subverts both the boxing and media industries and metaphorically outwits other social institutions. While the believability of the play might be suspect, the theme of a fictional audience performing and participating in a confidence scheme against an institution would have resonated with Depression audiences. For workers and audience members used to the swindles of capitalism, the staged narrative of workers flaunting their own cons to industries and institutions that had been swindling them for ages must have been a pleasurable experience.

Yet if the reactions of the boxing fans in *The Milky Way* are read in terms of the performances of professional wrestling, the fans' embrace of Sullivan speaks to their need to find meaning in his bouts. The fans' embrace of the obvious swindling in front of them signals that they read these performances not as an athletic competition but as a staged narrative, like professional wrestling, that holds mythological implications. And the myth that *The Milky Way* is wrestling with is the American Dream. Like plays of the Children's Theatre Unit of the FTP that Leslie Elaine Frost argues balanced ideals of model citizenry with an increasing apprehension over declining American fortunes, *The Milky Way* illustrates both the idealized and problematic American Dream through its portrayal of Sullivan. In one sense, his story is a near-perfect representation of the American Dream, as Sullivan achieves fame and fortune and uses his winnings to purchase a dairy and provide jobs to his former con artists. Yet the model actions of Sullivan, as well as his procurement of the American Dream, is undercut by the play. Despite his pluck and hard work as a milkman, the play provides us no sense that Sullivan would have been able to maintain his station in life by working for the dairy; indeed, given the nature of many other FTP plays that addressed economic issues, it is likely that audiences would have understood Sullivan's hold on his employment as tenuous at best. Moreover, Sullivan is only able to achieve the American Dream through a confidence scheme that not only requires the assistance of trainers, boxers, media members, and complicit national audience but also his willingness to gamble on a staged fight rather than working hard and saving his winnings. While the play outwardly showcases a model American who achieves the American Dream, *The Milky Way* also illustrates the public's fear over the "viability of the American . . .economic system" and the American Dream itself.[66]

Help Yourself

In her memoir of the FTP, Hallie Flanagan does not mention comic plays all that often. However, she does detail a few plays that drew her attention in her section on the New York City unit. In between mention of *Horse Eats Hat*, Orson Welles's first production for the program, and *Dance of Death*, she also mentions a text which she finds outrageous: a play by Paul Vulpius entitled *Help Yourself*, which "created comedy from its situation of the unemployed young man brightly hanging up his hat in a bank where he had no job and becoming the leading expert in a land deal that never existed in fact."[67] Flanagan's mention of the play was certainly due to a couple factors: one, it was one of the most performed plays produced by the program. And two, it was a play that garnered controversy and criticism, being noted by her as a play criticized by members of Congress for its satirical take on business ethics and the performances embedded in the business environment.[68]

These congresspersons were not necessarily wrong. *Help Yourself* is a satire of business performances and unethical banking practices at its root. The play, which as Flanagan lays out, follows an unemployed young man named Chris Stringer who shows up at the bank of his old college friend and declares that he too now works at the bank and concocts a land deal out of (relatively) thin air. But as I argue here, *Help Yourself* is not simply calling attention to the reckless banking and business practices that helped bring on the Great Depression nor the performative elements of the business space. The play also reinforces the Roosevelt administration's attempts to reform the banking industry but also points to the limitations of those reforms. While the play certainly celebrates its main character as a heroic confidence artist who is able to pull a fast one on those who should know better, the play also serves as a warning about the tolerance of confidence artists in certain industries—and reminds audiences that swindlers still exist.

Help Yourself takes place in the Mutual Trust Bank, where Fred Bittlesby works as a bank clerk. One morning, he is surprised by the appearance of an old college friend, Gerhardt Stringer—a Swiss man who is now going by Chris Stringer. Stringer reveals to Bittlesby that he is in dire financial straits and has not had steady employment in a long time. However, Stringer details that he recently happened upon a group of movers and decided to just join them. After helping move boxes and furniture from a house, the foreman gave Stringer half a dollar. Inspired by this, Stringer decides to "take work," and he declares that he is just going to work at the Mutual Trust—right in the empty desk across from Bittlesby. When his friend raises a series of objections over this scheme, Stringer responds that he has done extensive homework into the routine of the bank president, of banking principles, and of how people interact at the bank. If someone questions his employment, he will simply deflect or obscure his background. And Stringer then begins to draft a series of letters and make phone calls to various people to the rival Park Avenue Bank about a random company he finds listed in an outdated financial yearbook, the Kubinski Cement and Brick Works. Bittlesby tells his friend that he will go to jail, but Stringer is undaunted.

Stringer's deception results in a meeting between the heads of both the Mutual Trust and the Park Avenue Bank. Stringer confesses to Bittlesby that he never intended for the con to get this far, presuming that the bank president—Schuyler Danforth—would simply dismiss the plan and place Stringer onto another project. To curry favor with the president, Stringer has also begun dating Danforth's daughter, Peggy. Bittlesby declares that if they are going to get fired, they might as well go out with style, and he and Stringer throw themselves into preparing for the meeting. As the heads of the Park Avenue Bank arrive and await Danforth and Stringer, they determine that they will not approve of the Kubinski account unless their fears about the project have been allayed and the project's original records can be found. Stringer hears this news and panics: he confesses his deception to Peggy— who, after initially thinking that Stringer was here to rob the bank, understands his need to simply work—and she joins in the confidence scheme by telling her father that *he* lost the original proposal for the Kubinski account. She and Stringer then cajole Danforth into "remembering" details of the Kubinski account and satisfied with his progress, the president and Stringer head to the meeting. Stringer then takes charge of the meeting, deciding to not "bore" the assembled with details of the Kubinski account but instead to urge their action on passage of the project with a series of hollow yet uplifting speeches that play to the emotions of the bank heads, who wholeheartedly approve the plan.

Work is about to begin on the Kubinski brick factory, as both banks have agreed to the proposal, and they have also received funding from a government grant to reopen the brick factory. Peggy reveals to both Bittlesby and Stringer that her father wants to name Stringer as the general manager of the factory. Stringer then panics, realizing that since there is no record of him working at the bank in an official capacity, he cannot be transferred to the new post. At a meeting with the heads of the banks, Stringer confesses that the entire business proposal was a fake and that he has never worked at the bank. The bankers are astonished—some claiming that "they never recognized Stringer in the first place"—and then Peggy announces that Bittlesby has found Stringer's employment record (Peggy has convinced her father to name Bittlesby the personal manager for the bank and the two of them forged Stringer's employment records). Stringer—holding his employment record—then declares that he was lying about being a fraud or swindler and he said it to test the loyalty of the bank board members. They all apologize for doubting Stringer, and he agrees to be made general manager of the factory.[69]

Help Yourself was originally written by two Hungarian playwrights, Ladislas Fodor and Laszlo Lakatos, under their joint pen name of Paul Vulpius, and in 1933, the play entitled *Youth at the Helm* was translated into German by the playwright and poet Hans Adler who also used the name Paul Vulpius.[70] The play was then translated into English for a 1934 production at London's Westminster Theatre and was then staged several times throughout England through the end of the decade, culminating in a loose film adaptation entitled *Jack of All Trades* in 1936. In the United States, the FTP commissioned the writer John J. Coman to revise *Youth at the Helm* for an American audience, and the newer play, *Help Yourself*, premiered in 1936 at the Manhattan Theater on Broadway, which housed the FTP. The production starred Curt Bois, who had recently emigrated from Germany to escape Nazi anti-Semitism.

Nationally, *Help Yourself* was the most-staged production examined in this project and, insofar as I can tell, the most produced comedy of the FTP.[71] In addition to its stage productions, the play was also produced by the FTP Radio Division as an adaptation penned by Barry Williams and was performed in 1939 on various commercial stations.[72] As such, the play left a significant record of audience and press reactions. Writing in the *Peoria Star*, a reporter covering the opening of the play at that city's Majestic Theatre noted that "Sally after unrelenting sally of laughter" filled the auditorium and many of the attendees commented that the performance was the best offering the local unit had offered; incidentally, the performance of *Help Yourself* in the central Illinois city was the first to take place outside of New York.[73] And *Help Yourself* did not simply "play in Peoria." Positive reactions were found in other midwestern cities and in larger coastal cities. In its report to the FTP, the Omaha production stated the audience reaction was "very favorable,"[74] while the Des Moines report notes that many audience members left the theater repeating Stringer's refrain of "up she goes!"[75] In Boston, a writer for the *Christian Science Monitor* noted that there were "a great many unfunny passages" and the play's humor dependent too much on "situations and too little on clever lines," but *Help Yourself* was "the brightest if also the slightest" play undertaken by the Boston Unit. A writer for the *Boston Herald* declared *Help Yourself* to be a "featherweight variation of the fairy tale about the Emperor's New Clothes."[76] Similarly, audience members of the Los Angeles production found the play to have provided some relief from the economic climate of the Depression but demonstrated the limitations of theater. As one reviewer noted, "This is an amusing way of presenting a social problem. But I don't see the trials of the new generation being solved in this way except in the theatre."[77] Commenting on the production of the play by FTP Seattle, a writer for the University of Washington newspaper finds the play to be highly enjoyable but imbued with a very serious message. She writes, "The spirit of 1929 is on the way back. The catch line of the play is 'up she goes.' . . . The play was not produced in the same era as *Waiting for Lefty* and *Awake and Sing*."[78]

The play is straightforward with its satirical take on the banking industry. Both banks are hardly stalwarts of professionalism as the bankers are gullible and shown to be less than concerned with concrete details. Stringer himself believes that the banking industry is so simple that after he "introduces" himself to Danforth and the other bankers at the end of the first act, he tells Bittlesby that he is headed to the library to "study banking" and "train myself" for his new job with a "thorough education in finance" and "industry economics" and he will "be back in half an hour."[79] While the line is played for laughs, the bankers who are portrayed in the play do not demonstrate much demonstratable skill beyond a certain point; to be fair, there are bankers—especially A. B. Alexander, the chairman of the board at the Mutual Trust, who grows suspicious of Stringer's Kubinski plan, noting there's "nothing definite" in any of the materials about the account.[80] Yet whatever concerns the skeptical members of the bank have of Stringer's proposal, they do not act professionally. They simply resort to politicking and jealousy: at several points Alexander claims the project was his idea or decries the favoritism the bank president is showing Stringer or how Alexander cannot get Stringer to open up to him despite all the dinners he bought the con artist. There is—without question—a view of the banking industry as obsessed with a work environment that rewards superficiality in performance and short-term thinking. This is best illustrated with an admission from President Danforth, who reveals an exceptionalism to both his position and to the nature of the industry. After Stringer "apologizes" for his quirks and reaccepts the position of general manager of the brick factory, Danforth asks Stringer "Why do you think I'm president of this bank?" After Stringer says he does not know, Danforth answers: "I'd have been kicked out of any little job long ago. No little fellow could be as undependable as I am. I lost the Kubinski minutes, I sign important letters without reading them—the only excuse for me is that once a year I have an inspiration and the bank can live on that for ten years. Take this Kubinski business, for instance. That will keep me going for another year" (see Figure 5.3).[81]

Stringer is also able to deflect any concern over the "details" of the Kubinski project by evoking emotional rhetoric that appeals to the bankers by giving them a fiery, performative speech that mythologizes the bankers'

Figure 5.3 The bankers shouting, "Up she goes!" in response to Stringer's manipulation. From the Springfield, Massachusetts, production of *Help Yourself*. *(Box 570, Folder 3, FTP LC.)*

views of their social and moral worth. First Stringer compels the bankers to action by critiquing their inaction, arguing that they can be "leaders of industry" by rejecting the "inactivity . . . of laissez faire" and that the two banks "can set an example to the banks of the world and inspire them to follow your lead in reopening the highways to economic peace and happiness."[82] After making a direct parallel between the potential of the Kubinski project with divine rebirth—"What would happen, gentlemen, if the power above should suddenly say 'This year I won't have any spring. I'll wait until better times come along.'"—Stringer urges the bankers to go on working, not to contemplate and "ponder, but work . . . pick up the first packing-case you see with a shout of *up she goes!*" As he begins to conclude his speech, he evokes the image of the movers hoisting a piano that inspired him at the beginning of the play:

> Yes, gentlemen, that's how we must begin today—"Up she goes." This happy cry of the simple workman should be our slogan. Workers and employers, bakers and carpenters—"Up she goes!" Statesmen and politicians—Europe and America—"Up she goes!" In the mountains where the coal is buried, in the ground where the treasures are hidden—up she goes—Out there, machines lying cold—"Up she goes."

Rusty shovels lie in the engine rooms—"Up she goes!" Damn it gentlemen, bang on the table—Forget about your positions—put aside your official expressions.[83]

As the scene ends, the bankers dance out of the conference room shouting "up she goes" in unison. There is an irony to the fact that the actions of manual laborers compel the bankers (as well as Stringer) to act, and the play satirizes how proponents of traditional work ethics promoted the idea that work could provide workers with upward mobility when, ultimately, many workers would never achieve such aims. As such, the bankers are convinced to work by Stringer's usage of language that parodies traditional work rhetoric but also, again, is completely devoid of any actual solution. At this point, Stringer sells his marks on the narrative of the individualistic, forward-thinking capitalist—but the satire lies in how easily he can convince them of their own mythology through evoking a sort of reactionary mythology of the benevolent, important businessman, an ascetic connection to work, and the bankers' view of their labor as analogous with the work of the laborer.

Moreover, Stringer can maintain the illusion of his labor by understanding the performative elements of the business world, aligning in several respects with the emphasis on workplace performance becoming increasingly mainstream during the 1930s. While there was certainly no shortage of self-help books in the 1930s, the most prominent during the latter half of the decade was Dale Carnegie's *How to Win Friends and Influence People*. First published in 1936, the book became a hugely popular bestseller. Karen Halttunen argues that Carnegie's manual is a de facto guidebook to swindling one's professional colleagues. According to Halttunen, "Carnegie's purpose was to train men in a very special type of corporate salesmanship, 'the salesmanship of the system selling itself to itself.'"[84] While Carnegie's manual demonstrated how businesspeople should perform to other businesspeople, it also taught its readers how to convince themselves that they were performing their roles properly. In other words, Carnegie was also selling to his readers the spectacle of selling themselves to themselves, as if a reader were both the mark and the confidence man at the same time. This insincere performance is essential to Stringer's con of the bank. By studying the "bank inside and out," he has learned how to craft business proposals so ensconced in vague rhetoric that the bankers reading the proposal are inclined to accept it as is. In addition, Stringer manipulates his coworkers by evoking workplace rhetoric that persuades the other workers to react per the norms of the business world.[85] When someone asks Stringer if he is a new employee, Stringer replies that he has been at the bank for years but had been working in another department. Stringer also provides vague details about himself, such as "I was the guy in the corner" or "I always ate ham and cheese sandwiches."[86] Invariably, the other bank employees, after a brief pause, acknowledge that they remember Stringer. At points, Stringer is even able to tell "inside jokes" that his colleagues laugh at not because they understand, but because they are supposed to laugh at such jokes per the performance norms of the business world.

While *Help Yourself* critiques banking culture and its embedded, manipulatable performance norms, it also suggests that these performative elements in work extend beyond the banking industry and into society at large. While much of Stringer's con succeeds due in large part to the false persona and performative expectations of the banking industry, the play also suggests the allure of Stringer's con is the combination of play and performance. In stating part of his rationale for engaging in his con, Stringer claims that adopting a false persona is a game that everyone plays at. When Bittlesby asks him why he is undertaking this scam, Stringer explains, "Just the illusion of working does something for you. Everyone plays at something—children play at being policemen—politicians at being statesmen.... Why shouldn't I play at working?"[87] In a sense, this is a subtle metacommentary on acting as a con—actors playing roles—but in another, it is an acknowledgment from Stringer that there is an inherent appeal for people to don new roles once their participation in those roles loses their luster. Nor is this impulse restricted to work roles as Stringer performs his own nationality: upon first meeting his old college friend, Bittlesby addresses Stringer by his German name, Gerhardt, to which Stringer corrects him by noting he has changed it to the more Anglo-American "Christopher." When his friend asks him why the change, Stringer responds that "nobody could pronounce" his name and further, Gerhardt Stringer would hardly "be" American.[88] In declaring his new national identity, Stringer then suggests his nationality is more authentic than Bittlesby's, as he has had to *learn* a new performance and, again, evokes language borrowed from confidence schemes: "I am an American. I am more American than you. You are American because your parents, over whom you had no control, at the time—happened to—But I chose my nation—after studying in it, after studying *it*. I know all about it."[89] The play gives us no indication—aside from one moment where Stringer pronounces his birth name in German—that Stringer's Germanness is ever performed, and as such, the act of being "American" is something else that can simply be performed; at the same juncture, the play likely is even asking us whether Stringer's own Germanic backstory is legitimate or if this is just another role Stringer has adopted.[90] In this vein, the play questions any notion of authentic performance in any aspect of society.

Yet it is evident through the play that Stringer may himself be just as much of a mark as the bankers he is swindling. For starters, there is the matter of Stringer's relationship to his labor: it is not until the end of the play where he is guaranteed any compensation (and even then, it is through the forgery of Bittlesby and Stringer's girlfriend). One could correctly assert that one of the biggest marks in the play is Stringer himself, as he is perfectly willing to labor for free. He becomes a character so imbued with the rhetoric of traditional work norms that he is willing to forgo salary or compensation to subsist off the "feeling" that work provides him. And he consistently evokes language and positions found in the mythology of the self-made man and those who condemned idleness. Detailing his philosophy of work—and again highlighting his own indoctrination as a character—Stringer declares that his solution to his work situation was grabbing the initiative. He declares that he "changed from the unemployed to the employed not because I asked for work, but because I took it."[91] At this point, Stringer evokes the same language and general approach of the self-made man as the confidence artist is, in essence, telling his friend (and the audience) to pull themselves up by their bootstraps and find their own employment rather than waiting for a job to be given to them. Yet while he gains free lunches from other bankers trying to curry his favor, by the end of the play, Stringer is in such poor financial shape that he is being threatened with eviction from his landlord and constantly hungry. In this regard, it is the system that has conned Stringer.

Of course, it bears stating that the play also serves to remind audiences of the fraud and deception that precipitated much of the Depression—the failure of the national banking system that spurred New Deal banking reforms. Despite a series of piecemeal reforms, the number of commercial banks fell to fewer than twenty-five thousand by 1929. A great many of these banks were small institutions with assets under $1 million and mainly located in small communities and overbanked areas, especially in the South Atlantic and North Central states where agriculture was failing and were often doomed due to both national structural problems and their own mismanagement. Without the adequate reserves or branches to draw capital from, "when one country unit bank could not meet its depositors' demands, its failure undermined confidence in other banks, starting an epidemic run which frequently pulled down all the banks in the neighborhood, the sound along with the weak."[92] Adding to this were prominent examples of banking fraud in the country at the beginning of the Depression. Perhaps the most prominent example was the scandal involving the Bank of the United States in New York City. There two bank heads, Bernard Marcus and Sal Singer, had embezzled millions of dollars for their own real estate dealings and produced a staggering number of false claims. When the bank closed in December 1930, it created a wave of panic and bank runs across the country.

Moreover, the play and its radio version were staged at a time that there was a growing reactionary movement to reembrace older, more dangerous economic and baking policies. As William Bird details, the Great Depression era saw large corporations engaged in the promotion of anti–New Deal propaganda. One of the catalysts for this engagement of anti–New Deal rhetoric was the advertising executive Bruce Barton, who advocated for the "whig theory" of history—the idea that progress was inevitable. Already decried as fallacious by historians in the 1930s, Barton and other business leaders clung to the idea that economic policies prior to 1929 should be restored and New Dealers were the real enemies of progress. Embracing historical revisionism, Barton promoted the idea of the "flush times" of the 1920s, the importance of consumption, and how industries like the food industry, the chemical industry, and the electrical industry had provided genuine comfort for the average American while New Dealers were putting the "brakes" on the expansion of future prosperity with their taxes and pseudo-socialism.[93] As William Bird shows, business leaders as part of the American Liberty League began to realize that radio programs could promote a more capitalist-friendly vision of history and American society, and a show like *Cavalcade of America* could help rehabilitate business as a whole as well as individual companies wracked by corporate scandal. A case in point was the DuPont company, which came under fire for alleged munitions privateering during the First World War. By promoting the *Cavalcade of America*'s democratic narratives and values—at odds with the problematic structure of the company—the show partially helped rehabilitate the broader image of Dupont in the public's mind. In this context, both the play and the radio version of *Help Yourself* are directly engaging with audiences on the issue of corporate reactionary views. While the play version is centered in New York, the radio broadcast does change the implied scope and scale of the bank. While the bank in the play could be seen as a more local branch or a smaller organization, the FTP radio broadcast paints the Mutual Bank as a much bigger entity as the narrator details: "You know the Mutual Trust Company, of course. Probably the biggest bank in the country . . . branches all over the world . . . international loans, and all that sort of thing. A tremendous organization. This happened at the main office in Wall Street."[94] Emphasizing the location of the bank's main office as Wall Street certainly would have connected the Mutual Trust with Wall Street fraud and nefarious banking practices of the 1920s and perhaps the National Bank and Charles Mitchell.

While the play seems to suggest that understanding a role gives you believability, *Help Yourself* also appears to assert that this form of conning is endemic in all institutions—not just banking or other businesses. Echoing the ideological stances of some of the living newspaper plays, *Help Yourself* suggests to audiences that they need to be aware of the dangers of the con Stringer pulled. While Stringer may have demonstrated daring in swindling the banks and procured jobs for other unemployed people, he nevertheless operated a far more dangerous confidence scheme than seen in *The Milky*

Figure 5.4 Stringer (Curt Bois) and Bittlesby (Walter Burke) debate one another on the set of the New York production of *Help Yourself*. Note how the set design, specifically the intimidating scale of the bank's dollar signs, dwarf the actors and signals the power of the institution to the audience. *(Box 1216, FTP LC. Retrieved from https://www.loc.gov/item/musftpphotoprints.200222853/.)*

Way: while Sullivan and his cohorts engage in a scheme in the entertainment world (although they do risk their own savings and the money of gamblers), Stringer's swindle involves two separate banks and their respective investors as well as the government, and failure of this scheme would have likely endangered the money and jobs of other people. The danger of Stringer's con is reinforced to the audience by how the play utilizes them. Whereas the real and fictional audiences of *The Milky Way* are (for the most part) in on the con, the bankers in *Help Yourself* are mainly unaware of how Stringer operates, while FTP audience members would have understood how little he knows about the banking industry and how his con succeeds through a considerable amount of chance. As such, when Stringer is promoted at the conclusion of the play, audiences are, on the one hand, encouraged to enjoy his success, but on another, unnerved by the bank's inability to engage in due diligence with a powerful employee and left with the sense that Stringer or one of his colleagues might try another risky proposal in the future. Just as *The Milky Way* questioned the stability of the American Dream, *Help Yourself* presented to its audiences a terrifying idea: that bankers—despite New Deal reforms—would engage in the same careless and risky practices that occurred in "the spirit of 1929" (see Figure 5.4).

Epilogue

Over the last decade, I have had the privilege of teaching several courses on the Great Depression. Each time I have taught such a course, I have spent a couple weeks on the WPA. Often, one of my assignments for students is for them to research the physical legacies of the New Deal and the WPA in their hometowns by finding what projects were built by the CWA, CCC, or FAP. They are often rather surprised to learn that a mural in their local post office was done by an FAP artist or a pavilion in the park where they played as a kid was built by CCC workers. For many of them, these places and objects give them an immediacy to studying an event—the Great Depression—that seems far more distant in the past than it is.

The first few times I taught my Great Depression course, I included a section on the FTP. But unlike a post office mural in their small town in Illinois or a park pavilion in Green Bay, students had a harder time connecting to the plays we studied. Some of this, I have often suspected, is in the increasing lack of access to theater in many communities. In another sense, it is just a symptom of the ephemeral nature of theater, especially, I would argue, the FTP. While we do have playscripts and photos of many of the productions and some film of Orson Welles's production of *Macbeth* in Harlem, the discussion of plays that were, at best, unfamiliar to them paled in relationship to the tangible spaces in their communities they could interact with. In several ways, this aligns with some of the historical criticism of the FTP, as it simply could not resonate with Americans as could the other arts programs. As Jane De Hart Matthews argues, while the FTP had strong regional support, it could simply never obtain the national, grassroots support that an organization like the FAP could, both in terms of organizational outreach and the providing communities tangible products from the labor of Federal One.

In the summer of 2016, I decided to attempt once again to do a lesson on the FTP, and I had students read the adaptation of Sinclair Lewis's *It Can't Happen Here*. Admittedly, my choice of play text was inspired by the tone of Donald Trump's campaign, and I was far from alone in making the parallel between his candidacy and the content of Lewis's novel and play. On the day we discussed the play, I simply opened the floor to reactions to the text, and after a pause, a student said, rather bluntly: "This is Trump. That is pretty clear."[1] And for that student, and as I recall all the students in that class, the FTP suddenly had an immediacy to them that I had not seen before. And I certainly understood that student's connection and angst from the parallels she and her classmates saw in the play to the then current political and social climate.

I think about that class quite often, and I certainly do not bring up that anecdote to diminish the fear that group of students had in the summer of 2016 about the political climate. But in thinking about this project—one that I have been wrestling with since the summer of 2010—I have found the content of these plays to continually remind me of their immediacy. The diminishing stability of the middle class in the United States has become a standard talking point in election cycles, while economists openly worry about the rampant and reckless speculation in digital economies. And confidence artists in all manner of situations—politics, economics, art—still dominate news cycles and gain adherents. Discussions of work relief still dominate political discourse, as, for instance, was illustrated in the debate over direct payments to Americans during the height of the COVID-19 pandemic. Similar debates have occurred over what productions theaters and other places of art should show, and calls for broader, federalized funding for artists have generally been ignored in Western societies (with some exceptions, like in Germany). Moreover, there have been calls for a new, national theater program not unlike the FTP. In a 2021 piece for *American Theatre*, Jerald Raymond Pierce argued for the federal government to take the lead on establishing such an initiative to "send the message that the arts, and the people who make them, are worthy of support on par with our national parks . . . or public education." Such a move, he reasons, will inspire new investment in theater from foundations and private donors, but he notes that the "drumbeat for a new Federal Theatre Project isn't just about helping this industry survive the pandemic." "There is a profound interest," he asserts, "in revolutionizing how theatre functions, how it interacts with its communities, and how it can create healing art. This rallying cry goes beyond getting back to normal—a 'normal' that wasn't already working for so many artists and audiences. True, dedicated, extensive government support has the potential to fundamentally change the theatrical landscape forever."[2]

The legacy of the FTP has long focused on its guiding ethos of "free, adult, and uncensored"; the program's influence on American theater; and its sincerely noble mission to both disseminate theater to Americans across the country and radically change the nature of theatrical art. Of course, its legacy has also often focused on the political troubles the FTP faced in lieu of conservative hostility to its works, especially its more radical texts. But *All Play and No Work* I hope has illustrated that some of the most radical texts the FTP produced were not part of the living newspaper tradition or radical polemics from academic playwrights. Indeed, I would argue that many of these plays more than fulfilled Flanagan's goals for the program in that they represented the ideal of free, adult, and uncensored drama. Despite the view that comedy is not as serious as tragedy, these plays often examined the complex issues of work and labor in complicated ways and, at times, addressed issues of labor more fully than more "serious" texts. Moreover, these plays portrayed issues that were complimentary or critical of many New Deal and FTP policies. At times, these plays would act as de facto propaganda for New Deal policies; other times, they would defend or advocate for reform to the FTP; and, at other times, openly challenge their audiences about the political space, reminding them of the dangers of capitalism. Within the comedy and resistance of these plays, often dismissed as mere entertainment, are serious analyses of the nature of work. And if there is a new federalized theatre program on the horizon, it bears noting that sometimes the texts that provide the most agency and opportunities for resistance for audiences are the ones that do not bear the hallmarks of doing so.

Notes

INTRODUCTION

1. David Kennedy, *Freedom From Fear: The American People in Depression and War, 1929–1945* (Oxford: Oxford University Press, 1999), 176.

2. Max Weber, *The Protestant Ethic and the Spirit of Capitalism*, 1905, trans. Talcott Parsons, 1930 (London: Routledge, 2001), 123.

3. Weber, *Protestant Ethic*, 124.

4. Max Weber, "Politics as a Vocation," in *Max Weber: The Vocation Lectures*, ed. David Owen and Tracy Strong (Indianapolis: Hackett, 2004), 85.

5. John Frick, "A Changing Theatre: New York and Beyond" in *The Cambridge History of American Theatre*, vol. 2, *1870–1945*, ed. Don Wilmeth and Christopher Bigsby (Cambridge: Cambridge University Press, 1999), 230.

6. Michael North, *Machine-Age Comedy* (Oxford: Oxford University Press, 2009), 13.

7. Henri Bergson, *Laughter: An Essay on the Meaning of the Comic*, trans. Cloudesly Berereton and Fred Rothwell (New York: Macmillan, 1911), 197.

8. North, *Machine-Age Comedy*, 16.

9. James C. Scott, *Weapons of the Weak: Everyday Forms of Peasant Resistance* (New Haven, CT: Yale University Press, 1985), 41.

10. Scott, *Weapons of the Weak*, 349.

11. Scott, *Weapons of the Weak*, 350.

12. Lauren Krueger, *The National Stage: Theatre and Cultural Legitimation in England, France, and America* (Chicago: University of Chicago Press, 1992), 184.

13. North, *Machine-Age Comedy*, 13.

CHAPTER 1

1. For an analysis of the economic and social resentment toward more contemporary federalized arts programs, see Donna Binkiewicz, *Federalizing the Muse: United States*

Arts Policy and the National Endowment for the Arts, 1965–1980 (Chapel Hill: University of North Carolina Press, 2014).

2. Hallie Flanagan, *Arena* (New York: Duell, Sloan, and Pearce, 1940), 28.

3. Scholarship on the New Deal programs is rather vast but works like Arthur Schlesinger Jr.'s *The Age of Roosevelt* trilogy and Ellis Wayne Hawley's *The New Deal and the Problem of Monopoly* (Princeton, NJ: Princeton University Press, 1966) help cement this historical view—not without merit—that the New Deal's broader struggles in alleviating the concerns of capitalist influences while advocating for market controls and economic reform creating a pragmatic and ideologically inconsistent system. Recently, Ira Katznelson in *Fear Itself: The New Deal and the Origins of Our Time* (New York: Liveright, 2013) has shown that the impulse for security from fear drove New Deal policy, a system in contrast to dictatorships elsewhere in the world, but the administration's political and economic compromises cemented racial and social issues for contemporary America.

4. David Kennedy, "What the New Deal Did," *Political Science Quarterly* 124, no. 2, 2009: 251–68.

5. "Democratic Convention Acceptance Speech," FDR Presidential Library & Museum, accessed April 5, 2022, https://www.fdrlibrary.org/dnc-curriculum-hub.

6. "White House Statement on Relief for the Unemployed," White House Statement on Relief for the Unemployed, American Presidency Project (American Presidency Project, February 28, 1934), https://www.presidency.ucsb.edu/documents/white-house-statement-relief-for-the-unemployed.

7. "Annual Message to Congress," Annual Message to Congress, American Presidency Project, January 4, 1935, https://www.presidency.ucsb.edu/documents/annual-message-congress-3.

8. "Excerpts from the Press Conference in Hyde Park, New York," American Presidency Project, June 28, 1938, https://www.presidency.ucsb.edu/documents/excerpts-from-the-press-conference-hyde-park-new-york-3.

9. David Wagner, *The Poorhouse: America's Forgotten Institution* (New York: Rowan and Littlefield, 2005). 49.

10. Wagner, *Poorhouse*, 49.

11. Nancy E. Rose, *Put to Work: The WPA and Public Employment in the Great Depression* (New York: Monthly Review, 2009), 18

12. Theda Skocpol, *Protecting Soldiers and Mothers: The Political Origins of Social Policy in the United States* (Cambridge, MA: Harvard University Press, 1992), 526.

13. For an overview of this political and cultural exchange, see Daniel Rodgers, *Atlantic Crossings: Social Politics in a Progressive Age* (Cambridge, MA: Harvard University Press, 1998).

14. George Steinmetz, *Regulating the Social: The Welfare State and Local Politics in Imperial Germany* (Princeton, NJ: Princeton University Press, 1993), 160.

15. Steinmetz, *Regulating the Social*, 159–60.

16. Edwin Amenta, *Bold Relief: Institutional Politics and the Origins of Modern American Social Policy* (Princeton, NJ: Princeton University Press, 1998), 74.

17. William F. McDonald, *Federal Relief Administration and the Arts* (Columbus: Ohio State University Press, 1969), 5.

18. Amenta, *Bold Relief*, 74.

19. Rodgers, *Atlantic Crossings*, 418.

20. Rodgers, *Atlantic Crossings*, 418–19.

21. Nancy E. Rose, "Production-for-Use or Production-for-Profit?: The Contradictions of Consumer Goods Production in 1930s Work Relief," *Review of Radical Political Economics* 20, no. 1 (March 1988): 46–61.

22. Amenta, *Bold Relief*, 74. For an analysis of the intersection between labor and environment, see Neil Maher, *Nature's New Deal: The Civilian Conservation Corps and the Rise of the American Environmental Movement* (Oxford: Oxford University Press, 2008).

23. Amenta, *Bold Relief*, 75.

24. Amenta, *Bold Relief*, 84.

25. McDonald, *Federal Relief Administration and the Arts*, 59.

26. "$3,187,000 Relief Is Spent to Teach Jobless to Play; $19,658,512 Voted for April; 'Boon Doggles' Made," *New York Times*, April 4, 1935. While the etymology of the term is a little more complicated, this appears to be the first major reference in media of the term *boondoggle* meaning "a wasted effort" or "useless task" of "waste."

27. The article details a rather lurid hearing by the aldermen of the five boroughs of New York wherein the expenditures of the Emergency Relief Act were investigated. As the aldermen discovered, the unemployed were being taught "hobby" classes on elementary Latin, euthymic dancing, and an overview of historic time pieces of New York City. As witnesses testify to the usefulness of their classes, they are constantly berated by grandstanding city fathers; as one woman notes how her class emphasized craft, an alderman condescendingly retorts, "Did you say graft?" Another witness was forced to exhaustingly explain his class on boondoggles, which was simply a Midwestern term for gadgets, "things men and boys do that are useful in their everyday operations or about their home."

28. Rodgers, *Atlantic Crossings*, 479.

29. Richard Pells, *Radical Visions and American Dreams: Culture and Social Thought in the Depression Years* (Middletown, CT: Wesleyan University Press, 1973), 85.

30. Harold Ickes, *The Secret Diary of Harold L. Ickes*, vol. 1, *The First Thousand Days: 1933–1936* (New York: Simon and Schuster, 1953), 435.

31. McDonald, *Federal Relief Administration and the Arts*, 112–13.

32. Amenta, *Bold Relief*, 8.

33. Linda Gordon, *Pitied but Not Entitled: Single Mothers and the History of Welfare, 1890–1935* (Cambridge, MA: Harvard University Press, 1995).

34. Amenta, *Bold Relief*, 158–59.

35. Harry Hopkins, *Spending to Save: The True Story of Relief* (New York: Norton, 1936), 174.

36. Hopkins, *Spending to Save*, 174.

37. Hopkins, *Spending to Save*, 174.

38. Richard Wright, *American Hunger* (New York: Harper and Row, 1977), 114–16.

39. Jonas Barish, *The Antitheatrical Prejudice* (Berkeley: University of California Press, 1981), 165.

40. Rena Fraden, *Blueprints for a Black Federal Theatre, 1935–1939* (Cambridge: Cambridge University Press, 1994). 31.

41. Thomas Postlewait, "The Hieroglyphic Stage: American Theatre and Society, Post–Civil War to 1945," in *The Cambridge History of American Theatre*, ed. Don B. Wilmeth and Christopher Bigsby, 2:107–95 (Cambridge: Cambridge University Press, 1999), 156.

42. Postlewait, "Hieroglyphic Stage," 159.

43. Postlewait, "Hieroglyphic Stage," 160.

44. Postlewait, "Hieroglyphic Stage," 161.

45. Benjamin McArthur, *Actors and American Culture* (Iowa City: University of Iowa Press, 2000), 144.

46. Mark Franko, *The Work of Dance: Labor, Movement, and Identity in the 1930s* (Middletown, CT: Wesleyan University Press, 2002).

47. See Robert Maland, *Chaplin and American Culture: The Evolution of a Star Image* (Princeton, NJ: Princeton University Press, 1991).

48. McArthur, *Actors and American Culture*, 236.

49. Dorothy Chansky, *Composing Ourselves: The Little Theatre Movement and the American Audience* (Carbondale: Southern Illinois University Press, 2004), 165.

50. Martin Puchner, *Stage Fright: Modernism, Anti-Theatricality, and Drama* (Baltimore: Johns Hopkins University Press, 2002), 9–11.

51. James Fisher. "The Man Who Owned Broadway: George M. Cohan's Triumph in Eugene O'Neill's '*Ah, Wilderness!*'," *Eugene O'Neill Review* 23, no. 1/2 (Spring/Fall 1999): 109.

52. Henry Jenkins, *What Made Pistachio Nuts? Early Sound Comedy and the Vaudeville Aesthetic* (New York: Columbia University Press, 1992), 67–68.

53. Fraden, *Blueprints for a Black Federal Theatre*, 32–33.

54. McDonald, *Federal Relief Administration and the Arts*, 484.

55. Even Hollywood—which was receptive to more gag-based and avant-garde styles of comedy—was beginning to change during the Depression years; 1934 was the apex of the anarchistic comedy tradition in cinema. Henry Jenkins notes that box office returns for this type of comedy declined precipitously throughout the year, a fact that then contemporary observers attributed to "overexposure of the comic stars, the inconsistent quality of individual vehicles, the exhaustion of familiar stage material, and public distaste for the films' scatological content." Hollywood was willing to entertain new forms of comedy provided those forms proved profitable, and with complaints from audiences and exhibitors as well as poor box office returns, studios placed many comic vehicles "in line with the dominant forms of the classical Hollywood cinema . . . more formally a thematically conservative style of comedian comedy" (Jenkins, *What Made Pistachio Nuts?*, 280–81).

56. Karen Blair, *The Torchbearers: Women and Their Amateur Arts Associations in America, 1890–1930* (Bloomington: Indiana University Press, 1994), 159–60.

57. Lauren Rebecca Sklaroff, *Black Culture and the New Deal: The Quest for Civil Rights in the Roosevelt Era* (Chapel Hill: University of North Carolina Press, 2009), 38.

58. Flanagan, *Arena*, 43–44.

59. Flanagan, *Arena*, 372.

60. Flanagan, *Arena*, 20.

61. Hallie Flanagan, "Speech to New York City Project Production Supervisors," *Federal Theatre* 2, no. 1 (June 1936): 5–6.

62. Sklaroff, *Black Culture and the New Deal*, 40.

63. Sklaroff, *Black Culture and the New Deal*, 40–41.

64. McDonald, *Federal Relief Administration and the Arts*, 526–27.

65. McDonald, *Federal Relief Administration and the Arts*, 509.

66. Sklaroff, *Black Culture and the New Deal*, 40–41.

67. Sidney Howard to Hallie Flanagan, October 25, 1935, quoted in McDonald, *Federal Relief Administration and the Arts*, 581.

68. Franko, *Work of Dance*, 151.

69. Jane De Hart Matthews, *The Federal Theatre, 1935–1939: Plays, Relief, and Politics* (Princeton, NJ: Princeton University Press, 1967), 329.

70. Fraden, *Blueprints for a Black Federal Theatre*, 40.

71. Fraden, *Blueprints for a Black Federal Theatre*, 39–40.

72. Malcom Goldstein, *The Political Stage: American Drama and Theater of the Great Depression* (New York: Oxford University Press, 1974), 336.

73. Franko, *Work of Dance*, 148.

74. Franko, *Work of Dance*, 149.

75. A corollary to this dynamic is found with the FWP as commentators often disparaged its workers as "plumbers," and while many leftists saw this as flattery, other members of the program worried it would devalue their labor. See Christine Bold, *Writers, Plumbers, and Anarchists: The WPA Writer's Project in Massachusetts* (Amherst: University of Massachusetts Press, 2006).

76. Fraden, *Blueprints for a Black Federal Theatre*, 41.

77. Leslie Elaine Frost, *Dreaming America: Popular Front Ideas and Aesthetics in Children's Plays of the Federal Theatre Project* (Columbus: Ohio State University Press, 2013), 13–14.

78. Flanagan, *Arena*, 158.

79. Flanagan, *Arena*, 158–59.

80. Flanagan, *Arena*, 159.

81. Flanagan, *Arena*, 178.

82. Matthews, *Federal Theatre*, 148–49.

83. Flanagan, *Arena*, 286.

84. Michael Szalay, *New Deal Modernism: American Literature and the Invention of the Welfare State* (Durham, NC: Duke University Press, 2000). 68.

85. Szalay, *New Deal Modernism*, 72.

86. Szalay, *New Deal Modernism*, 74.

87. Matthews, *Federal Theatre*, 311.

88. Sheila Collins and Naomi Rosenblum, "The Democratization of Culture: The Legacy of the New Deal Arts Programs," in *When Government Helped: Learning from the Successes and Failures of the New Deal*, ed. Sheila Collins and Gertrude Schaffner Goldberg, 207–32 (Oxford: Oxford University Press, 2013), 224.

89. Barry Witham, *The Federal Theatre Project: A Case Study* (Cambridge: Cambridge University Press, 2003), 80.

90. Frost, *Dreaming America*, 15.

CHAPTER 2

1. Elizabeth A. Osborne, *Staging the People: Community and Identity in the Federal Theatre Project* (New York: Palgrave Macmillan, 2011), 29–31.

2. Phillip Charig, Ray Golden, and Sid Kuller, *O Say Can You Sing*, Box 1048, Chicago *O Say Can You Sing* Folder, FTP LC.

3. Jane Feuer, "The Self-Reflexive Musical and the Myth of Entertainment," in *Film Genre Reader II*, ed. Barry Keith Grant, 441–55 (Austin: University of Texas Press, 1995), 443.

4. Feuer, "Self-Reflexive Musical," 453.

5. For an analysis of the diegetic audience and musical number's role in backstage musicals, see Scott McMillian, *The Musical as Drama: A Study of the Principles and Conventions behind Musical Shows from Kern to Sondheim* (Princeton, NJ: Princeton University Press, 2006).

6. Part of the interest in many backstage musicals/shows of the era was no doubt fueled by the erotic gaze and fascination with chorus women in these shows. See Angela

J. Latham, "The Right to Bare: Containing and Encoding American Women in the Popular Theater," in *Posing a Threat: Flappers, Chorus Girls, and Other Brazen Performers of the American 1920s* (Hanover, NH: Wesleyan/University Press of New England, 2000).

7. Rick Altman, *The American Film Musical* (Bloomington: Indiana University Press, 1987), 205.

8. Altman, *American Film Musical*, 206.

9. Gina Bombola, "From 'There's Magic in Music' to 'The Hard-Boiled Canary': Promoting 'Good Music' in Prewar Musical Films," *Journal of the Society for American Music* 12, no. 2 (May 2018): 159.

10. Barry Keith Grant, *The Hollywood Film Musical* (Oxford: Blackwell, 2012), 30.

11. In addition to the backstage plays examined in this chapter, the FTP also staged Kauffman and Connelly's *Merton at the Movies*, Samuel Raphaelson's *Accent on Youth*, and Kaufman and Edna Ferber's *Stage Door*. The film adaptation of *Stage Door*, directed by Gregory La Cava with a screenplay written by Morrie Rysklund and starring Katherine Hepburn, Ginger Rodgers, Ann Miller, and Lucile Ball, shares very little with the Kaufman and Ferber original play. Kaufman allegedly referred to the changes to the play somewhat derisively as changing the film from *Stage Door* to "Screen Door" although Malcom Goldstein notes that, publicly at least, Kaufman preferred the film. See Goldstein, *Political Stage*, 269.

12. Bombola, "From 'There's Magic in Music,'" 159.

13. Altman, *American Film Musical*, 160.

14. Altman, *American Film Musical*, 235.

15. Sheri Chinen Biesen, *Music in the Shadows: Noir Musical Films* (Baltimore: Johns Hopkins University Press, 2014). 10.

16. Adrienne L. McLean, *Being Rita Hayworth: Labor, Identity, and Hollywood Stardom* (New Brunswick, NJ: Rutgers University Press, 2004), 141.

17. McLean, *Being Rita Hayworth*, 140–41.

18. Wendy Leigh, *True Grace: The Life and Death of an American Princess* (New York: St. Martin's Press, 2007), 25. According to Leigh, George Kelly advised his niece to never judge anyone who was a homosexual, and the family referred to George Kelly's longtime companion as his valet. William Waley, with whom Kelly had a fifty-five-year relationship, was not invited to his lover's funeral and apparently snuck in into the ceremony and wept quietly in the back.

19. Boze Hadleigh, *Broadway Babylon: Glamour, Glitz, and Gossip of the Great White Way* (New York: Back Stage Books, 2013), 121. While hardly an academic resource, this book is one of the few—if only—studies of Kelly's career that details the dearth of primary textual documents from the playwright.

20. George Kelly, *Three Plays: "The Torch-Bearers," "The Show-Off," "Craig's Wife,"* biographical and critical essays by William Lynch, foreword by Wendy Wasserstein (New York: Limelight, 1999), 4.

21. Bosley Crowther, "Home, Sweet Broadway," *New York Times*, September 27, 1936. Of course, in the same interview, Kelly would still harbor a negative view of amateur theater (and whether or not this was him still maintaining his contrarian persona, I am not sure): "One of his pet aversions which Mr. Kelly still cherishes is what he calls the 'professional amateurs'—the people from 'little theaters' and 'Summer stocks' who have no real talent or even sincere inclination for the theatre, but who manage to push themselves in and get jobs along Broadway. They are a menace, he opines, with all the conviction of a genuine professional."

22. Karen J. Blair, *The Torchbearers: Women and Their Amateur Arts Associations in America, 1890–1930* (Bloomington: Indiana University Press, 1994), 7.

23. Alexander Woolcott, "The Play: Joy in West 48th Street," *New York Times*, August 30, 1922.

24. Foster Hirsch, *George Kelly* (Boston: GK Hall, 1975), 57.

25. Chansky, *Composing Ourselves*, 144–45.

26. Chansky, *Composing Ourselves*, 145.

27. Chansky, *Composing Ourselves*, 145.

28. Staff of the Fenwick Library, George Mason University, *The Federal Theatre Project: A Catalog-Calendar of Productions* (New York: Greenwood Press, 1986), 161.

29. Dan Rush, review of *The Torch-Bearers* for the Bureau of Research and Publication, June 8, 1936, Box 333, *The Torch-Bearers* (Kelly) Folder, FTP LC.

30. Osborne, *Staging the People*, 86–88.

31. Osborne, *Staging the People*, 91.

32. Guy Munger, *Curtain Up! Raleigh Little Theatre's First 50 Years* (Raleigh, NC: Raleigh Little Theatre, 1985), https://raleighlittletheatre.org/about/curtain-up-rlt-first-50-years/.

33. Cecelia Moore, *The Federal Theatre Project in the American South: The Carolina Playmakers and the Quest for American Drama* (New York: Lexington Books, 2017), 68.

34. Quoted in Munger, *Curtain Up!*.

35. Kelly, *Torch-Bearers*, in *Three Plays*, 56.

36. There is at least one example of the FTP alluding to the head of the program. As Elizabeth Osborne argues, in the first draft of *O Say Can You Sing*, there is a character named Augustus Hamfield, the newly appointed secretary of entertainment who oversees the various plays within the play, who bears a striking resemblance to Hallie Flanagan in terms of not only his position, but the former's lack of experience in commercial theater (Osborne, *Staging the People*, 28).

37. Kelly, *Torch-Bearers*, in *Three Plays*, 37.

38. As Cecelia Moore argues, the production before *The Torchbearers* in Raleigh was a satirical take of *The Drunkard*, portraying that temperance play as broad farce and, in turn, providing the unit the opportunity to mock the Old South by incorporating costumes and scenery from a production of *Jefferson Davis*. See Moore, *Federal Theatre Project*, 56.

39. Originally titled *The Little Theater, Too Busy to Work* centers on the patriarch of the Jones family, John, being elected mayor of Maryville. As he neglects his family and his drugstore, his wife, Louise, decides to give her husband some payback by neglecting her own household chores and getting involved in an amateur theater production (I should note the rest of the film devolves into a convoluted narrative about drugstore competitors, missing bank safes, and money, and I do not know if I fully comprehend the plot). Whether this film is a direct adaptation of Kelly's play is up for some debate: marketing materials, copyright records, and many contemporary reviews of the film credit Kelly's *The Torch-Bearers* as the basis for the film (along with *Your Uncle Dudley*, a 1929 play written by Howard Lindsay and Bertrand Robinson), the plays are not credited in many of the internal documents of 20th Century Fox, yet the narrative point of Louise Jones joining an amateur troupe seems to be at the least inspired by Kelly's play.

40. Henry Clayton Anderson, *Will Rogers and "His" America*, Library of American Biography Series (Boston: Pearson, 2011), 195.

41. Anderson, *Will Rogers*, 196.

42. Anderson, *Will Rogers*, 186.

43. Anderson, *Will Rogers*, 194.

44. Kelly, *Torch-Bearers*, in *Three Plays*, 139.

45. Kelly, *Torch-Bearers*, in *Three Plays*, 140.

46. Kelly, *Torch-Bearers*, in *Three Plays*, 159 60.

47. Chansky, *Composing Ourselves*, 146.

48. For an analysis of the impact of the speech, see Ann George and Jack Selzer, "What Happened at the First American Writers' Congress? Kenneth Burke's 'Revolutionary Symbolism in America,'" *Rhetoric Society Quarterly* 33, no. 2 (2003): 47–66.

49. Kenneth Burke, "Revolutionary Symbolism in America," in *The Legacy of Kenneth Burke*, ed. Herbert Simons, 267–80 (Madison: University of Wisconsin Press, 1989), 271.

50. Patrick McGilligan and Paul Brule, eds., "Allen Boretz Interview," in *Tender Comrades: A Backstory of the Hollywood Blacklist* (New York: St. Martin's Press, 1997), 121.

51. Brooks Atkinson, "Stage Lunacy: Room Service as Further Evidence of George Abbott's Mastery of Fooling," *New York Times*, May 30, 1937, 121.

52. "*Room Service*: Play Bureau File, August 20, 1937," Box 298, *Room Service* (Murray, John and Boretz, Allen) folder, FTP LC.

53. "*Room Service* Report, Marion Murray. August 17, 1937," Box 298, *Room Service* (Murray, John and Boretz, Allen) folder, FTP LC.

54. "*Room Service* Report, Jo Eisinger. Sept. 7, 1937," Box 298, *Room Service* (Murray, John and Boretz, Allen) folder, FTP LC.

55. Staff of the Fenwick Library, George Mason University, *Federal Theatre Project*, 135. The six performances took place in Wilmington, North Carolina (October 1938); San Francisco (November 1938); San Diego (December 1938); New Orleans (May 1939); Denver (January 1939); Miami, Florida (January 1939).

56. Andrew Slane, "Director's Report," Box 1067, Denver *Room Service* Production Report, FTP LC.

57. "Audience Survey," Box 1067, Denver *Room Service* Production Report, FTP LC.

58. Joe Adamson, *Groucho, Harpo, Chico, and Sometimes Zeppo: A History of the Marx Brothers and a Satire on the Rest of the World* (New York: Touchstone, 1973), 344.

59. Martin Gardner, *The Marx Brothers as Social Critics: Satire and Comic Nihilism in Their Films* (Jefferson, NC: McFarland, 2009), 23.

60. Boretz himself seems to have cared little for the RKO film, although he maintained something of a friendship with Groucho Marx in the 1930s. Marx, according to Boretz, considered himself a Social Democrat, and he and the playwright would often have a "kind of bout going" over their divergent politics. Boretz recalled that one day he confronted Groucho about what the Marx brother wanted from society, and allegedly Groucho responded, "I don't want anything to change." See McGilligan and Buhle, *Tender Comrades*, 119.

61. Sebastian Trainor, "'It Sounds Too Much Like *Comrade*': The Preservation of American Ideals in *Room Service*," *Journal of American Drama and Theater* 20, no. 2 (2008): 41–42.

62. Joe Adamson, *Groucho, Harpo, Chico, and Sometimes Zeppo: A Celebration of the Marx Brothers* (New York: Simon and Schuster, 1973). 345.

63. Trainor, "It Sounds Too Much Like *Comrade*," 41–42.

64. Trainor, "It Sounds Too Much Like *Comrade*," 39.

65. Trainor, "It Sounds Too Much Like *Comrade*," 42.

66. John Murray and Allen Boretz, *Room Service* (New York: Samuel French, 1936), 31.

67. Murray and Boretz, *Room Service*, 63.

68. Murray and Boertz, *Room Service*, 35.

69. Burke, "Revolutionary Symbolism in America," 271.

70. Murray and Boertz, *Room Service*, 23.

71. Murray and Boretz, *Room Service*, 70.

72. Murray and Borertz, *Room Service*, 71–72.

73. *Back to the Woods*, accessed November 21, 2021, https://www.youtube.com/watch?v=Eiw49qhNiAQ.

74. Portions of this section were previously published in my essay "No Security in Acting: A Moral Entertainment and the Conflict Over Theatrical Labor in the Federal Theatre Project," *LATCH: A Journal for the Study of the Literary Artifact in Theory, Culture, or History* 8 (2015), © 2015 Open Latch Publications. Published under a CC-BY-SA 3.0 License, http://creativecommons.org/licenses/by-nc-sa/3.0/us/. My kind appreciation for their permission for its inclusion here.

75. *Ransom!* focuses on the struggles of family and police dealing with the moral and ethical issues associated with a kidnapping; *Bigger Than Life* deals with a schoolteacher father whose life spirals out of control after becoming addicted to cortisone pills.

76. Richard Maibaum, "On the New Drama, the New Play," in *Speaking of Writing*, ed. Sylvia Maibaum (New York: Page, 2019), 45.

77. Maibaum, "On the New Drama, the New Play," 45.

78. Maibaum, "On the New Drama, the New Play," 42.

79. Richard Maibaum, "On the Dedication of the EC Mabie Theater," in Maibaum, *Speaking of Writing*, 90.

80. Staff of the Fenwick Library, George Mason University, *Federal Theatre Project*, 106. The five productions occurred in Roslyn, New York (April 1938); Bryn Mawr (June 1938); San Francisco (October 1938); Boston (December 1938); Hartford (April 1939). The FTP LC archive also lists a performance in Oakland, California, aligned with the San Francisco production in October 1938.

81. "*A Moral Entertainment* report, Converse Tyler," January 10, 1938, Box 260, *A Moral Entertainment* (Maibaum) Folder, FTP LC.

82. "Preview of the *A Moral Entertainment* at the Avery Memorial Theatre, Wednesday evening, April 19, 1939, Hartford, Conn," Grace Fisher, April 19, 1939, Box 260, *A Moral Entertainment* (Maibaum) Folder, FTP LC.

83. Review of *A Moral Entertainment*, *Philadelphia Bulletin*, June 19, 1938, Box 1040, Bryn Mawr *A Moral Entertainment* Production Report, FTP LC.

84. William Kennedy, "*A Moral Entertainment*: Good Entertainment Too," Box 1040, Roslyn *A Moral Entertainment* Production Report, FTP LC.

85. Osborne (*Staging the People*, 52–53) shows how WPA workers in Boston were subjected to routine unemployment checks in the city's Charity Building as well as police hazing in investigating relief workers and their accounts.

86. Elinor Hughes, "Review of 'A Moral Entertainment,'" *Boston Herald*, December 28, 1938, Box 14, Richard Maibaum Papers (Iowa City: University of Iowa Special Collections).

87. Review of *A Moral Entertainment*, *Boston American*, December 28, 1938, Box 14, Richard Maibaum Papers (Iowa City: University of Iowa Special Collections).

88. David D. Hall, "Narrating Puritanism," in *New Directions in American Religious History*, ed. Harry S Stout and D.G. Hart, 51–83 (Oxford: Oxford University Press, 1997).

89. H. L. Mencken, "Puritanism as a Literary Force," in *Book of Prefaces*, 197–285 (New York: Knopf, 1917).

90. Richard Maibaum, *A Moral Entertainment*, Box 14, Richard Maibaum Papers, University of Iowa Library, Iowa City, Iowa, I:10. Note: the copy of *A Moral Entertain-*

ment here is divided by Roman numeral–numbered acts, so I will use that formatting here for the play.

91. Maibaum, *Moral Entertainment*, I:12.

92. Maibaum, *Moral Entertainment*, II:4.

93. Maibaum, *Moral Entertainment*, IV:25.

94. Maibaum, *Moral Entertainment*, IV:26.

95. Maibaum, *Moral Entertainment*, IV:20.

96. Maibaum, *Moral Entertainment*, IV:20.

97. Frost, *Dreaming America*, 14.

98. Judith Edith Brussell, "Government Investigations of Federal Theatre Project Personnel in the Works Progress Administration (The Show Must NOT Go On!)" (PhD diss., City University of New York, 1993), 141–42.

99. Brussell, "Government Investigations," 218.

100. Brussell, "Government Investigations," 4.

CHAPTER 3

1. Charles Maland, *Chaplin and American Culture: The Evolution of a Star Image* (Princeton, NJ: Princeton University Press, 1989), 153.

2. Maland, *Chaplin and American Culture*, 154.

3. Morris Dickstein, *Dancing in the Dark: A Cultural History of the Great Depression* (New York: W. W. Norton and Company, 2009), 244.

4. Lewis Corey, *The Crisis of the Middle Class* (New York: Covici-Friede, 1935), 11.

5. Corey, *Crisis of the Middle Class*, 10.

6. Corey, *Crisis of the Middle Class*, 10.

7. Corey, *Crisis of the Middle Class*, 281.

8. Marina Moskowitz, "'Aren't We All?' Aspiration, Acquisition, and the American Middle Class," in *The Making of the Middle Class*, ed. A. Ricardo Lopez and Barbara Weinstein, 75–86 (Durham, NC: Duke University Press, 2012), 80.

9. See Alfred Bingham, *Insurgent America: Revolt of the Middle Classes* (New York: Harper and Brothers, 1935).

10. Max Weber, "Bureaucracy," in *Max Weber: Essays in Sociology*, ed. Hans Gerth, and C. Wright Mills, 196–244 (New York: Oxford University Press, 1975), 241.

11. Tom Lutz, "'Sweat or Die': The Hedonization of the Work Ethic in the 1920s," *American Literary History* 8, no. 2 (1996): 261.

12. Daniel Rodgers, *The Work Ethic in Industrial America, 1850–1920* (Princeton, NJ: Princeton University Press, 1988), 75.

13. Lutz, "Sweat or Die," 264.

14. Lutz, "Sweat or Die," 274.

15. Lutz, "Sweat or Die," 276.

16. Roland Marchand, *Adverting the American Dream: Making Way for Modernity, 1920–1940* (Berkley: University of California Press, 1985), 118.

17. Marchand, *Adverting the American Dream*, 119. The AT&T campaign would eventually focus more on an elite market, as the ads promoted the notion that multiple phone lines would permit more private communication with servants in other areas of the home as well as keeping servants from the privacy of family phone conversations.

18. Rita Barnard, *The Great Depression and the Culture of Abundance: Kenneth Fearing, Nathanael West, and Mass Culture in the 1930s* (Cambridge: Cambridge University Press, 1995), 24–25.

19. Barnard, *Great Depression*, 24–25.

20. C. Wright Mills, *White Collar: The American Middle Classes* (Oxford: Oxford University Press, 1951).

21. Tom Lutz, *Doing Nothing: A History of Loafers, Loungers, Bums, and Slackers in America* (New York: Farrar, Straus and Giroux, 2006), 206.

22. Dickstein, *Dancing in the Dark*, 217.

23. Joanna Scutts, *The Extra Woman: How Marjorie Hillis Led a Generation of Women to Live Alone and Like It* (New York: Liveright, 2018), 108.

24. Susan Edmonds, *Grotesque Relations: Modernist Domestic Fiction and the U.S. Welfare State* (Oxford: Oxford University Press, 2008), 28.

25. Edmunds, *Grotesque Relations*, 30.

26. Lawrence B. Glickman, *A Living Wage: American Workers and the Making of Consumer Society* (Ithaca, NY: Cornell University Press, 1997), 148–49. Glickman also charts how much of the political discussion of the living wage intersected with this overall promotion of consumption as an antidote to economic calamity.

27. See Tracey Deutsch, *Building a Housewife's Paradise: Gender Politics and American Grocery Stores in the Twentieth Century* (Chapel Hill: University of North Carolina Press, 2010).

28. Lizabeth Cohen, "The New Deal State and the Making of Citizen Consumers," in *Getting and Spending: European and American Consumer Societies in the Twentieth Century*, ed. Susan Strasser, Charles McGovern, and Matthias Judt (Cambridge: Cambridge University Press, 1998), 121–23.

29. Cohen, "New Deal State," 124.

30. Rodgers, *Atlantic Crossings*, 462.

31. Robert S. Lynd and Helen Merrell Lynd, *Middletown in Transition: A Study in Cultural Conflicts* (New York: Harcourt, Brace, 1937), 142.

32. Lynd and Lynd, *Middletown in Transition*, 487–88.

33. Quoted in Flanagan, *Arena*, 193.

34. Staff of the Fenwick Library, George Mason University, *Federal Theatre Project*, 5–6. O'Neill's play was staged in Des Moines, Iowa (October 1937); Cincinnati (October 1937); Peoria, Illinois (November 1937); Miami, Florida (December 1937); Los Angeles (January. 1938); San Diego (January 1938); Salem, Massachusetts (January 1938); Newark, New Jersey (March 1938); New Orleans (May 1938); Holyoke, Massachusetts (June 1938); and Seattle (March 1938).

35. Leslie White, "Eugene O'Neill and the Federal Theatre Project," *Resources for American Literary Study* 17, no. 1 (1990): 68.

36. "*Ah Wilderness* by Eugene O'Neill Report," Box 137, *Ah, Wilderness* (O'Neill) Folder, FTP LC.

37. "*Ah Wilderness*," Box 137, *Ah, Wilderness* (O'Neill) Folder, FTP LC.

38. "Comment" Box 137, *Ah, Wilderness* (O'Neill) Folder, FTP LC.

39. Thomas Ewing Dabnzy, "Federal Theater Players Give Retrospect in '*Ah Wilderness*,'" *New Orleans States*, May 26, 1938, Box 969, New Orleans *Ah, Wilderness* Production Report, FTP LC.

40. "Director's Report," 1937, Box 969, Des Moines *Ah, Wilderness* Production Report, FTP LC.

41. *The American Citizen*, "St. Anthony's Sponsor Federal Theatre Play," October 22, 1937, Box 969, Des Moines *Ah, Wilderness* Production Report, FTP LC.

42. Audience Survey, 1938, Box 969, Los Angeles *Ah, Wilderness* Production Report, FTP LC.

43. James Fisher. "The Man Who Owned Broadway: George M. Cohan's Triumph in Eugene O'Neill's '*Ah, Wilderness!*,'" *Eugene O'Neill Review* 23, no. 1/2 (Spring/Fall 1999): 98–126.

44. Fisher, "Man Who Owned Broadway," 118.

45. See Greg Mitchell, *The Campaign of the Century: Upton Sinclair's Race for Governor of California and the Birth of Media Politics* (New York: Random House, 1992).

46. The Andy Hardy films are representative of a shift at MGM under the auspices of Mayer to produce more formulaic, B pictures that were both cheap to produce but also more financially rewarding for the studio. Focused mainly on the sentimental journey of Mickey Rooney's Andy Hardy character through his teenage years, college, and adulthood, the films with such titles as *Andy Hardy Gets Spring Fever* (1939), *Life Begins for Andy Hardy* (1941), and *Andy Hardy's Blonde Trouble* (1944), projected a generally sentimental view of American life not unlike many of the readings of O'Neill's play.

47. Eugene O'Neill, *Ah Wilderness!: A Comedy of Recollection in Three Acts* (New York: Samuel French, 1933), 21.

48. O'Neill, *Ah Wilderness!*, 22.

49. John Patrick Diggins, *Eugene O'Neill's America: Desire under Democracy* (Chicago: University of Chicago Press, 2007), 78.

50. O'Neill, *Ah Wilderness!*, 96.

51. O'Neill, *Ah Wilderness!*, 121.

52. O'Neill, *Ah Wilderness!*, 118.

53. Diggins, *Eugene O'Neill's America*, 146.

54. Diggins, *Eugene O'Neill's America*, 254.

55. O'Neill, *Ah Wilderness!*, 73.

56. Lynd and Lynd, *Middletown in Transition*, 142.

57. Eoin F. Cannon, *The Saloon and the Mission: Addiction, Conversion, and the Politics of Redemption in American Culture* (Amherst: University of Massachusetts Press, 2013), 139.

58. Cannon, *Saloon and the Mission*, 141.

59. Cannon, *Saloon and the Mission*, 142–43.

60. O'Neill, *Ah Wilderness!*, 40.

61. O'Neill, *Ah Wilderness!*, 61.

62. O'Neill, *Ah Wilderness!*, 40.

63. Cannon, *Saloon and the Mission*, 222.

64. Joy Elizabeth Hayes, "White Noise Performing the White, Middle-Class Family on 1930s Radio," *Cinema Journal* 51, no. 3 (2012), 97–118.

65. Hayes, "White Noise," 112.

66. Hayes, "White Noise," 112.

67. Hayes, "White Noise," 113.

68. Malcom Goldstein, *George S. Kaufman: His Life, His Theater* (New York: Oxford University Press, 1979), 75.

69. Goldstein, *George S. Kaufman*, 76.

70. Goldstein, *George S. Kaufman*, 77.

71. Alexander Wollcott, "The Play: By the Authors of '*Dulcy*,'" *New York Times*, February 21, 1922.

72. Nina Miller argues that since the purpose of the Round Table was to garner praise and promote public consumption of the wits' performances, logrolling was necessary to achieve the group's aims. She suggests that the discourse of the Round Table was one of blatant publicity, one designed to sell their personas. See Nina Miller, *Making Love*

Modern: The Intimate Public Worlds of New York's Literary Women (New York: Oxford University Press, 1999), 94.

73. "Play Reader Report, *To the Ladies*, Harold Callen," June 19, 1936, Box 332, *To the Ladies* (Kaufman and Connelly) Folder, FTP LC.

74. "Play Reader Report, *To the Ladies*, Henry Bennett," May 7, 1937. Box 332, *To the Ladies* (Kaufman and Connelly) Folder, FTP LC.

75. "Play Reader Report, *To the Ladies*, Reader Byrne," May 12, 1937, Box 332, *To the Ladies* (Kaufman and Connelly) Folder, FTP LC.

76. Staff of the Fenwick Library, George Mason University, *Federal Theatre Project*, 159–160. The locations were Omaha, Nebraska (January 1936); San Bernardino, California (June 1937); San Diego (June 1938); and Los Angeles (July 1938).

77. Robert Holcomb, "The Federal Theatre in Los Angeles," *California Historical Society Quarterly* 41, no. 2 (June 1962): 134.

78. Flanagan, *Arena*, 274.

79. Amy Brady, "'They're Sufferin' the Same Things We're Sufferin': Ideology and Racism in the Federal Theatre Project's The Sun Rises in the West," *Theatre Survey* 56, no. 1 (January 2015): 54.

80. Based on the available documents in the FTP archives at the Library of Congress and George Mason University, there do not appear to have been any major changes made to the playscripts of the productions of the play performed in California.

81. Brady, "They're Sufferin'," 52.

82. Connelly himself would be impressed with the FTP production of Arnold Sungaard's *Everywhere I Roam* to collaborate with the playwright for a short Broadway production in 1938 and 1939.

83. Garret Eisler, "Kidding on the Level: The Reactionary Project of *I'd Rather Be Right*," *Studies in Musical Theatre* 1, no. 1 (2007): 9.

84. Eisler, "Kidding on the Level."

85. Eisler argues this is a subtle and not-so-subtle jab at Orson Welles's Project 891. 17.

86. George Kaufman and Moss Hart, *I'd Rather Be Right* (New York: Random House, 1937), 53.

87. "Director's Report," Box 1081, San Diego *To the Ladies* Production Report, FTP LC.

88. *Los Angeles Times* Review of *To the Ladies*, July 20, 1938, Box 1081, Los Angeles *To the Ladies* Production Report, FTP LC.

89. "Los Angeles Herald & Express Review of To the Ladies," July 20, 1938, Box 1081, Los Angeles To the Ladies Folder, FTP LC. McIntyre is perhaps best known for her work with the Three Stooges in several of their short films. Often appearing as the blond object of one or more of the Stooges' romantic affections, McIntyre was a brunette in most of her early stage and film work in the later 1930s.

90. Audience Reaction Report, 1937, Box 1081 San Bernardino *To the Ladies* Production Report, FTP LC.

91. Review of *To the Ladies, San Bernardino Sun Telegram*, June 17, 1937, Box 1081, San Bernardino *To the Ladies* Production Report, FTP LC.

92. "Audience Reaction Report, San Diego *To the Ladies*," Box 1081, San Diego *To the Ladies* Folder, FTP LC; "Audience Reaction Report," Los Angeles *To The Ladies*, Box 1081, Los Angeles *To the Ladies* Folder, FTP LC.

93. George Kaufman and Marc Connelly, *To the Ladies* (New York: Samuel French, 1922), 40.

94. Stephanie Coontz, *The Way We Never Were: American Families and the Nostalgia Trap* (New York: Basic Books, 1992), 157.

95. Lutz, "Sweat or Die," 276.

96. Coontz, *Way We Never Were*, 158.

97. Coontz, *Way We Never Were*, 158.

98. Kaufman and Connelly, *To the Ladies*, 74.

99. Kaufman and Connelly, *To the Ladies*, 18

100. Barnard, *Great Depression*, 189–91.

101. Kaufman and Connelly, *To the Ladies*, 12.

102. Viki Howard, *From Main Street to Mall: The Rise and Fall of the American Department Store* (Philadelphia: University of Pennsylvania Press, 2015), 87.

103. Howard, *From Main Street to Mall*, 89.

104. Andrew Sarris, *You Ain't Heard Nothing Yet: The American Talking Film, History & Memory, 1927–1949* (New York: Oxford University Press, 1998), 93.

105. Olympia Kiriakou, *Becoming Carole Lombard: Stardom, Comedy, and Legacy* (New York: Bloomsbury Academic, 2020), 77.

106. Heather Gilmour, "Different, Except in a Different Way: Marriage, Divorce, and Gender in the Hollywood Comedy of Remarriage," *Journal of Film and Video* 50, no. 2 (1998): 31.

107. Gilmour, "Different, Except in a Different Way," 38.

108. Gilmour, "Different, Except in a Different Way," 27–28.

109. Kaufman and Connelly, *To the Ladies*, 69–70.

CHAPTER 4

1. An important caveat: Lears focuses a great deal on extending his definition of speculation to confidence artists, and while there is some overlap between the two, I differentiate between speculation, gambling, and just being lucky as actions, all of which I believe Aubrey Piper and Henry Washington engage in, and the deliberate and extensive labor that exists in the confidence schemes outlined in both *The Milky Way* and *Help Yourself* in Chapter 5.

2. Jackson Lears, *Something for Nothing: Luck in America* (New York: Penguin, 2003), 19.

3. Lears, *Something for Nothing*, 4.

4. Ann Fabian, *Card Sharps and Bucket Shops: Gambling in Nineteenth Century America* (New York: Routledge, 1999).

5. Jason Puskar, *Accident Society: Fiction, Collectivity, and the Production of Chance* (Stanford: Stanford University Press, 2012), 2–3.

6. Gerda Reith, *The Age of Chance: Gambling in Western Culture* (London: Routledge, 1999), 176. Emphasis in text.

7. Reith, *Age of Chance*, 178.

8. Reith draws on Dostoevsky's musings on the nature of aristocratic and bourgeois styles of play and argues that a broader acceptance of risk that some of the "abandonment of reason embodied in Dostoevsky's plunging parodied the bourgeois style of play; a style eternally constrained by the discipline of self-consciousness over oblivion and restraint over excess. By not risking all, such gamblers will never lose all, but nor will they ever gain anything of value. Their greatest reward will be a few pennies, carefully won in an eternity of sensible, cautious play" (*Age of Chance*, 154).

9. Rodgers, *Work Ethic in Industrial America, 1850–1920*, 12.

10. Rodgers, *Work Ethic in Industrial America, 1850–1920*, 116.

11. By the time of the First World War, many academics and business leaders began to promote an idea of the business cycle, "periodic fluctuations in production, employment,

and other economic activity" that revealed more causality to economic downturns than simply rampant speculation. See Walter Friedman, *Fortune Tellers: The Story of America's First Economic Forecasters* (Princeton, NJ: Princeton University Press, 2013), 11.

12. See Friedman for an in-depth discussion of the broad interest in fortune-telling and astrology promotion of stocks as well as the professionalization of stock forecasting.

13. Franklin Roosevelt, "Inaugural Address," *American Presidency Project,* March 4, 1933, https://www.presidency.ucsb.edu/documents/inaugural-address-8.

14. Lears, *Something for Nothing,* 235.

15. John Maynard Keynes, *The General Theory of Employment, Interest, and Money* (1936; repr., Amherst: Prometheus Books, 1997), 380–81.

16. Rodgers, *Atlantic Crossings,* 445.

17. Rodgers, *Atlantic Crossings,* 444.

18. Jackson Lears argues that one of the more surprising desires for rational security amid an unsecure time was the rise of scientific polling, which "provided an apparently scientific basis for belief in a homogeneous American Way of Life—a transcendent collective identity for a society in search of security, a vision of classless cultural nationalism that informed everything from Popular Front rhetoric to Frank Capra films" (*Something for Nothing,* 235).

19. Lawrence W. Levine, "American Culture and the Great Depression," *Yale Review* 74, no. 2 (1985): 203.

20. Tino Balio, *Grand Design: Hollywood as a Modern Business Enterprise, 1930–1939* (Berkley: University of California Press, 1996), 28.

21. Edward Maisel, "The Theater of George Kelly," *Theater Arts* 31 (February 1947): 42.

22. Maisel, "Theater of George Kelly," 43.

23. Brooks Atkinson, "Portrait of a Talker," *New York Times,* December 13, 1932, 10.

24. Kelly, *The Show-Off,* in *Three Plays,* 269.

25. Kelly, *The Show-Off,* in *Three Plays,* 212–13.

26. Kelly, *The Show-Off,* in *Three Plays,* 212.

27. Hirsch, *George Kelly,* 63.

28. Hirsch, *George Kelly,* 62.

29. Carol Bird, "Interview with George Kelly," *Theater* 43 (August 1924), 24, quoted in Hirsch, *George Kelly,* 62.

30. In addition to the productions in Harlem (March 1937) and Chelsea (February 1938), *The Show-Off* was performed in Miami, Florida (March 1936); Cambridge, Massachusetts (June 1936); Holyoke, Massachusetts (November 1936); New York City (December 1937); Detroit (June 1938); and in a Tent Production in Sterling, Illinois (July 1938).

31. Inge first worked with the FTP in its Translations Department where he and his staff translated plays from Italian, Russian, Spanish, French, German—including *Help Yourself,* which I discuss in Chapter 5—and Yiddish.

32. Among the other projects Inge commissioned were Yiddish versions of Eugene O'Neill's *The Hairy Ape,* Elmer Rice's *Street Scene,* Mike Gold's *Money,* Clifford Odet's *Awake and Sing,* as well as an adaptation of Scolem Asch's novel *Three Cities* (among other projects).

33. Joel Schechter, *Messiahs of 1932: How American Yiddish Theatre Survived Through Satire* (Philadelphia: Temple University Press, 2008), 92.

34. Director's Report, Chelsea *The Show-Off* folder, Box 1072, FTP LC.

35. Macki Braconi, *Harlem's Theaters: A Staging Ground for Community, Class, and Contradiction,* 1929–39 (Evanston, IL: Northwestern University Press, 2015), 126–27.

36. Braconi, *Harlem's Theaters*, 128.

37. Braconi, *Harlem's Theaters*, 124.

38. Braconi, *Harlem's Theaters*, 130.

39. Braconi, *Harlem's Theaters*, 131.

40. Kelly, *The Show-Off*, in *Three Plays*, 248,

41. Kelly, *The Show-Off*, in *Three Plays*, 251.

42. Ken Dornstein, *Accidentally on Purpose: The Making of a Personal Injury Underworld in America* (New York: St. Martin's Press, 1996), 94.

43. Elliot Arnold, "Faking Car Accidents," *The Nation*, November 21, 1936, 602.

44. Kelly, *The Show-Off*, in *Three Plays*, 229.

45. Kelly, *The Show-Off*, in *Three Plays*, 228.

46. Kelly, *The Show-Off*, in *Three Plays*, 229.

47. The insurance agent details Piper's interest, and there is a clear implication that the insurance agent is unaware of Piper's own sordid history with risk and a sense of individualized interest. "Why, it's a little explanation of some of the features of a very attractive accident policy that our company has brought out—and I was talking to Mr. Piper about it the day called for Mr. Fisher's policy. He seemed to be very much interested. In fact, I find that people are usually a little more susceptible to the advantages of a good insurance policy when they actually see it being paid to somebody else. Now, that particular policy there—is a kind of combination of accident and life insurance policy—as well as disability and dividend features. In fact, we contend that there is no investment on the market today that offers the security or return that that particular policy described there does. The thing is really almost benevolent" (Kelly, *The Show-Off*, 249–50).

48. Puskar, *Accident Society*, 220.

49. Puskar, *Accident Society*, 221.

50. Puskar, *Accident Society*, 222.

51. Kelly, *The Show-Off*, in *Three Plays*, 272.

52. Kelly, *The Show-Off*, in *Three Plays*, 125–26.

53. Kate Dossett, *Radical Theatre in the Black New Deal* (Chapel Hill: University of North Carolina Press, 2020), 11.

54. Dosset, *Radical Theatre*, 11.

55. Dosset, *Radical Theatre*, 11.

56. Dosset, *Radical Theatre*, 13–14.

57. In addition to the Chicago performance, Brownell's play was also staged in Cleveland (April 1936); Seattle (January 1938); New York City (March 1938); Hartford, Connecticut (April 1938); Newark, New Jersey (May 1938); Harlem (June 1938); and Cedar Grove, New Jersey (January 1939). Like *Help Yourself* that I will discuss in Chapter 5, the play was also featured during a broadcast of the Federal Theatre Project Radio productions in 1938 that featured the actor Walter Brogsdale, who had worked as a rail porter before beginning work as an actor in film and theater in the 1910s, as the voice of Henry Washington and Julian Costello, who would also appear in several other FTP Negro Unit plays at the Lafayette Theatre, as Reverend Tatum.

58. Dossett, *Radical Theatre*, 8–9.

59. Sklaroff, *Black Culture and the New Deal*, 53.

60. Sklaroff, *Black Culture and the New Deal*, 54–55.

61. Sklaroff, *Black Culture and the New Deal*, 60.

62. "Play Reader Report of *Mississippi Rainbow*, William Stone," February 26, 1937, Box 258, *Mississippi Rainbow* (Brownell) Folder, FTP LC.

63. "Play Reader Report of *Mississippi Rainbow*, Samuel Kreiter," December 17, 1937, Box 258, *Mississippi Rainbow* (Brownell) Folder, FTP LC.

64. "Play Reader Report of *Mississippi Rainbow*, Alfred B. Kuttner," March 5, 1937, Box 258, *Mississippi Rainbow* (Brownell) Folder, FTP LC.

65. "Bureau of Research and Publication, Special Play Reader Report of *Mississippi Rainbow*, C.C. Lawrence," Box 258, *Mississippi Rainbow* (Brownell) Folder, FTP LC.

66. Letter from Richard J. Madden to John C. Brownell, May 13, 1936, Box 132, Folder 1, John C. Brownell Papers, Beinecke Rare Book and Manuscript Library, Yale University, New Haven [hereafter referenced as John C Brownell Papers].

67. Cleveland Neighborhood Association Letter, February 1, 1936, Box 132, Folder 1, John C. Brownell Papers.

68. Based on several letters and telegrams in the Brownell archive, by 1936 editions of the play were still circulating with the three different titles: *Nothing but Trouble, Brain Sweat*, and *Mississippi Rainbow*.

69. Vanita Marian Vactor, "A History of the Chicago Federal Theatre Project Negro Unit" (PhD diss., New York: City University of New York, 1998), 74.

70. Two of the actors who appeared in the *Brain Sweat* Broadway production were instrumental in establishing the Negro Unit of the FTP: Rose McClendon who played Carrie Washington and Dick Campbell who played Jake Johnson. It is not clear if they had any sway over the play's selection, and McClendon had died before *Mississippi Rainbow*'s staging by the agency.

71. Letter from Brownell to Susan Glaspell, July 13,1937, Box 132, Folder 1, John C. Brownell Papers.

72. In the letter, Brownell notes, "*Mississippi Rainbow* called for Bert Williams and there are no more of his caliber. What Bert Williams would have done for our play *Mississippi Rainbow* would have been nobody's business. In that pantomime scene in the first act, I saw Williams. It had to be cut out because—well—Bert Williams was dead. I can only think of one man who could do this and that man is Paul Robeson" (John Brownell to George Kondolf, July 28, 1937, Box 132, Folder 4, John C. Brownell Papers).

73. John C. Brownell to Theodore Ward, May 11, 1937, Box 132, Folder 4, John C. Brownell Papers.

74. John C. Brownell to Shirley Graham, May 11, 1937, Box 132, Folder 4, John C. Brownell Papers.

75. Shirley Graham letter to John C. Brownell, May 12, 1937, Box 132, Folder 4, John C. Brownell Papers.

76. Vactor, "History of the Chicago Federal Theatre Project," 77.

77. Charles Collins, "Review of *Mississippi Rainbow*," March 8, 1937, Box 258, *Mississippi Rainbow* folder (Brownell), FTP LC.

78. "Review of *Mississippi Rainbow*," *Chicago Daily News*, March 8, 1937, Box 258, *Mississippi Rainbow* folder (Brownell), FTP LC.

79. Shirley Graham to Black Organizations, form letter, February 23, 1937, Box 132, Folder 3, John C. Brownell Papers.

80. Claude A. Barnett to John Brownell, May 26, 1937, Box 132, Folder 4, John C. Brownell Papers.

81. Dossett, *Radical Theatre*, 170.

82. Review of *Mississippi Rainbow*, *Chicago Defender (National Edition)*, May 8, 1937, ProQuest Historical Newspapers: *Chicago Defender*, 10.

83. James Grant, "Welcome Federal Theatre," *Chicago Defender (National Edition)*, April 17, 1937, ProQuest Historical Newspapers: *Chicago Defender*, 17.

84. Julie Burrell, *The Civil Rights Theatre Movement in New York, 1939–1966: Staging Freedom* (New York: Palgrave/Macmillan, 2019), 33.

85. Burrell, *Civil Rights Theatre Movement*, 33–34. Ward's play also drew some negative responses from Black Chicagoans. Burrell notes that several audience members wrote complaints noting their own experiences and condemning Ward's work as too narrow in its focus.

86. Theodore Ward to John Brownell, May 20, 1937, Box 132, Folder 3, John C. Brownell Papers.

87. Fabian, *Card Sharps and Bucket Shops*, 143–44.

88. Fabian, *Card Sharps and Bucket Shops*, 145.

89. Fabian, *Card Sharps and Bucket Shops*, 145.

90. Fabian, *Card Sharps and Bucket Shops*, 146.

91. John C. Brownell, *Mississippi Rainbow* (New York: Samuel French, 1935), 23.

92. Lawrence Levine, *Black Culture and Black Consciousness: Afro-American Folk Thought from Slavery to Freedom* (New York: Oxford University Press, 1977), 327.

93. Pearl Bowser and Louise Spence, *Writing Himself into History: Oscar Micheaux, His Silent Films, and His Audiences* (New Brunswick, NJ: Rutgers University Press, 2000), 191.

94. Bowser and Spence, *Writing Himself into History*, 185.

95. Brownell, *Mississippi Rainbow*, 36.

96. Brownell, *Mississippi Rainbow*, 51.

97. Brownell, *Mississippi Rainbow*, 80. Italics in text.

98. Brownell, *Mississippi Rainbow*, 86.

99. Brownell, *Mississippi Rainbow*, 29.

100. Brownell, *Mississippi Rainbow*, 28. Emphasis in text.

101. Brownell, *Mississippi Rainbow*, 29. Emphasis in text.

102. See Fabian, *Card Sharps and Bucket Shops*, 134, for a discussion of the failure of the Freedman's Bank in the Reconstruction period; also see Lears, *Something for Nothing*, 261.

103. Brownell, *Mississippi Rainbow*, 29.

104. Brownell, *Mississippi Rainbow*, 29.

105. Brownell, *Mississippi Rainbow*, 29. Emphasis in text.

106. Brownell, *Mississippi Rainbow*, 20.

107. Brownell, *Mississippi Rainbow*, 49.

108. Brownell, *Mississippi Rainbow*, 88.

109. Brownell, *Mississippi Rainbow*, 106.

110. Brownell, *Mississippi Rainbow*, 111–12.

111. Braconi, *Harlem's Theaters*, 134.

CHAPTER 5

1. Roland Barthes, *Mythologies*, trans. Annette Lewis (1952; repr., New York: Hill and Wang, 1972), 15.

2. Sharon Mazar, *Professional Wrestling: Sport and Spectacle* (Oxford: University Press of Mississippi, 1998).

3. Portions of this chapter were first published in "The Illusion of Work: The Con Artist Plays of the Federal Theatre Project," *Journal of American Drama and Theatre* 30, no. 1 (Fall 2017), ISNN 2376–4236. © 2017 by Martin E. Segal Theatre Center. Used with permission of the journal and the Martin E. Segal Theatre Center. My sincere appreciation for their permission for its inclusion here.

4. Grantland Rice, "Rasslin' Gets a Toe Hold," *Collier's*, March 14, 1931, 65. Rice's piece is one of the first major exposés of professional wrestling, but it appears to have already been something of an open secret among wrestling fans that professional wrestling was staged. For a general overview of the history of wrestling and the complicit audiences of it, see David Shoemaker, *The Squared Circle: Life, Death and Professional Wrestling* (New York: Gotham, 2013).

5. I use the terms *swindler*, *con artist*, and *confidence artist*, as well as *confidence scheme*, *con*, and *con game* interchangeably throughout this essay. Rather than *con man*, I mainly rely on the gender-neutral term *confidence artist* in these pages.

6. Edward J. Balleisen, *Fraud: An American History from Barnum to Madoff* (Princeton, NJ: Princeton University Press, 2017), 245–46.

7. Balleisen, *Fraud*, 249.

8. Balleisen, *Fraud*, 250–51.

9. Balleisen, *Fraud*, 263.

10. Balleisen, *Fraud*, 264.

11. Balleisen, *Fraud*, 264.

12. Karen Halttunen, *Confidence Men and Painted Women: A Study of Middle-Class Culture in America, 1830–1870* (New Haven, CT: Yale University Press, 1982), 45.

13. Halttunen, *Confidence Men*, 14–17.

14. Halttunen, *Confidence Men*, 20.

15. For example, in the post–Civil War era, the confidence artist became "either a heroic or villainous deceiver, his actions judged solely by simplified political and ethical criteria" (149).

16. Gary Lindberg, *The Confidence Man in American Literature* (New York: Oxford University Press, 1982), 7.

17. Lindberg, *Confidence Man*, 9.

18. William Lenz, *Fast Talk and Flush Times: The Confidence Man as Literary Convention* (Columbia: University of Missouri Press, 1985), 21.

19. Halttunen, *Confidence Men*, 201–2.

20. Halttunen, *Confidence Men*, 202.

21. I can personally attest to the required skill needed for three-card monte. During a teaching observation of a class where we were discussing Susi Lori-Parks's *Topdog/Underdog*, I tried to demonstrate a "con" of three-card monte given its prominence in the play. I failed miserably in my attempt to do a successful three-card monte game (much to the delight of both students and the colleague observing me).

22. David Maurer, *The Big Con: The Story of the Confidence Man* (1940; repr., New York: Doubleday, 1999), 158.

23. "Fool's Gold: How I Sold You Your Fake Mining Stock: As Told to Edward H. Smith," *Collier's Illustrated Weekly*, December 3, 1921, 7.

24. "Fool's Gold: How I Sold You Your Fake Mining Stock," 8.

25. "Fool's Gold: How I Sold You Your Fake Mining Stock," 19.

26. W. T. Brannon, *Yellow Kid Weil: The Autobiography of America's Master Swindler* (Chicago: Ziff-Davis, 1948), 18. Weil himself gained notoriety for a series of short cons, such as selling "talking dogs," selling erroneous mine claims, and staging fake boxing fights.

27. Brannon, *Yellow Kid Weil*, 11.

28. Brannon, *Yellow Kid Weil*, 12.

29. Lindberg, *Confidence Man*, 206.

30. Stephen Mihm, *A Nation of Counterfeiters: Capitalists, Con Men, and the Making of the United States* (Cambridge, MA: Harvard University Press, 2007), 13.

31. Lenz, *Fast Talk and Flush Times*, 199.

32. Lenz, *Fast Talk and Flush Times*, 198.

33. Lenz, *Fast Talk and Flush Times*, 200.

34. While the overall narrative of *Nothing Sacred* moves toward the main characters' marriage, Olympia Kiriakou argues that several of the physical comedy sequences in the film presents Lombard's character in a transgressive lens, moving toward an egalitarian model of physical comedy that allows her to both fight back and desexualize the comedy, thereby being the physical equal of her male counterpart (*Becoming Carole Lombard*, 112).

35. The overlap between gambling and the perception of boxing as a lower-class and disreputable sport led to not only the outlawing of prizefighting in most of the United States—save for Nevada—from the 1890s to the 1920 passage of the Walker Law in New York State but also the censoring of boxing pictures (the filmed recordings of significant fights) throughout the United States. See Barak Orbach, "Prizefighting and the Birth of Movie Censorship," *Yale Journal of Law and the Humanities* 21 (2009): 251, Arizona Legal Studies Discussion Paper no. 09-08, https://ssrn.com/abstract=1351542.

36. Peter Benson. *Battling Siki: A Tale of Ring Fixes, Race, and Murder in the 1920s* (Fayetteville: University of Arkansas Press, 2008), 59.

37. Jake LaMotta, *Raging Bull* (Englewood Cliffs: Prentice Hall, 1970), 162. LaMotta is referring to Madison Square Garden here.

38. Probably the most famous work between the two writers was Root's book for the 1940, all-Black musical *Cabin in the Sky*.

39. Lynn Root's copy of *The Cheese Champion*, Lynn Root Papers, Box 8, Folder 3, American Heritage Center, University of Wyoming.

40. "Playreader Report of *The Milky Way*, Koby Kohn," 1936, Box 256, *The Milky Way* (Root and Clork) Folder, FTP LC.

41. *Three Men on a Horse* was also produced by the FTP for one production, while the play *Personal Appearance*, written by Lawrence Riley, was a Broadway smash in 1935 and would later be the basis for the Mae West vehicle *Go West, Young Man* (Henry Hathaway, 1936). *June Moon* refers to the George S. Kaufman and Ring Lardner musically themed comedy that premiered on Broadway in 1929 (with several revivals throughout the 1930s).

42. "Playreader Report of *The Milky Way*, B. Sim," 1936, Box 256, *The Milky Way* (Root and Clork) Folder, FTP LC, Washington, DC.

43. "Play Reader Report of *The Milky Way*, Gus Winberg," March 10, 1936. Box 256, *The Milky Way* (Root and Clork) Folder, FTP LC.

44. "The Milky Way Playreader Report, Arthur Bond," June 4, 1936, Box 256, *The Milky Way* (Root and Clork) Folder, FTP LC.

45. Staff of the Fenwick Library, George Mason University, *Federal Theatre Project*, 103. The locations of the performances were Manchester, New Hampshire (February 1938 and July 1938); Holyoke, Massachusetts (March 1938); Salem, Massachusetts (1938); New York City (June 1938); Los Angeles (August 1938); Denver (1938); San Diego (1938); Portland, Oregon (1939).

46. "Audience Survey," Box 1040, Portland *The Milky Way* Production Report, FTP LC.

47. Review of *The Milky Way*, *San Diego Union*, August 26, 1938, Box 1040, San Diego *The Milky Way* Production Report, FTP LC.

48. "Review of *The Milky Way*," *Los Angeles Evening News*, August 5, 1938, Box 1040, Los Angeles *The Milky Way* Production Report, FTP LC.

49. The film had a relatively high budget and something of a troubled production history, with several actors becoming seriously ill during its production. The film did man-

age a small return on its budget, and while not a major financial success, it did have a significant profile.

50. Richard Schickel, *Harold Lloyd: The Shape of Laughter* (New York: Time Life Books, 1974), 123.

51. Adam Reilly, *Harold Lloyd: The King of Daredevil Comedy* (New York: Collier Books, 1977), 138.

52. Alan Bilton, *Silent Film Comedy and American Culture* (Basingstoke, UK: Palgrave Macmillan, 2013), 159.

53. Bilton, *Silent Film Comedy*, 160.

54. Bilton, *Silent Film Comedy*, 159.

55. Bilton, *Silent Film Comedy*, 160.

56. Bilton, *Silent Film Comedy*, 160.

57. Lynn Root and Harry Clork, *The Milky Way* (New York: Samuel French, 1934), 65.

58. Root and Clork, *Milky Way*, 94.

59. Root and Clork, *Milky Way*, 69.

60. Root and Clork, *Milky Way*, 84.

61. Edward J. Balleisen, *Fraud: An American History from Barnum to Madoff* (Princeton, NJ: Princeton University Press, 2017), 249.

62. Root and Clork, *Milky Way*, 60.

63. Roland Marchand, *Advertising the American Dream: Making Way for Modernity, 1920–1940* (Berkley: University of California Press, 1985), 315.

64. Root and Clork, *Milky Way*, 97.

65. Root and Clork, *Milky Way*, 99.

66. Frost, *Dreaming America*, 14.

67. Flanagan, *Arena*, 77.

68. Flanagan notes that *Help Yourself* was criticized by Congress for its satire of high-pressure business methods, see Flanagan, *Arena*, 433.

69. There is also an odd subplot in the play concerning an older man who continually seeks employment. At the play's conclusion, a woman appears at the bank angry that the Kubinski project is proceeding, and it is revealed that the older male job seeker was her husband who has been faking his death for two years (for reasons). Mr. Kubinski is then shoved into the board meeting of the banks to be named a new director.

70. Not to be confused with H. G. Adler, Adler was also a published poet in the German humor/satire journal *Simplicissimus*, writing poems/stories, such as "The Juror," "The Bride," and "Suburban Ballad," throughout the 1910s and 1920s. See the *Simplicissimus* website, http://www.simplicissimus.info/index.php?id=5. The German language version of *Youth at the Helm/Help Yourself* was entitled *Hau-rack (Heave Ho!)*. According to Anselm Heinrich, a theater group sympathetic to the Nazi Party wrote to the Prussian Theatre Council in 1933 and inquired as to whether "Vulpius" was Jewish. Initially, the theater council informed the group that Vulpius's lawyer had informed them that Vulpius was Aryan. However, in 1934, the Prussian Theatre Council declared Vulpius to be a "non-Aryan" (Anselm Henrich, *Entertainment, Propaganda, Education: Regional Theatre in Germany and Britain Between 1918 and 1945* [Herefordshire, UK: University of Herefordshire Press, 2007], 121–22).

71. Staff of the Fenwick Library, George Mason University, *Federal Theatre Project*, 71–72. The play was produced in the following cities: New York City (July 1936 and July 1937); Syracuse, New York (September 1936); White Plains, New York (September 1936); San Bernardino, California (October 1936); Peoria, Illinois (December 1936); Los Angeles (January 1937); Springfield, Massachusetts (January 1937); Denver (February 1937);

Omaha, Nebraska (March 1937); Cincinnati (March 1937); San Francisco (March 1937); Wilmington, Delaware (April 1937); Des Moines, Iowa (April 1937); Salem, Massachusetts (1937); Boston (August 1937); Bridgeport, Connecticut (August 1937); Philadelphia (September 1937); Drexel Hill, Pennsylvania (October 1937); Seattle (September 1937); and Atlanta (April 1938).

72. Radio script of *Help Yourself* by Paul Vulpius, adapted by Barry Williams, 1939, Box 280, Folder 1, Federal Theatre Project Collection, George Mason University, Fairfax, Virginia.

73. "Help Yourself," *Peoria Star*, Box 1015, Peoria Production Report, FTP LC.

74. "Audience Reaction Report," Box 1016, Omaha *Help Yourself* Production Report, FTP LC.

75. "Audience Reaction Report," Box 1016, Des Moines Production Report, FTP LC.

76. "Review of *Help Yourself*," *Boston Herald*, January 27, 1937, Box 1015, Boston *Help Yourself* Production Report, FTP LC.

77. "Audience Reaction," Box 1015, Los Angeles *Help Yourself* Production Report, FTP LC.

78. Mary Sayler, "*Help Yourself*," *University of Washington Daily*, November 6, 1937, Box 1016, Seattle Help Yourself Production Report, FTP LC.

79. Paul Vulpius, *Help Yourself: A Farce in Three Acts*, trans. John Coman (New York: Samuel French), 1936, 39.

80. Vulpius, *Help Yourself*, 50.

81. Vulpius, *Help Yourself*, 76.

82. Vulpius, *Help Yourself*, 62.

83. Vulpius, *Help Yourself*, 63.

84. Halttunen, *Confidence Men*, 209.

85. Vulpius, *Help Yourself*, 19.

86. Vulpius, *Help Yourself*, 16.

87. Vulpius, *Help Yourself*, 22–23.

88. Vulpius, *Help Yourself*, 15.

89. Vulpius, *Help Yourself*, 15.

90. Special thanks to Jason Puskar who suggested the idea of Stringer "pretending to be German" as a way of the play complicating the notion of authentic performance during my dissertation defense on April 21, 2015.

91. Vulpius, *Help Yourself*, 18.

92. Susan Estabrook Kennedy, *The Banking Crisis of 1933* (1973; repr., Lexington: University Press of Kentucky, 2021), 17–18.

93. William Bird, *"Better Living": Advertising, Media, and the New Vocabulary of Business Leadership, 1935–1955* (Evanston, IL: Northwestern University Press, 1999), 22.

94. Radio script of *Help Yourself* by Paul Vulpius, 1.

EPILOGUE

1. I detailed this student's comment and this particular class also in an essay I wrote for *Howlround* entitled "It Happened Here: Looking Back on the Revivals of Sinclair Lewis's Play during the Election of 2016," February 19, 2017, https://howlround.com/it-happened-here.

2. Jerald Raymond Pierce, "So What Could a 'New Federal Theatre Project' Actually Look Like?," *American Theatre*, October 3, 2021, https://www.americantheatre.org/2021/02/03/so-what-could-a-new-federal-theatre-project-actually-look-like/.

Bibliography

BOOKS, ESSAYS, NEWSPAPER REPORTS

Adamson, Joe. Groucho. *Harpo, Chico, and Sometimes Zeppo: A Celebration of the Marx Brothers*. New York: Simon and Schuster, 1973.

Altman, Rick. *The American Film Musical*. Bloomington: Indiana University Press, 1987.

Amenta, Edwin. *Bold Relief: Institutional Politics and the Origins of Modern American Social Policy*. Princeton, NJ: Princeton University Press, 1998.

Anderson, Henry Clayton. *Will Rogers and "His" America*. Library of American Biography Series. Boston: Pearson, 2011.

Arnold, Elliot. "Faking Car Accidents." *Nation*, November 21, 1936, 601–2.

Atkinson, Brooks. "Portrait of a Talker." *New York Times*, December 13, 1932, 10.

Balio, Tino. *Grand Design: Hollywood as a Modern Business Enterprise, 1930–1939*. Berkley: University of California Press, 1996.

Balleisen, Edward J. *Fraud: An American History from Barnum to Madoff*. Princeton, NJ: Princeton University Press, 2017.

Barnard, Rita. *The Great Depression and the Culture of Abundance: Kenneth Fearing, Nathanael West, and Mass Culture in the 1930s*. Cambridge: Cambridge University Press, 1995.

Barthes, Roland. *Mythologies*. Translated by Annette Lewis. 1952. Reprint, New York: Hill and Wang, 1972.

Benson, Peter. *Battling Siki: A Tale of Ring Fixes, Race, and Murder in the 1920s*. Fayetteville: University of Arkansas Press, 2008.

Bentley, Joanne. *Hallie Flanagan: A Life in the American Theatre*. New York: Knopf, 1988.

Bergson, Henri. *Laughter: An Essay on the Meaning of the Comic*. Translated Cloudesly Berereton and Fred Rothwell. New York: Macmillan, 1911.

Bieson, Sheri Chinen. *Music in the Shadows: Noir Musical Films*. Baltimore: Johns Hopkins University Press, 2014.

Bilton, Alan. *Silent Film Comedy and American Culture.* Basingstoke, UK: Palgrave Macmillan, 2013.

Bingham, Alfred. *Insurgent America: Revolt of the Middle Classes.* New York: Harper and Brothers, 1935.

Binkiewicz, Donna. *Federalizing the Muse: United States Arts Policy and the National Endowment for the Arts, 1965–1980.* Chapel Hill: University of North Carolina Press, 2014.

Bird, William. *"Better Living": Advertising, Media, and the New Vocabulary of Business Leadership, 1935–1955.* Evanston, IL: Northwestern University Press, 1999.

Blair, Karen J. 1994. *The Torchbearers: Women and Their Amateur Arts Associations in America, 1890–1930.* Philanthropic Studies. Bloomington: Indiana University Press.

Bold, Christine. *Writers, Plumbers, and Anarchists: The WPA Writer's Project in Massachusetts.* Amherst: University of Massachusetts Press, 2006.

Bombola, Gina. 2018. "From 'There's Magic in Music' to 'The Hard-Boiled Canary': Promoting 'Good Music' in Prewar Musical Films." *Journal of the Society for American Music* 12, no. 2: 151–78.

Bowser, Pearl, and Louise Spence. *Writing Himself into History: Oscar Micheaux, His Silent Films, and His Audiences.* New Brunswick, NJ: Rutgers University Press, 2000.

Braconi, Macki. *Harlem's Theaters: A Staging Ground for Community, Class, and Contradiction, 1923–1939.* Evanston, IL: Northwestern University Press, 2015.

Brady, Amy. "'They're Sufferin' the Same Things We're Sufferin': Ideology and Racism in the Federal Theatre Project's 'The Sun Rises in the West.'" *Theatre Survey* 56, no. 1 (January 2015): 51–70.

Brinkley, Alan. *Liberalism and Its Discontents.* Cambridge: Harvard University Press, 1998.

Brownell, John C. *Mississippi Rainbow.* New York: Samuel French, 1935.

Brussell, Judith Edith. "Government Investigations of Federal Theatre Project Personnel in the Works Progress Administration (The Show Must NOT Go On!)." PhD diss., City University of New York, 1993.

Burrell, Julie. *The Civil Rights Theatre Movement in New York, 1939–1966: Staging Freedom.* New York: Palgrave/Macmillan, 2019.

Cannon, Eoin F. *The Saloon and the Mission: Addiction, Conversion, and the Politics of Redemption in American Culture.* Amherst: University of Massachusetts Press, 2013.

Chansky, Dorothy. *Composing Ourselves: The Little Theatre Movement and the American Audience.* Carbondale: Southern Illinois University Press, 2004.

Charney, Maurice. *The Comic World of the Marx Brothers' Movies: "Anything Further Father?"* Madison, NJ: Fairleigh Dickinson University Press, 2007.

Chicago Defender (National Edition). Review of *Mississippi Rainbow,* May 8, 1937, ProQuest Historical Newspapers: *Chicago Defender,* 10.

Cohen, Lizabeth. "The New Deal State and the Making of Citizen Consumers." In *Getting and Spending: European and American Consumer Societies in the Twentieth Century,* edited by Susan Strasser, Charles McGovern, and Matthias Just, 111–27. Cambridge: Cambridge University Press, 1998.

Coontz, Stephanie. *The Way We Never Were: American Families and the Nostalgia Trap.* New York: Basic Books, 1992.

Corey, Lewis. *The Crisis of the Middle Class.* New York: Covici-Friede, 1935.

Crowther, Bosley. "Home, Sweet Broadway." *New York Times,* September 27, 1936.

Davis, Robert. "Is Mr. Euripides a Communist? The Federal Theatre Project's 1938 'Trojan Incident.'" *Comparative Drama* 44/45, no. 1 (2010): 457–76.

Decker, Todd. *Showboat: Performing Race in an American Musical*. New York: Oxford University Press, 2013.

Deutsch, Tracey. *Building a Housewife's Paradise: Gender Politics and American Grocery Stores in the Twentieth Century*. Chapel Hill: University of North Carolina Press, 2010.

Dickstein, Morris. *Dancing in the Dark: A Cultural History of the Great Depression*. New York: Norton, 2010.

Diggins, John Patrick. *Eugene O'Neill's America: Desire under Democracy*. Chicago: University of Chicago Press, 2007.

Dornstein, Ken. *Accidentally on Purpose: The Making of a Personal Injury Underworld in America*. New York: St. Martin's Press, 1996.

Dossett, Kate. *Radical Black Theatre in the New Deal*. Chapel Hill: University of North Carolina Press, 2020.

Edmonds, Susan. *Grotesque Relations: Modernist Domestic Fiction and the U.S. Welfare State*. Oxford: Oxford University Press, 2008.

Eisler, Garret. "Kidding on the Level: The Reactionary Project of *I'd Rather Be Right*." *Studies in Musical Theatre* 1, no. 1 (2007): 8–24.

Fabian, Ann. *Card Sharps and Bucket Shops: Gambling in Nineteenth Century America*. New York: Routledge, 1999.

Feuer, Jane. "The Self-Reflexive Musical and the Myth of Entertainment." In *Film Genre Reader II*, edited by Barry Keith Grant, 441–55. Austin: University of Texas Press, 1995.

Fisher, James. "The Man Who Owned Broadway: George M. Cohan's Triumph in Eugene O'Neill's 'Ah, Wilderness!'" *Eugene O'Neill Review* 23, no. 1/2 (1999): 98–126.

Flanagan, Hallie. *Arena*. New York: Duell, Sloan, and Pearce, 1940.

———. "Speech to New York City Project Production Supervisors." *Federal Theatre* 2, no. 1 (June 1936): 5–6.

"Fool's Gold: How I Sold You Your Fake Mining Stock: As Told to Edward H. Smith." *Collier's Illustrated Weekly*, December 3, 1921, 7–8, 19, 24.

Fraden, Rena. *Blueprint for a Black Federal Theatre, 1935–1939*. Cambridge: Cambridge University Press, 1994.

Franko, Mark. *The Work of Dance: Labor, Movement, and Identity in the 1930s*. Boston: Wesleyan University Press, 2002.

Frick, John. "A Changing Theatre: New York and Beyond." In *The Cambridge History of American Theatre*, vol. 2, *1870–1945*, edited by Don Wilmeth and Christopher Bigsby, 196–232. Cambridge: Cambridge University Press, 1999.

Friedman, Walter. *Fortune Tellers: The Story of America's First Economic Forecasters*. Princeton, NJ: Princeton University Press, 2013.

Frost, Leslie Elaine. *Popular Front Ideals and Aesthetics in Children's Plays of the Federal Theatre Project*. Columbus: Ohio State University Press, 2013.

Gagliardi, Paul. "The Illusion of Work: The Con Artist Plays of the Federal Theatre Project." *Journal of American Drama and Theatre* 30, no. 1 (2017), https://jadtjournal.org/2017/12/11/the-illusion-of-work-the-con-artist-plays-of-the-federal-theatre-project/.

———. "No Security in Acting: A Moral Entertainment and the Conflict over Theatrical Labor in the Federal Theatre Project." *LATCH: A Journal for the Study of the Literary Artifact in Theory, Culture, or History* 8, no. 1 (2015): 1–15.

Garcia, Desirée J. "Toil behind the Footlights: The Spectacle of Female Suffering and the Rise of Musical Comedy." *Frontiers: A Journal of Women Studies* 40, no. 1 (2019): 122–45.

Gardner, Martin A. *The Marx Brothers as Social Critics: Satire and Comic Nihilism in Their Films.* Jefferson: McFarland and Company, 2009.

George, Ann, and Jack Selzer. "What Happened at the First American Writers' Congress? Kenneth Burke's 'Revolutionary Symbolism in America.'" *Rhetoric Society Quarterly* 33, no. 2 (2003): 47–66.

George Mason University. *The Federal Theatre Project: A Catalog-Calendar of Productions.* New York: Greenwood Press, 1986.

Gilmour, Heather. "Different, Except in a Different Way: Marriage, Divorce, and Gender in the Hollywood Comedy of Remarriage." *Journal of Film and Video* 50, no. 2 (1998): 26–39.

Glickman, Lawrence B. *A Living Wage: American Workers and the Making of Consumer Society.* Ithaca, NY: Cornell University Press, 1997.

Goldstein, Malcom. *George S. Kaufman: His Life, His Theater.* Oxford: Oxford University Press, 1979.

———. *The Political Stage: American Drama and Theater of the Great Depression.* New York: Oxford University Press, 1974.

Gordon, Linda. *Pitied but Not Entitled: Single Mothers and the History of Welfare, 1890–1935.* Cambridge, MA: Harvard University Press, 1995.

Grant, Barry Keith. *The Hollywood Film Musical.* Oxford: Blackwell, 2012.

Grant, James. "Welcome Federal Theatre," *Chicago Defender (National Edition),* April 17, 1937, ProQuest Historical Newspapers: *Chicago Defender,* 17.

Hadleigh, Boze. *Broadway Babylon: Glamour, Glitz, and Gossip of the Great White Way.* New York: Back Stage Books, 2013.

Hall, David D. "Narrating Puritanism." In *New Directions in American Religious History,* edited by Harry S. Stout and D. G. Hart, 51–83. Oxford: Oxford University Press, 1997.

Halttunen, Karen. *Confidence Men and Painted Women: A Study of Middle-Class Culture in America, 1830–1870.* New Haven, CT: Yale University Press, 1982.

Hayes, Joy Elizabeth. "White Noise Performing the White, Middle-Class Family on 1930s Radio." *Cinema Journal* 51, no. 3 (2012): 97–118.

Heinrich, Anselm, *Entertainment, Propaganda, Education: Regional Theatre in Germany and Britain between 1918 and 1945.* Herefordshire, UK: University of Herefordshire Press, 2007.

Hirsch, Foster. *George Kelly.* Boston: GK Hall, 1975.

Holcomb, Robert. "The Federal Theatre in Los Angeles." *California Historical Society Quarterly* 41, no. 2 (1962): 131–47.

Hopkins, Harry. *Spending to Save: The True Story of Relief.* New York: Norton, 1936.

Hopkins, June. *Harry Hopkins: Sudden Hero, Brash Reformer.* New York: St. Martin's Press, 1999.

Howard, Viki. *From Main Street to Mall: The Rise and Fall of the American Department Store.* Philadelphia: University of Pennsylvania Press, 2015.

Hurt, Melissa. "Oppressed, Stereotyped, and Silenced: Atlanta's Black History with the Federal Theatre Project." *Theatre Symposium* 11 (January 1, 2003): 74.

Ickes, Harold. *The Secret Diary of Harold L. Ickes.* Vol. 1, *The First Thousand Days: 1933–1936.* New York: Simon and Schuster, 1953.

Inness, C. D. *Modern German Drama: A Study in Form.* Cambridge: Cambridge University Press, 1979.

Jarvis, Arthur R. "The Living Newspaper in Philadelphia, 1938–1939." *Pennsylvania History: A Journal of Mid-Atlantic Studies* 61, no. 3 (1994): 332–55.

Jenkins, Henry. *What Made Pistachio Nuts? Early Sound Comedy and the Vaudeville Aesthetic*. New York: Columbia University Press, 1992.

J.K.H. "Help Yourself Is Given By WPA." *New York Times*, July 15, 1936, 15.

Kaufman, George, and Marc Connelly. *To the Ladies*. New York: Samuel French, 1922.

Kaufman, George, and Moss Hart. *I'd Rather Be Right*. New York: Random House, 1937.

Kelly, George. *Three Plays: "The Torch-Bearers," "The Show-Off," "Craig's Wife."* Biographical and critical essays by William Lynch. Foreword by Wendy Wasserstein. New York: Limelight, 1999.

Kennedy, David. *Freedom from Fear: The American People in Depression and War, 1929–1945*. Oxford: Oxford University Press, 1999.

———. "What the New Deal Did." *Political Science Quarterly* 124, no. 2 (2009): 251–68.

Kennedy, Susan Estabrook. *The Banking Crisis of 1933*. 1973. Reprint, Lexington: University Press of Kentucky, 2021.

Keynes, John Maynard. *The General Theory of Employment, Interest, and Money*. 1936. Reprint, Amherst: Prometheus Books, 1997.

Kim, Sung Ho. *Max Weber's Politics of Civil Society*. Cambridge: Cambridge University Press, 2004.

Kimmel, Michael S. *Manhood in America: A Cultural History*. Oxford: Oxford University Press, 2006.

Kiriakou, Olympia. *Becoming Carole Lombard: Stardom, Comedy, and Legacy*. New York: Bloomsbury Academic, 2020.

Kloppenberg, James. *Uncertain Victory: Social Democracy and Progressivism in European and American Thought, 1870–1920*. Oxford: Oxford University Press, 1988.

Krueger, Lauren. *The National Stage: Theatre and Cultural Legitimation in England, France, and America*. Chicago: University of Chicago Press, 1992.

LaMotta, Jake. *Raging Bull*. Englewood Cliffs: Prentice Hall, 1970.

Latham, Angela J. *Posing a Threat: Flappers, Chorus Girls, and Other Brazen Performers of the American 1920s*. Hanover, NH: Wesleyan/University Press of New England, 2000.

Lears, Jackson. *Something for Nothing: Luck in America*. New York: Penguin, 2003.

Lehnhof, Kent R. "Antitheatricality and Irrationality: An Alternative View." *Criticism* 58, no. 2 (2016): 231–50.

Leigh, Wendy. *True Grace: The Life and Death of an American Princess*. New York: St. Martin's Press, 2007.

Lenz, William E. *Fast Talk & Flush Times: The Confidence Man as a Literary Convention*. Columbia: University of Missouri Press, 1985.

Levine, Lawrence W. "American Culture and the Great Depression." *Yale Review* 74, no. 2 (1985): 196–223.

———. *Black Culture and Black Consciousness: Afro-American Folk Thought from Slavery to Freedom*. Oxford: Oxford University Press, 1978.

Lindberg, Gary. *The Confidence Man in American Literature*. Oxford: Oxford University Press, 1982.

Louvish, Simon. *Monkey Business: The Lives and Legends of the Marx Brothers: Groucho, Chico, Harpo, Zeppo, with Added Gummo*. New York: Faber and Faber, 1999.

Lutz, Tom. *Doing Nothing: A History of Loafers, Loungers, Bums, and Slackers in America*. New York: Farrar, Straus and Giroux, 2006.

———. "'Sweat or Die': The Hedonization of the Work Ethic in the 1920s." *American Literary History* 8, no. 2 (1996): 259–83.

Lynd, Robert S., and Helen Merrell Lynd. *Middletown in Transition: A Study in Cultural Conflicts*. New York: Harcourt, Brace, 1937.

Maibuam, Richard. "On the Dedication of the EC Mabie Theater." In *Speaking of Writing*, edited by Sylvia Maibaum, 86–91. New York: Page, 2019.

———. "On the New Drama, the New Play." In *Speaking of Writing*, edited by Sylvia Maibaum, 41–53. New York: Page, 2019.

Maisel, Edward. "The Theater of George Kelly." *Theater Arts* 31 (February 1947): 42–50.

Maland, Charles J. *Chaplin and American Culture: The Evolution of a Star Image*. Princeton, NJ: Princeton University Press, 1989.

Marchand, Roland. *Adverting the American Dream: Making Way for Modernity, 1920–1940*. Berkley: University of California Press, 1985.

Matthews, Jane De Hart. *The Federal Theatre, 1935–1939: Plays, Relief, and Politics*. Princeton, NJ: Princeton University Press, 1967.

Maurer, David. *The Big Con: The Story of the Confidence Man*. New York: Merrill, 1940.

Mazer, Sharon. *Professional Wrestling: Sport and Spectacle*. Oxford: University Press of Mississippi, 1998.

McArthur, Benjamin. *Actors and American Culture*. Iowa City: University of Iowa Press, 2000.

McCann, Sean. *Gumshoe America: Hard-Boiled Crime Fiction and the Rise and Fall of New Deal Liberalism*. Durham, NC: Duke University Press, 2000.

McClendon, Rose. "As to a New Negro Stage." *New York Times*, June 30, 1935, 10:1.

McDonald, William F. *Federal Relief Administration and the Arts*. Columbus: Ohio State University Press, 1969.

McGilligan, Patrick, and Paul Brule, eds. "Allen Boretz Interview." In *Tender Comrades: A Backstory of the Hollywood Blacklist*, 112–28. New York: St. Martin's Press, 1997.

McLean, Adrienne L. *Being Rita Hayworth: Labor, Identity, and Hollywood Stardom*. New Brunswick, NJ: Rutgers University Press, 2004.

McMillin, Scott. *The Musical as Drama*. Princeton, NJ: Princeton University Press, 2006.

Mencken, H. L. "Puritanism as a Literary Force." In *Book of Prefaces*, 197–285. New York: Knopf, 1917.

Mihm, Stephen. *A Nation of Counterfeiters: Capitalists, Con Men, and the Making of the United States*. Cambridge, MA: Harvard University Press, 2007.

Miller, Nina. *Making Love Modern: The Intimate Public Worlds of New York's Literary Women*. New York: Oxford University Press, 1999.

Mills, C. Wright. *White Collar: The American Middle Classes*. Oxford: Oxford University Press, 1951.

Mitchell, Greg. *The Campaign of the Century: Upton Sinclair's Race for Governor of California and the Birth of Media Politics*. New York: Random House, 1992.

Mommosen, J. Wolfgang. *The Political and Social Theory of Max Weber*. Chicago: University of Chicago Press, 1989.

Moore, Cecelia. *The Federal Theatre Project in the American South: The Carolina Playmakers and the Quest for American Drama*. New York: Lexington Books, 2017.

Mordden, Ethan. *Sing for Your Supper: The Broadway Musical in the 1930s*. New York: Palgrave, 2005.

Moskowitz, Marina. "'Aren't We All?' Aspiration, Acquisition, and the American Middle Class." In *The Making of the Middle Class*, edited by A. Ricardo Lopez and Barbara Weinstein, 75–86. Durham, NC: Duke University Press, 2012.

Munger, Guy. *Curtain Up! Raleigh Little Theatre's First 50 Years*. Raleigh: Raleigh Little Theatre, 1985.

Murray, John, and Allen Boretz. *Room Service*. New York: Samuel French, 1936.

New York Times. "$3,187,000 Relief Is Spent to Teach Jobless to Play; $19,658,512 Voted for April; 'Boon Doggles' Made." April 4, 1935.

North, Michael. *Machine-Age Comedy*. Oxford: Oxford University Press, 2009.

O'Neill, Eugene. *Ah Wilderness!: A Comedy of Recollection in Three Acts*. New York: Samuel French, 1933.

Orbach, Barak. "Prizefighting and the Birth of Movie Censorship." *Yale Journal of Law and the Humanities* 21 (2009): 251. Arizona Legal Studies Discussion Paper no. 09-08, https://ssrn.com/abstract=1351542.

Osborne, Elizabeth. *Staging the People: Community and Identity in the Federal Theatre Project*. New York: Palgrave, 2011.

Pells, Richard. *Radical Visions and American Dreams: Culture and Social Thought in the Depression Years*. Middletown: Wesleyan University Press, 1973.

Postlewait, Thomas. "The Hieroglyphic Stage: American Theatre and Society, Post–Civil War to 1945." In *The Cambridge History of American Theatre*, edited by Don B. Wilmeth and Christopher Bigsby, 2:107–95. Cambridge History of American Theatre. Cambridge: Cambridge University Press, 1999.

Puchner, Martin. *Stage Fright: Modernism, Anti-Theatricality, and Drama*. Baltimore: Johns Hopkins University Press, 2002.

Puskar, Jason. *Accident Society: Fiction, Collectivity, and the Production of Chance*. Stanford: Stanford University Press, 2012.

Quinn, Susan. *Furious Improvisation: How the WPA and a Cast of Thousands Made High Art Out of Desperate Times*. New York: Walker, 2008.

Redd, Tina. "Birmingham's Federal Theater Project Negro Unit: The Administration of Race." In *African American Performance and Theater History: A Critical Reader*, edited by Harry J. Elam Jr. and David Krasner, 271–87. New York: Oxford University Press, 2001.

Reilly, Adam. *Harold Lloyd, The King of Daredevil Comedy*. New York: Collier Books, 1977.

Reith, Gerda. *The Age of Chance: Gambling in Western Culture*. London: Routledge, 1999.

Rice, Grantland. "Rasslin' Gets a Toe Hold." *Collier's*, March 14, 1931, 16, 65.

Rodgers, Daniel. *Atlantic Crossings: Social Politics in a Progressive Age*. Cambridge, MA: Harvard University Press, 1998.

———. *The Work Ethic in Industrial America, 1850–1920*. Princeton, NJ: Princeton University Press, 1988.

Root, Lynn, and Harry Clork. *The Milky Way*. New York: Samuel French, 1936.

Rose, Nancy E. "Production-for-Use or Production-for-Profit?: The Contradictions of Consumer Goods Production in 1930s Work Relief." *Review of Radical Political Economics* 20, no. 1 (March 1988): 46–61.

———. *Put to Work: The WPA and Public Employment in the Great Depression*. New York: Monthly Review, 2009.

Rubinow, I. M. *The Quest for Security*. New York: Holt and Company, 1934.

Sarris, Andrew. *You Ain't Heard Nothing Yet: The American Talking Film, History & Memory, 1927–1949*. New York: Oxford University Press, 1998.

Scarry, Elaine. *The Body in Pain*. Oxford: Oxford University Press, 1985.

Schaum, Melita. "H. L. Mencken and American Cultural Masculinism." *Journal of American Studies* 29, no. 3 (1995): 379–98.

Schechter, Joel. *Messiahs of 1932: How American Yiddish Theatre Survived through Satire*. Philadelphia: Temple University Press, 2008.

Schickel. Richard. *Harold Lloyd: The Shape of Laughter.* New York: Time Life Books, 1974.

Scott, James C. *Weapons of the Weak: Everyday Forms of Peasant Resistance.* New Haven, CT: Yale University Press, 1985.

Scruggs, Charles W. "Finding Out about This Mencken: The Impact of 'A Book of Prefaces' on Richard Wright." *Menckeniana,* no. 95 (Fall 1985): 1–11.

Scutts, Joanna. *The Extra Woman: How Marjorie Hillis Led a Generation of Women to Live Alone and Like It.* New York: Liveright, 2018.

Shandall, Jonathan. *The American Negro Theatre and the Long Civil Rights Era.* Iowa City: University of Iowa Press, 2018.

Shoemaker, David. *The Squared Circle: Life, Death and Professional Wrestling.* New York: Gotham, 2013.

Sklaroff, Lauren Rebecca. *Black Culture and the New Deal: The Quest for Civil Rights in the Roosevelt Era.* Chapel Hill: University of North Carolina Press, 2009.

Skocpol, Theda. *Protecting Soldiers and Mothers: The Political Origins of Social Policy in the United States.* Cambridge, MA: Harvard University Press, 1992.

Sotiropoulos, Karen. *Staging Race: Black Performers in Turn of the Century America.* Cambridge: Harvard University Press, 2008.

Steinmetz, George. *Regulating the Social: The Welfare State and Local Politics in Imperial Germany.* Princeton, NJ: Princeton University Press, 1993.

Sunstein, Cass. *The Second Bill of Rights: FDR's Unfinished Revolution.* New York: Basic, 2005.

Szalay, Michael. *New Deal Modernism: American Literature and the Invention of the Welfare State.* Durham, NC: Duke University Press, 2000.

Trainor, Sebastian. "'It Sounds Too Much Like *Comrade*': The Preservation of American Ideals in *Room Service.*" *Journal of American Drama and Theater* 20, no. 2 (2008): 29–48.

Vactor, Vanita Marian. "A History of the Chicago Federal Theatre Project Negro Unit." PhD diss., City University of New York, 1998.

Vulpius, Paul. *Help Yourself: A Farce in Three Acts.* Translated by John Coman. New York: Samuel French, 1936.

Wagner David. *The Poorhouse: America's Forgotten Institution.* New York: Rowan and Littlefield, 2005.

Weber, Max. "Bureaucracy." In *Max Weber: Essays in Sociology,* edited by Hans Gerth and C. Wright Mills, 196–244. New York: Oxford University Press, 1975.

———. *Economy and Society.* Edited by Guenther Roth and Claus Wittch. 1958. Reprint, Berkley: University of California Press, 1968.

———. "Politics as a Vocation." In *Max Weber: The Vocation Lectures,* edited by David Owen and Tracy Strong, 32–89. Indianapolis: Hackett, 2004.

———. *The Protestant Ethic and the Spirit of Capitalism,* 1905. Translated by Talcott Parsons, 1930. London: Routledge, 2001.

Weil, Yellow Kid. *Yellow Kid Weil: The Autobiography of America's Master Swindler; As told to W. T. Brannon.* Chicago: Zip Davis Publishing, 1948.

White, Leslie. "Eugene O'Neill and the Federal Theatre Project." *Resources for American Literary Study* 17, no. 1 (1990): 63–85.

Wilmeth, Don B., and Christopher Bigsby, eds. *The Cambridge History of American Theatre.* Vol. 2, *1870–1945.* Cambridge: Cambridge University Press, 1998.

Witham Barry B. *The Federal Theatre Project: A Case Study.* Cambridge: Cambridge University Press, 2003.

Wollcott, Alexander. "The Play: By the Authors of 'Dulcy.'" *New York Times,* February 21, 1922.

——. "The Play: Joy in West 48th Street." *New York Times*, August 30, 1922.

Wong, Edwin. *The Risk Theatre Model of Tragedy: Gambling, Drama, and the Unexpected*. Victoria: Friesen Press, 2019.

Wright, Richard. *American Hunger*. 1944. Reprint, New York: Harper and Row, 1977.

Young, James Harvey. *The Toadstool Millionaires: A Social History of Patent Medicines in American before Federal Regulation*. Princeton, NJ: Princeton University Press, 1961.

ARCHIVES

George Mason University, Special Collections, Federal Theatre Project

Radio script of *Help Yourself* by Paul Vulpius, adapted by Barry Williams, 1939, Box 280, Folder 1.

Radio script of *Mississippi Rainbow* by John C. Brownell, 1938, Box 280, Folder 7.

Library of Congress, Federal Theatre Project Collection

"Ah Wilderness." Box 137, *Ah, Wilderness* (O'Neill) Folder.

"Ah Wilderness by Eugene O'Neill Report." Box 137, *Ah, Wilderness* (O'Neill) Folder.

The American Citizen. "St. Anthony's Sponsor Federal Theatre Play." October 22, 1937, Box 969, Des Moines *Ah, Wilderness* Production Report.

"Audience Reaction." Box 1015, Los Angeles *Help Yourself* Production Report.

"Audience Reaction Report." Box 1016, Des Moines *Help Yourself* Production Report.

"Audience Reaction Report." Box 1016, Omaha *Help Yourself* Production Report.

"Audience Reaction Report, Los Angeles *To the Ladies*." Box 1081, Los Angeles *To the Ladies* Folder.

"Audience Reaction Report, San Diego *To the Ladies*." Box 1081, San Diego *To the Ladies* Folder.

"Audience Survey." Box 1040, Portland *The Milky Way* Production Report.

"Audience Survey." Box 1067, Denver *Room Service* Production Report.

"Audience Survey, 1938." Box 969, Los Angeles *Ah, Wilderness* Production Report.

"Bureau of Research and Publication, Special Play Reader Report of *Mississippi Rainbow*, C.C. Lawrence." Box 258, *Mississippi Rainbow* (Brownell) Folder.

Charig, Phillip, Ray Golden, and Sid Kuller. *O Say Can You Sing*. Box 1048, Chicago *O Say Can You Sing* Folder.

"Comment." Box 137, *Ah, Wilderness* (O'Neill) Folder.

Dabnzy, Thomas Ewing. "Federal Theater Players Give Retrospect in 'Ah Wilderness.'" *New Orleans States*, May 26, 1938, Box 969, New Orleans *Ah, Wilderness* Production Report.

"Director's Report." Box 1081, San Diego *To the Ladies* Production Report.

"Director's Report, 1937." Box 969, Des Moines *Ah, Wilderness* Production Report.

"Help Yourself." *Peoria Star*. Box 1015, Peoria Production Report.

Kennedy, William. "A Moral Entertainment: Good Entertainment Too." Box 1040, Roslyn *A Moral Entertainment* Production Report.

Los Angeles Herald & Express Review of *To the Ladies*, July 20, 1938. Box 1081, Los Angeles *To the Ladies* Folder.

Los Angeles Times Review of *To the Ladies*, July 20, 1938. Box 1081, Los Angeles *To the Ladies* Production Report.

"The Milky Way Playreader Report, Arthur Bond." June 4, 1936. Box 256, *The Milky Way* (Root and Clork) Folder.

"A Moral Entertainment report, Converse Tyler." January 10, 1938. Box 260, *A Moral Entertainment* (Maibaum) Folder.

"Playreader Report of *The Milky Way*, B. Sim." 1936. Box 256, *The Milky Way* (Root and Clork) Folder.

"Playreader Report of *The Milky Way*, Koby Kohn." 1936. Box 256, *The Milky Way* (Root and Clork) Folder.

"Play Reader Report of *The Milky Way*, Gus Winberg." March 10, 1936. Box 256, *The Milky Way* (Root and Clork) Folder.

"Play Reader Report of *Mississippi Rainbow*, Alfred B. Kuttner." March 5, 1937. Box 258, *Mississippi Rainbow* (Brownell) Folder.

"Play Reader Report of *Mississippi Rainbow*, Samuel Kreiter." December 17, 1937. Box 258, *Mississippi Rainbow* (Brownell) Folder.

"Play Reader Report of *Mississippi Rainbow*, William Stone." February 26, 1937. Box 258, *Mississippi Rainbow* (Brownell) Folder.

"Play Reader Report, *To the Ladies*, Harold Callen." June 19, 1936. Box 332, *To the Ladies* (Kaufman and Connelly) Folder.

"Play Reader Report, *To the Ladies*, Henry Bennett." May 7, 1937. Box 332, *To the Ladies* (Kaufman and Connelly) Folder.

"Play Reader Report, *To the Ladies*, Reader Byrne." May 12, 1937. Box 332, *To the Ladies* (Kaufman and Connelly) Folder.

"Review of *The Milky Way*." *Los Angeles Evening News*, August 5, 1938. Box 1040, Los Angeles *The Milky Way* Production Report.

Review of *The Milky Way*. *San Diego Union*, August 26, 1938. Box 1040, San Diego *The Milky Way* Production Report.

Review of *A Moral Entertainment*. *Philadelphia Bulletin*, June 19, 1938. Box 1040, Bryn Mawr *A Moral Entertainment* Production Report.

Review of *To the Ladies, San Bernardino Sun Telegram*, June 17, 1937. Box 1081, San Bernardino *To the Ladies* Production Report.

"*Room Service*: Play Bureau File, August 20, 1937." Box 298, *Room Service* (Murray, John and Boretz, Allen) Folder.

"*Room Service* Report, Jo Eisinger. Sept. 7, 1937." Box 298, *Room Service* (Murray, John and Boretz, Allen) Folder.

"*Room Service* Report, Marion Murray. August 17, 1937." Box 298, *Room Service* (Murray, John and Boretz, Allen) Folder.

Rush, Dan. "Review of *The Torchbearers* for the Bureau of Research and Publication." June 8, 1936. Box 333, *The Torchbearers* (Kelly) Folder.

Sayler, Mary. "*Help Yourself*," *University of Washington Daily*, November 6, 1937. Box 1016, Seattle *Help Yourself* Production Report, FTP LC.

Slane, Andrew. "Director's Report." Box 1067, Denver *Room* Production Report.

University of Iowa, Richard Maibaum Papers
Hughes, Elinor. "*Review of A Moral Entertainment*." *Boston Herald*, December 28, 1938, Box 14.

Maibaum, Richard. *A Moral Entertainment*, Box 14.

Review of *A Moral Entertainment*, *Boston American*, December 28, 1938, Box 14.

University of Wyoming, American Heritage Center, Lynn Root Collection
Lynn Root's copy of *The Cheese Champion*; Lynn Root Papers, Box 8, Folder 3.

Yale University, Beinecke Rare Book and Manuscript Library,
John Brownell Papers
Claude A. Barnett to John Brownell, May 26, 1937, Box 132, Folder 4.
Cleveland Neighborhood Association Letter, February 1, 1936, Box 132, Folder 1.
John C. Brownell to Susan Glaspell, July 13, 1937, Box 132, Folder 1.
John C. Brownell to Shirley Graham, May 11, 1937, Folder 3.
John C. Brownell to George Kondolf, July 28, 1937, Box 132, Folder 4.
John C. Brownell to Theodore Ward, May 11, 1937, Box 132, Folder 4.
Richard J. Madden to John C. Brownell, May 13, 1936, Box 132, Folder 1.
Shirley Graham to Black Organizations, form letter, February 23, 1937, Box 132, Folder 3.
Shirley Graham to John C. Brownell, May 12, 1937, Box 132, Folder 4.
Theodore Ward to John Brownell, May 20, 1937, Box 132, Folder 3.

Index

Accident fraud, 109

Advertising: consumerism, 71–72; intersection with swindling, 128, 137; middle-class promotion and anxiety, 70, 100–101; *The Milky Way*, 143–144; model for New Deal communication, 84; professional ethical divide, 143–44; promotion of gendered labor, 90; promotion of regulation, 143; solution to domestic problems, 90–91; *To the Ladies*, 90–91

Agricultural Adjustment Administration (AAA), 33, 74

Ah, Wilderness!, 6, 9, 25, 69–84, 95; conservative reception, 77–80; critique of middle-class politics, 81–82; critique of middle-class charity and work, 82–84; Des Moines production, 77–78; film adaptation, 79–80, 170n46; FTP reader reports, 77–78; New Orleans FTP production, 77; O'Neill's rationale for writing, 78; other FTP productions, 169n34; portrayal of alcoholism, 83–84; portrayal of the working class, 81–82; press coverage, 77–78; promotion of middle-class life, 80–81; summary, 76–77; touring productions, 78–79. *See also* O'Neill, Eugene

Albee, Edward, 22

Alcoholics Anonymous, 83

Alger, Horatio, 97, 130

Algonquin Round Table, 87

Alsberg, Henry, 32

Altars of Steel, 45

Amateur theater, 22, 60; effect of Great Depression on, 26; theatrical labor, 29, 41–42, 46. *See also* Little Theatre Movement

American Dream, 88, 145–146

American Writer's Congress, 50, 55

Antitheatricality, 22–24

Backstage narratives: appeal to Hollywood, 37–38; declining popularity, 38; diegetic audiences, 37; historical development, 37–38; labor in, 37–40; shift to realism, 38; self-reflexive musicals, 35–36. See also *A Moral Entertainment, Room Service, The Torch-Bearers*

Back to the Woods, 57

Baker, George Pierce, 47

Banking industry, 10, 15; *Help Yourself*, 146, 149–152, 153–155; New Deal reforms of, 108, 128; skepticism toward, 122, 155; unethical practices of, 122, 131, 146, 149, 153

Paul Gagliardi is a Teaching Associate Professor of English at Marquette University.